CW01202547

In commemoration of
"Industrial Heritage Year"
1993

Amalbrea Stamps, downstream from Amalveor Mine, worked by John James Curnow and photographed in the 1920s by A.K. Hamilton Jenkin. (Courtesy Royal Institution of Cornwall).

THE ST. IVES MINING DISTRICT

By
Cyril Noall

VOLUME TWO

Edited with a Foreword
By
Philip Payton & Leonard Truran

ISBN 185 022 0670 Paperback

First published 1993 by Dyllansow Truran, Redruth, Cornwall
Printed by St. George Printing Works Ltd., Commercial Centre, Wilson Way, Redruth, Cornwall
Telephone (0209) 217033

ACKNOWLEDGEMENTS

I wish to express grateful thanks to all those kind friends who willingly assisted during the compilation of this book. Charles Smith provided some notes on the geology of the district and was actively associated with the project in various ways. Many of the photos were made available by John H. Trounson, of Redruth, from his unique collection of Cornish mining views. To Justin Brooke, of Marazion, I am indebted for many kindnesses; he readily consented to read the manuscript, making several suggestions for its improvement; he also supplied information from his own extensive files on some of the more elusive local mines, and compiled the valuable list of mines arranged in order of parishes.

Information and help were also given by the following: G.C. Penaluna, Scorrier; Paul Stephens, Devoran; Alan Pearson, Redruth; H.L. Douch (former Curator) and Roger Penhallurick, Royal Cornwall Museum, Truro; P.L. Hull (former Archivist) and J.C. Edwards, County Record Office, Truro; Mrs. S. Balson, Librarian Penzance (Morrab Gardens) Library; staff of St. Ives Branch, Cornwall County Library; Terry Knight, Cornish Studies Library; the late W.T. Harry, Penzance; E.T. Berryman, Beagletodn, Towednack; St. Ives Museum Management Committee (for use of photos and other material); Jim Hodge, St. Ives; Dicon Nance, Carbis Bay; Arthur Dale, Lelant Downs; E.W.A. Edmonds, Perranwell.

Cyril Noall

PRINCIPAL SOURCES

Cann, F.C. 1917. "The Mines, Lodes and Minerals of the Stennack Valley, St. Ives." (*Trans. Corn. Inst. Min. Eng.*, vol x.)

Collins, J.H. 1912. "Observations on the West of England Mining Region." (*Trans. Roy. Geol. Soc. Corn.*, xiv.)

Dines, H.G., 1956. *The Metalliferous Mining Region of South-West England.*

Henwood, W.J. 1843. "On the Metalliferous Deposits of Cornwall and Devon." (*Trans. Roy. Geol. Soc. Corn.*, v.)

Henwood, W.J. 1865. "Observations on Providence Mines." (*Trans. Roy. Geol. Soc. Corn.*, vii.)

Hunt, R. 1884. *British Mining.*

Jenkin, A.K. Hamilton, 1961. *Mines and Miners of Cornwall, I. Around St. Ives.*

MacAlister, D.A. 1907. *The Geology of the Land's End District.*

Spargo, T. 1865. *The Mines of Cornwall and Devon.*

Williams, J. 1861, 1870. *Devon and Cornwall Mining Directory.*

Newspapers:

Sherborne Mercury; Royal Cornwall Gazette; West Briton; Cornubian; Penzance Gazette; Penzance Journal; Cornish Telegraph; Cornishman; St. Ives Weekly Summary; Western Echo; St. Ives Times.

ABBREVIATIONS

MSM	*Mining and Smelting Magazine*
MJ	*Mining Journal*
MW	*Mining World*
PRO	Public Record Office
SCR,CRO	Stannary Court Records, County Record Office, Truro
J.B.	Justin Brooke
A.K.H.J.	Dr. A.K. Hamilton Jenkin
J.H.T.	John H. Trounson

THE ST. IVES MINING DISTRICT

ALPHABETICAL LIST OF MINES, ARRANGED IN ORDER OF PARISHES
(USING MID-19th CENTURY PARISH BOUNDARIES)
LELANT

Wheal Adelaide 1905
Wheal Alice 1873-77
Balnoon before 1758
Balnoon (1827) - 1839
Balnoon Consols Mine (1845) - 1850
Balnoon Consols Mining Company 1852-58
Bennyon 1584
Boldstamps — before 1870
Wheal Fanny Adela (1868) — (1871)
Wheal Gilbert Consols 1875-76
Wheal Grace 1756-58
Hallywoone 1584
Hawke's Point 1949-54
Wheal Hope 1844-45
South Wheal Kitty 1860-74
Wheal Kitty 1852-76
Wheal Kitty and Mary United 1858-61
Lelant Consolidated Mines (1829) - 1840
Lelant Consols 1852-67
Lelant Consols Mining Company 1844-52
Lelant Mining Company, Limited 1905-09
Lelant Syndicate, Limited 1911
Lelant Towant (1710)
Lelant Towans (1820)
Wheal Locke 1892-94
West Wheal Lucy Tin and Copper Mine 1871-76
East Wheal Margaret 1902-03
South Margaret 1872-82   and Ludgvan
South Wheal Margaret 1854-57
                       and Ludgvan
West Margaret 1869-71
West Wheal Margaret 1857-62
Wheal Margaret 1790
Wheal Margaret Mining Company 1840-75
                       and Towednack
Wheal Margery 1853-69
East Wheal Mary 1871-73
Wheal Mary (1838) - 1875
Mount Tiack Tin and Copper Mining Company 1852-56
Nance Valley Lead and Copper Mine 1860-62
                       (location doubtful)
Wheal Nantz 1849
Wheal North 1904
Wheal Pencrom (1869) - 1870
Polpeor Mine 1873-75
East Providence 1872
East Providence Mine 1852 — before 1857

East Providence Mining Company 1857-77
Providence Mines 1832-78   and St. Ives
South Providence (1870) - 1889
South Providence Mine (1855) - 1857
Providence United Mining Company 1882-89
Wheal Providence Copper Mine (1821)
East Wheal Reeth 1868-71
East Wheal Reeth 1857-60
East Wheal Reeth Mining Company 1850-55
Wheal Reeth 1757
Wheal Reeth (1785) — before 1812
Wheal Reeth 1812-42
Wheal Reeth 1844-67
South Wheal Speed 1850-55
Old Tincroft Mine 1855-59
Towan Mine 1855
Trelyon Bounds 1836-58
Trembethow (1825)
Trencrob-ben (or Trencrom) Tin and Copper Mine 1871 - (1875)
Trencrom Mine 1857-66
Trevarrack 1911
Trevarrack Mining Company 1869-73
Trevarrack Mining Company, Limited 1873-76
Trewartha Tin and Copper Mine 1845-52

MORVAH

Carn Galver Mine 1851-59   and Zennor
Carn Galver Mine 1874 - (1882)
                       and Zennor
Garden Mine 1860 — before 1873
Garden Tin Mine 1853
Morvah and Zennor United Mines 1836-41
                       and Zennor
Morvah Consols 1851-54
Morvah Consols Tin Mining Company, Limited 1871-90
Rosemergy and Morvah Syndicate Limited 1908-15   and Zennor
Rosemergy Cliff about 1758
Wheal Widden 1849

ST. IVES

Wheal Ayr Mine 1847-50
North Battery Tin Mine 1821
British Radium Corporation, Limited 1908-21

vii

Carbisse 1584
Carrack Dews (1810-1838)
Carrack Dews Mine 1861-62
Carrack Dews United Mines 1853-60
Wheal Crack — before 1832
Wheal George 1832-39
Wheal Gift (1860)
Goole Pellas Mine 1876-81
Island Consols 1853
Ludgvan Lease Tin Mine Company 1853-57
Wheal Margery (1760)
Penolva Mine (1822)
Providence Mines 1907
North Wheal Providence Mining Company
1859-73
North Wheal Providence Tin and Copper
Mining Company, Limited 1862-82
Providence Tin Mines, Limited 1907-15
West Providence Mine 1881-91
Wheal Racer, Limited 1907-09
      and Towednack
Wheal St. Aubyn and Tregenna Mine 1847
St. Ives Consolidated Mines, Limited,
1908-25
St. Ives Consols 1818-82
St. Ives Consols (1875) - 1890
(St. Ives Copper Mines) 1687
St. Ives Mines, Limited 1917-22
      and Towednack
South Saint Ives Tin and Copper Mining
Company, (Limited) 1864-65
West St. Ives Mines 1866-72
St. Ives Wheal Allen 1860-68
Wheal Sarah 1838 St. Ives district; may be
      Gulval
Stennack Stamps — before 1876
Tasmanian Exploration Company, Limited
1904-12   and Tasmania
Thermo-Electric, Limited 1912-32
Trelyon Consolidated Mines 1849
Trenwith Mine 1905-08
Trenwith Mine 1917-20
Trenwith Stamps (1792)
Wheal Trenwith 1825-49
Wheal Trenwith 1853-57
Wheal Union 1836 and Towednack
Velenoweth Mine — before 1849 St. Ives
    district; may be Ludgvan
Wheal Venture 1836-39
Wheal Wellesley 1836
Western Worke 1585
Worvas Downs (1810) - (1817)
Worvas Downs 1905-09
Worvas Downs Mine 1860-72

TOWEDNACK
Billia Consols 1864-70
Bray Tin and Copper Mine (1838) - (1848)
Bray Tin Mine — 1822
Brea Consolidated Tin and Copper Mining
Company, Limited 1858-1901
Wheal Bussow 1852
Wheal Buzza (1880)
Wheal Conquer 1859-61
Wheal Conquer Consols 1857
Durlo Mine 1859-64
Georgia Consols 1847-48
Georgia Consols 1850-54
Georgia Consols 1871-73
Giew, opened after 1871, closed by 1909 and
      Lelant
Giew 1917-22
Giew Consolidated Mines 1869 - (1871)
Wheal Lady Down and Conquer 1836
West Wheal Margaret Mining Company,
Limited 1871-72
Wheal Margaret 1798
Wheal Montague Tin Mine 1851-56
Wheal Music 1844 (locations unconfirmed)
Wheal Music Mine 1839
Praed Consols 1850-54
Praed Consols 1860-62
South Providence 1869-72 and Lelant
South Providence 1873-89 and Lelant
Reeth Consolidated Mining Company 1836-52
Reeth Consols 1852-59
Wheal Rose 1854-55
Rosewall Hill and Ransom United Mines
1857-80
Rosewall Hill Mine (1808) - (1815)
Rosewall Hill Mine 1838-42
Rosewall Hill Mine 1876
Rosewall Hill Mining Company 1845-50
Rosewall Stamps 1680
Roswall 1584
West St. Ives Consolidated Tin Mining
Company, Limited 1868-83
Tincroft Consols 1836-41 and Ludgvan
New Tincroft United Mining Company,
Limited 1876-86   and Ludgvan
Old Tincroft Consols Mining Company,
Limited 1874-84
Trevega Mine 1909-15   and Zennor
Trevega Mine, Limited 1907-11 and Zennor
Trevesa and Brea Tin and Copper Mining
Company, Limited 1864-73
Trevidgia Mine 1841-42
Trewey Consolidated, Limited, 1907-10
      and Zennor
Trowan Consols Mine 1846-54
Tyringham Consols Mining Company
1860-64   and St. Ives

ZENNOR

Carn Galver Tin Mining Company, Limited
1871-74   and Morvah
Carnelloe 1862-66
Carnelloe Consols 1853 - (1856)
Carnelloe Mine 1871-74
Wheal Chance and Good Fortune 1844
Wheal Chance Tin Mine 1809
Cleveland Mining Company 1845-58
Wheal Dollar Mine 1823-25
Wheal Dollar Mine 1834-41
West Wheal Fanny Tin Mining Company
1852-53
North Grylls Tin Mining Company, Limited
1864
Wheal Grylls 1860-64
Gurnett's Head Mine 1843-44
Wheal Hope Mining Company 1845-48
Wheal Rose 1893
Rosevale Mine (1910) - 1912
Rosevale (Zennor) Tin Mine, Limited
1912-18
Wheal Sandwich 1836
Great Sperries Consols 1862
                    and Towednack
Wheal Sperries 1836   and Towednack
Great Sperries Consols Tin Mining Company
1853   and Towednack
Treen Copper mine — before 1821
Tregerthen Mine 1872
Treveal Tin and Copper Mine 1836
                    and Towednack
Trewey Downs Mining Company, Limited
1906-07
North United Mining Company 1843-48
Zennor Consols Tin Mine 1873-75

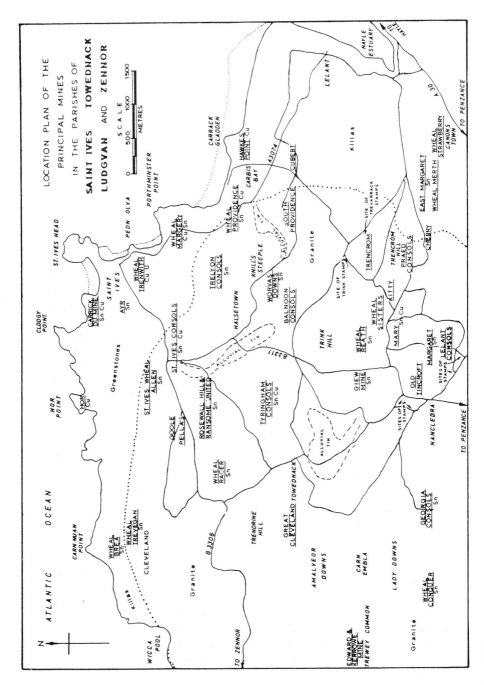

LOCATION PLAN OF THE
PRINCIPAL MINES
IN THE PARISHES OF
**SAINT IVES TOWEDNACK
LUDGVAN AND ZENNOR**

SCALE

0   500   1000   1500
METRES

x

FOREWORD

I

It is now more than a decade since the appearance of the first volume of Cyril Noall's major study, *The St. Ives Mining District*, and some eight years since his untimely death brought to an abrupt end that relentless pattern of research, writing and publication that had characterised his busy life. Inevitably, he had in hand a number of projects at the time of his passing, and in 1989 we collaborated (Philip Payton as editor, Leonard Truran as publisher) to complete and produce, from a manuscript he had left, his *Cornish Mine Disasters*. Although we embarked upon that project with some trepidation, anxious that our production should do Cyril justice and mindful of the inherent delicacy of working upon the fruits of those that have gone before, we were delighted in the response that the volume received. No less an authority than J.A. Buckley declared (in an edition of the Trevithick Society's *Newsletter*) that *Cornish Mine Disasters* was Cyril Noall's most important work, filling as it did a gap in the literature of Cornish mining and social history, while steady sales have attested to the book's popularity amongst the reading public.

Suitably encouraged, we then proceeded to work upon Cyril Noall's other major project left outstanding, his second volume of *The St. Ives Mining District*. And so here at last, some ten years on, we are pleased to present *The St. Ives Mining District: Volume II*, completing what Cyril Noall might himself have considered his most important work — the detailed, painstaking, perhaps definitive, mine-by-mine survey of that part of Cornwall which he knew and loved so well and was for him "home". Spanning the entire period from the eighteenth-century to the years after the Second World War, the book charts the rise and fall of numerous mining ventures, set against the wider fluctuations in copper, tin and other minerals, but also revealing the significance of local events, attitudes and personalities (including a barbed word or two regarding those conservationists who helped to prevent the spread of mining development in the 1960s!). As well as drawing upon the standard secondary sources, Cyril Noall undertook substantial primary research — not least in the files of local newspapers — and it is in his ability to marshall and evaluate the minutiae of mining detail that his scholarship is especially evident. In his introduction, reproduced here in full from Volume I, his ability to provide the overview is also apparent, painting his picture in words of the mining history of "...the old undivided parishes of St. Ives, Lelant, Towednack, Zennor and Morvah, bordering the north-western shore of the Penwith peninsula".

Following the pattern established in Volume I, this volume is organised into three distinct sections, based on the districts of St. Ives, Towednack and Zennor. The acknowledgements, list of abbreviations and sources, and alphabetical listings of mines by parish, are also reproduced here (with only minor adjustment) from Volume I. Additional acknowledgement is due in this

xi

volume to Gerald Williams, who offered encouragement and advice and who drew our attention to Cyril Noall's apparent confusion over the identity of West Providence, providing his own notes on the history of the mine to put the record straight. Assistance with photographic illustrations for Volume II was also provided by Roger Penhalurick at the Royal Institution of Cornwall, as acknowledged in the text.

II

That *The St. Ives Mining District: Volume II* should appear during this year is especially appropriate, for 1993 has been declared "Industrial Heritage Year". Indeed, this publication is a reminder of Cyril Noall's important contribution to the documentation of the industrial heritage of Cornwall, and is Dyllansow Truran's own contribution to the wide range of activity in Cornwall to mark "Industrial Heritage Year". What Cyril Noall would have made of "Industrial Heritage Year" we cannot know, but we do know that he placed great value upon the physical remains of Cornish mining, and we know too that he was a great believer in both the archival and educational functions of museums. And whilst he would have been deeply saddened by the demise of Geevor as a working tin-producer (he had, after all, written the standard history of that great mine), his sorrow at the final passing of mining in his beloved West Penwith may have been tempered by a realisation of the archaeological, educational and indeed economic opportunities offered by the Trevithick Trust enterprise which intends to construct a Cornwall-wide network of museum and interpretation sites of which Geevor is one.

The designation of 1993 as "Industrial Heritage Year" is a cue for people throughout the United Kingdom to celebrate Britain's eighteenth and nineteenth-century Industrial Revolution. In particular, it is an invitation to recognise the importance of the rich diversity of artifacts that have survived from that era, not least the multiplicity of industrial buildings and landscapes that still mark — often in a most striking manner — the old industrial regions of the United Kingdom. And in Cornwall we have a series of industrial landscapes, quite literally from the Tamar to Lands End, which are not only unique but are inextricably entwined in the sense of "Cornishness" and separate identity that pervades our land. The work of Cyril Noall reflects this link between mining heritage and cultural identity, and in his *The St. Ives Mining District: Volume II* we have an intimate, exhaustive account of the history that lies behind one of the most spectacular landscapes in the British Isles.

Philip Payton, Leonard Truran,
Redruth, Cornwall.
28th April, 1993, Trevithick Day

INTRODUCTION

The area covered by this survey embraces the old undivided parishes of St. Ives, Lelant, Towednack, Zennor and Morvah, bordering the north-western shore of the Penwith peninsula. Some of the most varied and beautiful scenery in Cornwall is to be found here, making it today a tourist's paradise, but in the past it was chiefly noted for its connection with the industries of fishing and mining. The district is bounded on the east by that part of St. Ives Bay extending from the ancient fishing port of St. Ives along an indented shore of dark headlands and contrasting golden beaches towards Lelant Towans and the western side of Hayle Estuary. The pleasant woodlands at Lelant, rising above the river, flourish in the shelter of Trencrom Hill, whilst in similar fashion Carbis Bay and St. Ives nestle below the heights of Worvas, Penbeagle and Rosewall. Beyond, the bleak moors and "high countries" of the western parishes sweep away under a wide sky towards the limits of Bolerium. To the north and west these moors command magnificent views of the Atlantic Ocean; but between them and the rugged shore lies a narrow fertile plain patterned with the complicated tracery of an ancient Celtic field system.

The area is rich in prehistoric remains, including hut circles, cromlechs and barrows. It is certain that from Bronze Age times onwards the inhabitants of West Penwith were engaged in the winning of tin, for which the district was very favourably endowed by Nature. Nearly the whole of the peninsula consists of granite; but along its shore runs a narrow band of metamorphosed killas[1] and greenstone, which attains its greatest width at Lelant, being there up to a mile and a half across, but at Rosemergy disappears altogether, the cliffs there being of granite. Around St. Ives, as at St. Just, heavily mineralised lodes traverse the killas and granite around their contact, material from which, eroded by swift-flowing streams, provided the earliest tinners with the alluvial or "stream" tin which they dug from shallow workings. In much later times deep mines were developed on these lodes, usually at or near the granite-killas junction.

In the immediate vicinity of St. Ives this contact zone occurs along an inclined plane sloping very irregularly to the E. and N.E., with an average strike of E. 20 deg. S. The killas overlies the granite, so that mines sunk at surface in the first rock often enter the second in depth. At Wheal Trenwith, for example, the contact is seen in Victory shaft 285′ below sea level; whilst at Cornish shaft and Sump shaft of St. Ives Consols, lying further to the west, it appears at 160′ and 280′ above sea level respectively. It has been calculated that the approximate dip of the granite is 15 deg. N.E. between the surface junction and Cornish shaft, and 33 deg. N.E. between Cornish shaft and Victory shaft; while below the 60 fm. level around Victory shaft the dip becomes much steeper and its strike more easterly. On one side of the contact are seen altered slates and greenstone and on the other quartz-tourmaline and greisen of various types graduating into moderately fine-grained granite. Further west, the granite becomes more coarsely crystalline with large crystals of pale pink and white felspar.

The lodes generally trend E.N.E., the cross-courses, locally termed "trawns," trending nearly N.—S. around St. Ives and a few degrees W. of N. elsewhere. Generally speaking, the lodes, when in granite, produced tin, and copper when in the overlying rocks; but there were some notable exceptions to this rule, as at Wheal Providence and Wheal Sisters, where large amounts of copper were produced from granite country. In addition to these metals, small quantities of uranium were found at Trenwith and South Providence, as well as nickel and cobalt, but except for uranium (for its associated radium) none of these was mined on a commercial scale.

The lodes in the western part of the district were relatively unimportant, and Morvah and Zennor consequently failed to develop any large mines. The principal lode systems were those which gave rise to the mines in the immediate vicinity of the town of St. Ives (Rosewall Hill, St. Ives Consols and Trenwith); south of St. Ives (Tyringham, Trelyon and Margery); Carbis Bay (Balnoon, Worvas and Providence); and the Billia-Giew-Reeth, Sisters and Merth series. In the northern part of the district the lodes cut the granite-killas junction nearly at right-angles, but in the south run sometimes nearly parallel with it. Certain of the coastal mines — notably Margery and Providence — had workings which extended beneath the sea, but were never prosecuted to any great degree there, owing, so it is said, to percolation of salt water through the sea bed, this being in marked contrast to the St. Just submarine mines, which were extremely dry. So far as these explorations went, however, they showed that the ore-shoots pitched eastwards, or away from the killas-granite contact.

An unusual feature of the district was the occurrence of large deposits of ore, quite different in character from the conventional lodes, known as "carbonas." They were found principally in Rosewall Hill, St. Ives Consols and Providence, and always in granite. The carbonas seemed to have but a tenuous relationship to the lode systems in these mines. At. St. Ives Consols, for example, the carbonas were found between the Standard lode and the Bahavella lode running parallel to it on the south. These carbonas were extremely rich and their material largely decomposed, enabling it to be easily removed.

Some authorities likened these carbonas to the irregular ore-bodies in the limestone country of the lead-mining districts; but Cann[2] insisted they were nothing more than a special type of peculiar form of ordinary lodes. In St. Ives Consols they were invariably connected with the Standard lode by a vein, although this vein was very small at the point of junction, sometimes no more than two or three inches wide. The irregularly-shaped portions of the carbonas were apparently formed by the contact of a series of branch veins and the intersection of approximately E. and W. running cross-lodes, with converging cross-courses. It is not clear whether these cross-lodes belong to a later period, as the junctions show only a jumbled mass of ore, from 50 to 70 ft. wide, shading off into the country rock without any distinct boundaries. Much of this material was formed as a replacement of the enclosing rock. The cross-courses were of a subsequent period, as they fault the carbonas, parallel lodes and cross-lodes. Near the cross-courses numerous veinlets rich in cassiterite branch off from the hanging and footwall sides of the carbonas at their junction.

It therefore seems that carbonas developed at points where several lodes intersected and where the nature of the resulting fracture zone allowed the ascending tin and copper-bearing fluids to replace the severely fractured granite. Thus carbonas possess the replacement features of ''pipes and flats'' in that extensive replacement of country rock which did occur, but in their overall attitudes they reflected that of the adjacent lodes. It is also relevant that carbonas tend to have developed close beneath the killas-granite contact, which suggests that the resistant nature of the overlying killas tended to ''bottle-up'' or impound the rising mineral-bearing fluids and force them to react and replace the fractured granite.

The most spectacular of these massive ore bodies was the ''Great Carbona'' of St. Ives Consols, which branched off from the Standard lode at the 77 fm. level, approximately 460 ft. below the surface. Cann's description of it is worth quoting: ''From the point of junction it has been worked about 900 ft. in a direction S. 40 deg. E. and has been followed downward on an incline from the horizontal of 75 deg. W. to a depth of about 600 ft. below the 57 fm. level. The character of the ore varies a good deal with depth. In the upper portion it consists of very hard and compact quartz-schorl rock with cassiterite disseminated in very minute particles. Below, it is composed of quartz and chlorite with a considerable amount of tourmaline. The cassiterite is fairly coarse and associated with a little copper pyrites and mispickel. There also occur, in the lower portions, alternate bands of fluorspar on the footwall side, highly impregnated with fairly large crystals of cassiterite.''[2]

In *British Mining* (1884) Dr. Robert Hunt went very thoroughly into the meaning and origin of this curious word ''carbona.'' Dismissing theories that it may have been derived from a Cornish (Celtic) source, he quoted the following passage from the New Testament published at the English College in Rheims, A.D. 1582, where St. Matthew, c.27, v. 6, is rendered: ''Principes, autem sacerdotum, acceptis argenteis dixerunt: Non licet eos mittere in carbonam'' (But the chief priests having taken the pieces of silver, said, It is not lawful to put them into the carbona, because it is the price of blood.) The carbona was, in fact, the Treasury of the Temple where the people put in their gifts or offerings, and was thus a very appropriate term to apply to unusually large and rich bunches of ore.

The history of the development of mining at St. Ives followed much the same pattern as in other mineralised areas of Cornwall, beginning with streaming for alluvial tin deposits in the valleys and moors. Probably the best known of the ancient stream works from which the local mining industry evolved lay along the valley which runs into the town of St. Ives from the western hills. Its very name, Stennack, means tin bearing ground, the earliest form of which, spelled *Steynek*, dates from as early as 1334.[3] This stream work extended southwards from Hallesveor Moors to Balnoon, taking in the lower part of the present vallage of Halsetown. Another followed the course of the little rivulet which runs from the higher part of the Belyars near Carnstabba Farm, through Tregenna estate and the steep, narrow Primrose Valley to Porthminster beach. The bottoms between Providence and South Providence, at Carbis Bay, and the Nancledra, Trink and Trencrom valleys were also turned over and over again by the ''old men'' with their primitive tools in search of the precious black stones. Further west, there were very ancient stream works at Trewey, in Zennor, and in some of the valleys running from the western moors to the sea. Nearly all traces of these workings have disappeared, and no description exists of them; but Henwood has left an account of one very late example which was being prosecuted in the lower part of Coldharbour Moor, Towednack, around 1872. Beneath a 2½' layer of peat appeared 3' of granitic gravel unequally fixed with blue clay to different depths. Under this lay another strata of gravel 6½' deep, brownish buff above and reddish brown below. The first contained small amounts of detrital cassiterite, and the second angular and fairly rounded masses of tin-bearing veinstone. The underlying bedrock was undulating and of varied hardness, moderate amounts of detrital ore being found in the depressions.[4]

The exploitation of these deposits eventually led to the discovery of the lodes from which their material had been derived, and so enabled true mining to begin. In the early years of underground mining the primitive workings were drained by adits driven from nearby valleys. As the levels began to go below adit buckets and rag-and-chain pumps were progressively used, but with continually increasing depth and extent of the workings the volume of water proved too much for such elementary forms of drainage, so water wheels were used to motivate the pumps, ''flat rods'' often being used to transmit their power over considerable distances.

Around the coast, lodes were readily discovered by their outcrops in the cliffs, on which adits were then driven. One of the earliest and most interesting of these was the ''Western Worke,'' a St. Ives copper mine dating from the year 1585. The famous ''Mines Royal'' had a considerable interest in Cornish copper mining at this time; and ore both from St. Ives and St. Just was shipped off to Neath for smelting from St. Ives. Norden mentions ''Carbisse,'' a mine at St. Ives in 1584; this was presumably located in the vicinity of Carbis Water, being a primitive working on the site of the later Providence Mines. Also working at that time were Bennyon and Hallywoone, in Lelant, and Roswall, in Towednack. Coffen (open cast) mining was extensively practised at this early period on Rosewall Hill, its summit being scored by deep trenches on the backs of the lodes, revealing very plainly the direction of their strike.

Around 1687 Sir Thomas Clarke and others worked copper mines in the St. Ives area. The technique of blasting was introduced into West Cornwall by a German expert about the year 1700 at Trevega Bal; whilst smelting was carried on at St. Ives in 1712 by Eswyn, and by Fayrehoven and Co. in 1714; also by Thomas Morgan. Hicks (the first St. Ives historian) writing in 1722 further mentions a copper house started by one Pollard. In those times, St. Ives was connected with St. Just by a packhorse trackway which ran more or less in a straight line over the moors and hills between; and it seems probable that these smelting works received ore from the far west as well as from the local mines.

As the mines grew deeper new techniques were developed to counter the increasing hardness of the rocks. Improved iron drills with finely tempered cutting edges were made to bore holes in the granite and overlying killas. Due to increasing harness below the zone of weathering, shafts were sunk along the dip of the lode or its "underlie"; thus until recent times shafts were narrow and crooked depending upon the varying attitude of the lode being followed. Lodes and cross-cuts were driven by hand drilling using a "drag round" pattern of holes and black powder. With the advent of machine drilling (the widow maker) and more powerful explosives, this drag round gave way to the "pyramid cut." Stoping of the lode was either "overhand" (with the lode in the roof or back) or "underhand" (with the lode in the floor), with or without stulls. Pillars of ground were left only when the lode was uneconomic; often the roof and floor of a drive would be removed and the track supported on wooden stulls. This timber has now long rotted away and the dangers of entering these old workings is now very great and should on no account be attempted.

Steam power for pumping was introduced into one or two mines in the mid 18th century, notably at Wheal Margaret and Wheal Reeth. It is interesting to note that the original name of the Engine Inn, at Cripple's Ease, near those mines, was the Fire Engine, showing what a great impression the Newcomen machine must have made in that neighbourhood. But steam did not really come into its own until about the 1820's, from which time the mines increased rapidly in depth and output. The middle years of the 19th century saw the industry at its zenith, several thousand persons being employed both above and below ground. Then it was that the lords, like the Praeds of Trevetho, and the adventurers, like James Halse (after whom the mining village of Halsetown took its name) practised the art of transmuting base tin and copper into pure gold, while the miners grubbed for a bare pittance in the bowels of the earth and thought themselves lucky to get an occasional "sturt."

Those were busy, bustling, hard-working times, such as the district never knew before and will never know again, and which lasted all too briefly. By the 1870's the mines were collapsing everywhere, victims of cheap imported Australian and Malaysian tin. Wrote one observer in 1879: "Nothing is plainer than that we are passing through a period of transition at St. Ives. Why, a miner going over the road now is almost as rare a sight as a kilted Highlander, though we used to meet them every day, going to and coming from bal, in droves. The ruins of mines in full work and paying dividends a few years ago, everywhere meet the eye, looking not as picturesquely but quite as forlorn, as the ruins of ancient cities. The old stamps, whose rattling sound was always dinning in your ears, morning, noon and night, are now as silent as the grave. Mines and miners have passed away like a dream, and the next generation will be asking the meaning of all those ruined houses and those monster piles of rubbish.''[5]

By about 1890 the industry was virtually dead in this area. Around 1905, however, an improved price for tin, and the introduction of electric pumping equipment led to a revival, several mines being restarted, but the only ones to make any appreciable returns were Trenwith (of radium) and St. Ives Consols and Giew (of tin.) Of these, only Giew survived the Great War; but it succumbed to economic and labour difficulties in 1922, and with its closing mining at St. Ives came to an end. Water wheels continued to be used to work small, eight-head sets of stamps in the deep valleys surrounding the Penwith granite. Many of these worked for years after the mines had fallen silent, crushing horse-drawn cart loads of tin ore which out-of-work miners laboriously hand-sorted from the great heaps of mine waste which scarred the landscape.

The levels and stopes from whence this material had come filled with water, and ladders and pitwork left in place may still be seen leading down into the crystal clear, blue-green depths of the silent flooded shafts. In place of the rhythmic thump of the hammers on iron drills swung by miners, many of whom ended their days in overseas graveyards, only the drip of water can be heard in the long-abandoned workings. Whether there will ever be a second resurgence must remain a matter for conjecture.

1. "Killas" is a general Cornish term for thermally altered clayey rocks.
2. Cann, F.C. The Mines, Lodes and Minerals of the Stennack Valley, St. Ives. *Trans. Corn. Inst. Min. Eng.*, vol. x, 1917.
3. Pool, P.A.S. *The Place-Names of West Penwith*, 1973.
4. *Jour. Roy. Inst. of Corn.*, vol. iv.
5. *Cornish Telegraph* May 13, 1879.

FIRST SECTION
ST. IVES DISTRICT

ST. IVES WHEAL ALLEN
WHEAL APPLIN
WHEAL AYR (WHEAL GEORGE, ST. IVES EAST CONSOLS)
BAHAVELLA MINE
NORTH BATTERY MINE
THE BELYARS ADIT AND CARNSTABBA HILL
WHEAL BROTHERS
CARRACK DEWS UNITED MINES
WHEAL DREAM
WHEAL FAT
WHEAL FOLLY
NORTH WHEAL FORTUNE
HOR BAL (MUNGREN'S HILL MINE)
ISLAND CONSOLS (WHEAL SNUFF)
LUDGVAN LEASE
WHEAL MARGERY
MURRISH'S, NANKERVIS'S AND TREGENNA STAMPS
PEDNOLVER MINE (NORTH WHEAL PROVIDENCE)
WHEAL QUEEN: WHEAL ST. AUBYN AND TREGENNA
WHEAL RACER
ST. IVES CONSOLS
ST. IVES HARBOUR BEACH WORK
SOUTH ST. IVES
WEST ST. IVES MINE
WHEAL TAVAS
TRELYON CONSOLS
WHEAL TRENWITH
TREVALGAN
TROWAN CONSOLS
WHEAL WELLESLEY
WESTERN WORKE

ST. IVES WHEAL ALLEN

In a field on the north side of the St. Ives—Land's End road, between Hellesveor and Folly Farms, stands an isolated minestack, all that now remains at surface of St. Ives Wheal Allen. It is said that the stack owes its preservation to Lady Hain, wife of Sir Edward Hain, the shipowner, on whose estate it stood, as she much admired its graceful proportions. In a photograph of Hellesveor Chapel, taken in the early 1900's, the old engine house may just be discerned, adjoining the stack on the N.

The mine derives its name from the Allen family of St. Ives, who worked it in 1730. A re-opening appears to have taken place in 1828 under the name of Wheal Folly, *q.v.*, but the principal phase of working commenced in June 1860. The deepest workings (50 fms.) were on a South lode or carbona, which had formerly been drained by a flat-rod from the western engine of St. Ives Consols. The new engine of 30″ cylinder was placed on a shaft on a lode 18 fms. to the N. sunk 19 fms. below shallow adit. In clearing this adit and cutting down the shaft a lode had been found in both ends of the shaft valued at £30 per fm. At this new engine shaft the deep adit would come in 11 fms. below shallow adit.[1]

St. Ives Wheal Allen, with Rosewall Hill in the background   (Noall Collection)

2

The agent's report, signed H. Taylor, of July 10 1862, stated that in Roderick's engine shaft, sinking below the 10, the lode was 9″ wide, worth £9 per fm. In the stones in the bottom of the 20 fm. level E. of Louisa's shaft on Roderick's lode, the lode was 12″ wide, worth £9.10s. per fm. In the 20 E. of Giesler's Flat-rod shaft, the lode was 6′ wide, worth £12 per fm. and still improving. In the winze sinking below the 40 E. of shaft the lode was 18″ wide, worth £8 per fm. They had not yet reached the bottom of the shaft in the shallow adit; it was still full of "attle" (waste rock left by the "old men.") They could see some of the former workings in the W. of the shaft.[2]

On December 29 1864 J. Daniel reported the stope below the 10 worth £4 per fm., and other stopes were valued around £4-5 per fm. The lode in the 40 W. was small, yielding a little tin. The 45 E. was worth £8 per fm. Frederick's stope was working on tribute.[3]

The financial results, meanwhile, had been disappointing, the adventurers being faced with a constant succession of calls. Eventually, at the quarterly meeting held at St. Austin Friars, London, in May 1865, with the cost book looking as cheerless as ever, it was urged that the prospective feature of success lay in sinking the mine to deeper levels. The best levels in the adjacent St. Ives Consols had been the 47 and 57 below adit, which would correspond to the 60 fm. level at Wheal Allen. The purser consequently recommended sinking 20 fms. deeper.[4] At about this time the mine employed 55 men, 8 women and 7 boys. Adit level was 18 fms. and the bottom 58 fms. There was an 18″ stamping engine, in addition to the 30″ pumping engine.[5]

All efforts to put the mine in a profitable state proved unavailing, the falling price of tin adding to the adventurers' difficulties. At the March meeting in 1867 a further call of 8s.8d. per 673rd share was made, bringing the total amount called up since commencement to about £14,000, or £19 per share. Hope springs eternal, however, and a recent discovery made in the adjoining Rosewall Hill mine induced them to believe that something good might be found in their property also, but it was not to be.[6]

Wheal Allen ceased work in 1868, having raised between 1862 and that date 116 tons of black tin. Though it must be classed as one of the more unsuccessful local mining speculations, its abandoned workings were put to new uses some years later. In November 1893 the St. Ives Borough Surveyor announced that he had examined the shaft there and found the water to be 43′ from surface, the flow being 8 gallons per minute. He was instructed to prepare an estimate for cutting an adit to bring the water to the main road and place pipes therein. Men were also to be engaged to explore the North Adit and ascertain the extent of the workings. Agreement was reached with Earl Cowley's trustees the following January to abstract water from the mine.[7]

Wheal Allen is in granite. The loads are known as Roderick's and Carbona; the shafts are Louisa's, Highburrow, Giesler's and New. This mine is identified as Wheal Mary on the O.S. map; Cann similarly refers to it; but no record can be traced of its ever being worked under this name.

1. *Mining Journal* June 30 1860
2. *Cornish Telegraph* July 16 1862
3. *Cornish Telegraph* January 1865
4. *Royal Cornwall Gazette* May 26 1865
5. Spargo, Thomas, *The Mines of Cornwall*, 1865
6. *Cornish Telegraph* March 6 1867
7. Dines, 1956, p.112

WHEAL APPLIN

About 900' S of the Standard lode of St. Ives Consols and Wheal Trenwith and parallel to it lies the Bahevella lode which courses E. 23 deg. N. underlying 5 deg. S. Although poorer in quality than the Standard lode, it was exploited for copper in the clay slate by Bahavella Mine, and for tin in the granite by Wheal Applin. The shafts at the latter were 20 fms. deep, but appear to have been filled in. It seems possible that this mine may have been named after Capt. Phillip Aplin, purser at St. Ives Consols in the 1860's.

WHEAL AYR (WHEAL GEORGE, ST. IVES EAST CONSOLS)

This mine, situated on the high ground to the north of the Stennack Valley, exploited the most northerly of the three great E.-W. mineral lodes which traverse the area, hence called the North lode. A plan dated 1860 also shows a number of lesser lodes coursing roughly E.N.E. and N.-S., but only one was actually worked, the Wheal Ayr lode, coursing E. 22 deg. N. and underlying S. Engine shaft, sited near the eastern end of Wheal Ayr Terrace, was sunk to the 65 fm. level below deep adit (20 fms.) Shallow adit level began at the shaft top and was carried some distance westwards with an air shaft near its western end. Deep adit level extended W. and E., with two air shafts, the drainage cross-cut being driven 100 fms. N. of one of these to the cliff at Porthmeor Beach (120 yards N.W. of Barnoon Cemetery chapel.)[1] Its workings lie principally in greenstone, the produce consisting of both tin and copper.

Wheal Ayr is a very ancient mine, but no record has been traced of its early working. However, the original adventurers bequeathed a valuable boon to the people of St. Ives in the stream of pure water which ran from higher adit level, and was widely used for a public supply. When, therefore, in August 1838 Capt. Charles Thomas inspected the mine, then called "Wheal George," with the object of putting it to work again, the inhabitants were greatly incensed, not only by the threatened loss of this stream, but also by the probable disappearance of an even more important supply at the ancient Venton Ia well above Porthmeor Beach, to which many of the "Downlong" housewives resorted daily with their "patticks," or earthenware water pitchers. On

4

September 8 Capt. J.T. Short noted in his diary: "Last evening at eight o'clock a great concourse of people paraded the streets with an effigy of 'Rover,' which they burnt in front of Richard Penrose's house, and at the same time a great many panes of glass were broken. It is conjectured that this affair took place on account of Richard Penrose bringing a number of miners to clear up an old mine, called Wheal Ayr. By so doing, it is thought that the present supply of water at Ventenear Well would be cut off, which happened at the previous working of the mine, and the well, which formerly gave an abundant supply, is now greatly diminished."

Wheal Ayr engine-house, following its conversion to a dwelling. The building was demolished in 1935 (Noall Collection)

Those residents likely to be affected by the loss of the shallow adit stream at Ayr also resorted to direct action to preserve their rights. More than forty years later, one of those involved — Peter Berriman, through whose land the stream partly flowed — described the event vividly and with pride, as an old soldier might recall a successful campaign of his younger days: "It" — the stream — "had existed as long as any could remember, and the people had been in the habit of supplying themselves from it by means of pitchers and barrels. When it failed, the people assembled and went in search of the stream. They explored Wheal Ayr in which it rose, and found it had gone from the shallow to the deep adit, and so reached the cliff without benefitting anyone. We brought it back, and the water once more flowed through its old course — a blessing to the neighbourhood.''[2] As a result of these determined actions, the attempt to re-open the mine was temporarily abandoned.

However, on May 8 1844 the first piped water supply was brought into St. Ives from the Tregenna stream, as a result of which the old well at Venton Ia was no longer resorted to as frequently by the women with their "patticks". With this difficulty removed, Wheal Ayr was put to work without further opposition, and seems to have been prosecuted on a fairly moderate scale for a few years. It was probably during this period that the very picturesque engine house, with ornamented stone chimney, was erected at Engine shaft to house the 25″ pumping engine. When the mine eventually ceased working, this building was converted to a three-storey dwelling house. It formed a conspicuous landmark, visible for some distance around, and much regret was expressed at its demolition in 1935 to make way for the present Wheal Ayr Terrace.

In August 1860 an attempt was made to re-open the western part of the mine under the name of "East St. Ives Consols," the invocation of that magical name doubtless being regarded as a certain talisman of success by the promoters, but unhappily it failed to have the desired effect. The mine was described as adjoining St. Ives Consols, which lay to the S. and W., St. Ives Wheal Allen to the W., Trenwith to the S., "Carrack Due" to the N., and by the town of St. Ives and the sea eastwards. The sett extended three quarters of a mile on the course of the lodes, held from the Earl of Mornington and Edwin Ley, Esq. The (principal) lode, which averaged 2′ wide, had yielded £700 worth of copper and £2,000 worth of tin when worked by the previous company, yet it did not appear that levels had been driven for any great distance from Engine shaft. Two other lodes, running N. and S., had been wrought on the backs to shallow depth, and the old workings filled in. It was not proposed to work the old mine, but to develop the lodes about 150 fms. further W., where a shallow adit had been brought up to the depth of 8 fms. The lode had been taken away above this level and a sink made below it, in which the lode was 15″ wide, worth 8s. per barrow of 22 gallons. The strata was greenstone on the junction of the granite. Capt. R.S. Bryant, in a report on the intended mine, considered it a "fair speculation."[4]

Meanwhile, the growing town of St. Ives was experiencing a need for an increased water supply. On May 22 1866 the newly formed St. Ives Water Committee decided at its first meeting "to take immediate Steps for the purpose of getting a Reservoir or Tank constructed at Ayr." This was to be fed from shallow adit level principally to serve some new houses built at Barnoon. The reservoir — actually an enclosed surface tank — was built on land leased from the Tregenna estate, the work being completed by Mr. F. Pascoe in 1868 at a cost of £4.4s.6d! Soon after this, the water rights at Ayr were acquired by Mr. Bower, who also owned the St. Ives gasworks at Porthmeor. In 1871, Bower, who at first demanded £20 per annum for the water, offered to supply the town with gas at the exorbitant price of 6s. per cubic feet and with water at 7½% on the income (rates) derived from it. The Council, being at his mercy, was obliged to submit under protest, but bickering between the two parties continued for some time after. The Council also found themselves involved in protracted quarrel with the Earl of Mornington's trustees and the Earl of Cowley regarding a drinking trough erected at Ayr and fed by the Ayr stream; this lasted from 1869 to 1881! and ended with a writ served by representatives of the Earl on the Council to stop them diverting the Ayr stream. A few fragments of this old water system may still be seen at the roadside adjoining the school playing field, whilst the former reservoir has been converted into a garage at the entrance to Parc Bean.

1. Dines, pp. 110-11.
2. *Cornish Telegraph* June 9 1881
3. Report Book, C.R.O., Truro
4. St. Ives Water Committee's Minute Book

BAHAVELLA MINE

This mine lay adjacent to Bahavella farmstead, and 300 fms. S. of Wheal Trenwith. It developed a lode running parallel to the Standard lode in St. Ives Consols and Trenwith, this lode also being opened on by an adit level just S. of Pednolver Point, and in Wheal Applin, S. of St. Ives Consols. In Applin, the lode was in granite, but in Pednolver and Bahavella in metamorphic rocks. Mr. George Treweeks stated in 1904 that small quantities of copper ore were raised at Bahavella.[1] The shafts are said to have had a depth of 60 fms. but their location had been forgotten until, between the wars, the farmer, when erecting a cart shed adjacent to Bahavella Lane, found that he had sited it squarely on top of one of them, the walls of the uncompleted building now serving as a protective fence to its mouth.

1. *St. Ives By The Sea.*

7

NORTH BATTERY MINE

Joseph Carne, writing in the *Transactions of the Royal Geological Society of Cornwall* in 1822 referred to this ancient mine, which was situated close to St. Ives Head. The 7 fm. level was driven 20 fms. beneath the sea. It had recently been set to work again, but with no useful result. The Island (St. Ives Head) is composed mainly of greenstone, through which run several lodes. Traces of early mining may be seen along the northern shore of the headland near the masonry three-gun emplacement completed in August 1860[1] on the side of an earlier fifteen-gun earth battery dating back to Napoleonic times.[2]

1. Capt. J.T. Short's *Diary*
2. Matthews, J.H., *History of St. Ives*, 1892, p.535.

THE BELYARS ADIT AND CARNSTABBA HILL

In the upper part of Belyars Lane, by the entrance to Carnstabba Farm, a stream emerges from an adit and flows by the roadside, through fields and Tregenna woods and down Primrose Valley to Porthminster Beach. The higher part of this stream is covered with large slabs of stone, a remarkable feature now obscured be dense vegetation. This work was ordered to be caried out by the St. Ives Water Committee on August 23 1866, when it was decided to "get a Covered Drain forthwith constructed to take the Stream of Water from the Mouth of the Adit in the Belyars to the Road leading to Corva or as far short of that spot as (we) shall see fit."[1] The object of this cover was presumably to prevent the water being fouled by cattle, as the Tregenna stream was the source of the town's first piped water supply, inaugurated in 1844. The adit itself drains an old mine lying just south of the Belyars — Halsetown footpath, of whose history nothing seems to be recorded.

North of the Halsetown footpath lies Carnstabba Hill, on top of which was a notable coffen, now overgrown and filled in; this led to a small tunnel which ran for some distance under the rocks. The names of the adjoining Bal Rock and Bal Field are said to be derived from the old working.[2]

1. St. Ives Water Committee Minute Book
2. *St. Ives By The Sea*

WHEAL BROTHERS

In January 1830 Mr. Eldred Roberts of St. Ives offered for sale by private contract 33/62nd shares in "Huel Brothers Tin Mine, situate in the parish of Saint Ives." The mine was said to exploit the Wheal Reeth lodes, which had been, and were still giving a great profit, and lay in the immediate vicinity of Balnoon, which was also making a good profit.[1] The sett was, in fact, located at Westaway, a tenement in the valley between Worvas and Trink Hills.

8

Wheal Brothers is an ancient mine, but nothing has been recorded of its early history. Its last known period of working ran from about 1824-30, a 22½" cylinder engine being installed at the close of 1828.[2]

1. *Royal Cornwall Gazette* January 9 1830
2. Jenkin, A.K.H., *Cornish Mines and Miners*, i

CARRICK DEWS UNITED MINES

The picturesque craggy headland at the western end of Porthmeor Beach, St. Ives, is popularly known as "Man's Head" from the fancied resemblance to that object of a large rock on its summit; but its old Cornish name is Carrack Dhu (Black Rock), often contracted in popular speech to Carthew. On rising ground just behind the headland there could be seen, until the early years of this century, the ruins of two engine houses belonging to an old copper mine which rejoiced in the somewhat eccentrically spelt name of "Carrack Dews," but only the base of their walls now remains. The adit portal is at the base of the cliff just west of the headland.

Operations appear to have commenced here at quite an early period, probably stimulated by the discovery of lodes in the cliff, as happened elsewhere around the Cornish coast. The sett is known to have been worked by a party of poor men in 1810 and again in 1824, who, without the aid of machinery,

Carrack Dews United Mines; sometimes spelt Carrick Du and known locally as Carthew
(Courtesy Royal Institution of Cornwall)

9

raised a considerable amount of copper over a depth of less than six fathoms from surface. It was again re-opened by a party of poor men in 1837-8, when more copper was broken from a greater depth, but the operation came to an end when water overwhelmed the workings.

Clearly, no further development was possible until a pumping engine had been installed; and with this object in view the property was taken over in 1853 by a concern known as "The Carrack Dews United Mines." This new enterprise was actually put on in the same week that witnessed the rebirth of two other old St. Ives mines — Wheal Trenwith and Wheal Margery.[1] In September, a meeting of shareholders in London was informed that, in addition to numerous lodes already discovered and opened upon, the captain had found a rich copper vein, specimens from which were displayed for their gratification. The captain stated that the work done by the previous miners was of such an extent as would materially lessen the expense of future working, while discoveries made during the short period he had been on the mine had so convinced him of its value that he had doubled his own interest in the undertaking. It was resolved to increase the number of miners forthwith, and to purchase an engine. Three tons of ore had already been raised in the brief time they had been at work. Engine shaft was sunk twenty fathoms and various buildings contracted for.[2]

An unusual incident which strikingly illustrates the character this little cliffside mine was reported in the Press in 1856. On September 17 the young son of Capt. William Grenfell of the brigantine *Union*, when bathing with other boys went out to the rock Gowna, in Porthmeor Cove to gather mussels, but when returning lost his footing, and the undertow began to carry him out to sea. By the cries of his companions, the alarm was carried to "Carrackdue Mine," and one of the miners named Trevorrow quickly descended the cliff and plunged into the water. Seizing the drowning boy, he brought him to shore and took him to the first neighbour's house, where medical assistance was soon secured and successfully employed. It was said that Trevorrow's gallant act deserved the award of the Royal Humane Society's medal.[3]

This period of working lasted seven years, during which time (actually from 1856-60) 1,120 tons of seven per cent copper ore and five tons of black tin were sold. The principal lode coursed about E.N.E. being in metamorphosed killas and greenstone.[4] The author has in his possession the whim drawing account book for this mine covering the period March 8 1856 to April 9 1860, when operations ceased. At the beginning of this period stuff was being raised from the 40, 50, 60 and 70 fm. levels; but after May 1859 only the 30 and 40 fm. levels on Eley's lode were producing ore, showing that the lower part of the mine had been abandoned. The mine was listed by J. Williams in 1861 in his *Directory* as "Carrack Dew." It was in 7,500 shares the secretary being C.J. Eley, purser W. Hollow and agent Martin Dunn; its office was at 4 Adams Court, Old Broad Street, London.

The sale of materials from this mine was advertised to take place on July

31 1861. These included "one excellent bright 36" cylinder Pumping Engine, with one Boiler, ten tons; one 24" Winding and Stamping Engine, with 10 ton Boiler, in first-class condition, perfect as new — 10 head Stamps attached; one powerful Crusher; 2 Capstans and 2 Shears; 3 Balance-bobs, one V-bob, complete; 120 fms. of 7" Pumps and 40 of 5" do; 70 fms. Flat Iron Rods; 50 fms. Wood Flat Rods; 70 do. Pitch Pine Main Rods and Plates and Faggotted Caps; 65 fms. Bucket Rods; 120 do. Bridge and Flat Railroad Iron; 80 fms.

Carrack Dews United Mines; a page from the Whim Drawing Account Book, 1858
(Noall Collection)

11

4″ Cast and Zinc Air Pipes; 350 do. Wood Air Pipes; Cast Iron Air Machine; 160 do. Iron and Wood Stave Ladders and Skip Road; 2 Horse Whims, Machine and Horse Whim Kibbles; 2 Iron Skips; 3 Iron Tram Waggons (good); and Wood Tin House and Flooring, nearly new, 47′ long, 21′ wide.''[5]

Half a century after its closing the mine gave an unexpected reminder of its almost forgotten existence when, in 1909, the ground near the pathway leading from Porthmeor Beach to Carthew Point subsided and disclosed an old shaft. Because of the danger to walkers, stops were at once taken to make it secure.[6]

1. *Cornish Telegraph* May 25 1853
2. *Cornish Telegraph* September 11 1853
3. *Royal Cornwall Gazette* September 19 1856
4. Dines, p.110.
5. *Royal Cornwall Gazette* July 26 1861
6. *St. Ives Weekly Summary* April 10 1909

WHEAL DREAM

This curious place name appears to have been humorously bestowed on that part of St. Ives lying between the New Pier and Bamaluz Point in allusion to a drainage adit driven from the northern end of the harbour below Quay Street to the boulder strewn beach at Bamaluz Cove. This adit formed part of the scheme devised by John Smeaton for sluicing accumulated sand from the harbour by means of a reservoir under the church, supplied by the Stennack River, and a series of wooden launders running along to the root of the Old or Smeaton's pier which he built in 1770. This work was not carried out until 1798, as the following entry from the account book of the Harbour Trustees shows: ''Making an adit, and building a reservoir, and laying sanders to clear the pier of sand, etc., £646.12s.6d.''[1] This proved highly effective at first, but was allowed to fall into disuse. In 1895, however, when the town was being sewered, the adit was cleared to permit an outfall pipe to be laid through it. This enabled an old salt to walk through Smeaton's adit for the second time in his life, the first being in 1825, when he was a boy of ten.[2] Tradition says that when it was first made, smugglers made frequent use of the adit to bring contraband to the inn on the harbour side of Quay Street undetected by the Preventive men, the goods being hauled up through an aperture resembling the flue of a fireplace. The adit was often referred to by the old people as ''Cocking's Hole,'' Porth Cocking being an alternative name for the Fore Sand. Needless to say, no output statistics are available for Wheal Dream; but one may safely assume that experienced Cornish miners were employed in driving this very *un*keenly little bal.

1. Quoted in *Report on St. Ives Bay, Cornwall*, by Capt. James Vetch, R.E., F.R.S., 1847
2. *St. Ives Weekly Summary* July 27 1895

WHEAL FAT

Several references to this mine are to be found in an account book kept by Nathaniel Anthony of St. Ives. Thus, on February 26th 1778: "Paid Wheal Fat cost 6s.11½d." On December 27th of that year a further sum of 11s.3d. was debited to "Wheal Fatt," the final call of 7s.11½d. being paid on February 6th 1781.

WHEAL FOLLY

The *Royal Cornwall Gazette* of November 22 1828 announced that a copper mine called "Wheal Folly," in the parish of St. Ives, was to be set to work immediately. Folly Farm adjoins the Land's End road about a mile west of the town. The mine cannot with certainty be identified, but may have been St. Ives Wheal Allen during an early phase of working.

NORTH WHEAL FORTUNE

In *Mines and Miners of Cornwall* Dr. Hamilton Jenkin records that during the 1920's small mine dumps could be seen adjoining the footpath leading from Trenwith Lane to Corva Farm (they are still there) and that a subsidence nearby had revealed the back of a shallow adit whose portal lay in a marshy field north of the (former) tennis courts — that is, at the southern end of Bahavella Farm. These remains are believed to mark the site of a small mine known as North Wheal Fortune. A cost book, formerly in the possession of Sir Edward Hain, of St. Ives, gives some interesting particulars of its history.

In 1823 Hayle Foundry supplied the adventurers with timber, whilst John Stevens and pare were employed in erecting the engine and dropping a lift. At a meeting held on May 19 1823 "at the sign of the Sheaf of Wheat, St. Ives," they resolved to case down the shaft, fork the water, clear up the mine, sink the south shaft and drive north to cut the lode.

On January 1 1824 Mr. William Smitham was appointed captain and manager, and instructions were given him to clear up the adit shafts and set tutwork bargains and tribute pitches. At their next meeting on April 13 it was decided immediately "to drive an addit to the mine to be taken up the eastern corner of the Field called the Billiards (Belyars) field in Bahavella Estate." Items of expenditure incurred between then and October 23 that year included: "To building and covering the Moor house, 10s. For searching for the Tail of the Addit, 7s. For boring pump, 14s. Sinking in the shaft in Mr. Rosewall's field. For 25 Sheafs of Reed. to Mr. Jno. Richards, Timber & Midsummer pole. (Presumably a pole supplied at Midsummer.) To Mr. James Nicholas for Reed & Rope, 7s.6d. To Thatching the Moor House, 4s.6d."

On August 22 1929 it was decided to make a call of 20s. per 1/64th share in order to clear up "the old Rag and Chain shaft (if the water will permit.)" When the bottoms had been cleared and examined another meeting would be convened "to prepare and regulate the future proceedings of the mine." Apparently the outcome of this exploration proved unsatisfactory, the cost book — and presumably also the mine — coming to an end soon after September 1829.

HOR BAL (MUNGREN'S HILL MINE)

At Hor Point, one of the famous "Five Points" comprising the beautiful westward view from Clodgy, there may still be seen some surface remains of an old mine which, by reason of its situation must have had a highly picturesque appearance. The old access road is still used by anglers and others visiting the headland, and the coastal footpath also passes close by it. A local farmer once informed the writer that he had been told by an old man called Boorman, who lived at Hellesveor, that Hor Bal (to give it its popular name) was also known as Mungren's Hill Mine. When they were erecting the engine, sixteen horses had to be employed to draw the boiler through Pednanvounder Lane to the site; it was not lashed to the wagon in the usual way, but left loose, so that if it overbalanced as they were descending the steep mine road the horses and men would not be dragged with it over the cliff. According to another version of the story collected by a St. Ives resident from an old man called Major, no less than 37 horses were used in the operation. They were accompanied by a gang of labourers who removed one stone hedge of the narrow lane in advance of their passage and rebuilt it after the task was complete.

See also under West St. Ives Mine.

ISLAND CONSOLS (WHEAL SNUFF)

The *Cornish Telegraph* of September 21 1853 carried the following news item: "Important Mineral Discovery at St. Ives — It appears that for some time past traditions have existed respecting the existence of a very rich lode somewhere on the shore at about *half-tide* on the beach at the back of St. Ives. Latterly, these have been revived, and the other day, a party, consisting of about forty working miners and mine agents, after securing the proper grants, combined to search for it. Very fortunately for them, they have been rewarded by discovering an extraordinarily rich east and west tin lode. It is composed pricipally of killas, about two feet wide, and is very similar to the lodes in West Providence, like which mine it is confidently expected this will turn out. By its direction it must run into Carrack Dhu sett, thereby considerably enhancing the value of that speculation. We are never better pleased than when we see a thing of this kind fall into the hands of working miners, who are very often the best judges of lodes. It is intended, we believe, to throw the mine open into a large number of shares, and to invite capitalists to join them in carrying out what appears to be the best speculation ever started in Cornwall. It is easy to see that however good such a thing may be, when it requires capital to commence operations, very little can be provided by working men, and this must be the case here, but every man is determined to retain as large a share as his means will afford, and each seems confident of the result. This mine is to be called 'The Island Consols.' "

The late Sir Edward Hain, in a footnote to his copy of this report, stated that he believed it to be "a mining joke of the period." No doubt humour was intended by the hyperbole with which it was garnished; but the Island Consols did actually exist, though better remembered locally under its alternative name of "Wheal Snuff," derived from the brownish-yellow colour of the cliff at the Island end of Porthmeor beach where the adit was located. Its entrance was covered by the incoming tide each day; and although they built a wood collar and smeared it with candle clay, the water found its way in, causing the mine to be abandoned.[1]

In 1907, when a new mine was put on at St. Ives widely suspected of being a fraudulent venture, the following snippet appeared alongside its flamboyant prospectus in the local paper: "Another 'Bal' to be Started! — We are informed, that a syndicate has been formed between the members of Mr. E. Daniel's basket shop, to acquire and work the old mine situate near Porthmeor, and known by the old people under the name of Wheal Snuff. The directors are Messrs. T. Richards, M. Andrews, T. Jacobs, M. Trevorrow, J. Freeman and R.D. Trevorrow. The capital is to be £5,000, all of which is subscribed, and operations will be started on the next neap tides."[2] Now, that really *was* a mining joke, and a witty piece of satire, to boot, aimed at Wheal R----, whose foolish shareholders would have done far better to have sunk *their* £5,000 in the sea off Porthmeor!

1. *St. Ives Times* September 9 1921.
2. *The Western Echo* January 26 1907.

LUDGVAN LEASE

This mine was worked by a scrip company with offices (in 1853) at 114 Bishopsgate Street, London, E.C.3., the secretary and purser (pro tem 1853) being Robert Hounsell and the manager (1854) Capt. Thomas Wallis. Its capital consisted of 20,000 10s. shares, the company issuing share certificates to bearer. The shares were offered for sale in October 1853 at 10s. each, "without further call or liability," supported by a favourable report from William Fitze and a claim that good stones of tin had been found in the three lodes opened.

The offer stated that "to prevent any but *bona fide* applicants applying for shares in this legitimate undertaking," scrip certificates had been prepared for delivery by the directors, so that applicants could receive the number of shares they wanted when applying. Shares were also obtainable from the secretary.

Although situated at St. Ives, the mine took its name from the Domesday manor of Ludgvan Lease in the parish of Ludgvan, but which manor held extensive lands and privileges in St. Ives. The workings lay in a piece of ground immediately west of St. Ives Consols, between the two roads leading to St. Just and Trevalgan, extending as far west as the lane leading to Trevesa (Trevega). The sett was held for 21 years at 1/18th dues, from the Dowager Countess of Sandwich and the Duke of Cleveland. In January 1854 a correspondent reported that one of the three lodes was being worked. It was three feet wide and produced ore (tin) worth £80 per ton, and it was hoped to pay a dividend the same year. Three weeks later the manager reported the clearing of an old shaft on the lode, adding that the ground was favourable for sinking.

The shares were listed in the *Mining Journal* among those of the producing mines from January 1854 to November 1856. In November 1857 it was reported that the mine was "still idle, or nearly so, nor does there seem much chance of it again soon resuming operations."[1]

1. *Mining Journal* October 29 1853, January 14 1854, January 21 1854, February 11 1854, March 4 1854, November 21 1857 (per Mr. Justin Brooke).

WHEAL MARGERY

One automatically associates submarine mines in Cornwall with St. Just, but several were located in other parts of the county. One such was Wheal Margery, at St. Ives, a very ancient mine, whose sett encompassed a stretch of cliff to the S. of Porthminster Point, extending inland through the grounds of the present Treloyhan Manor Hotel. An early reference to it occurs in a report drawn up in 1782 by the celebrated John Knill and others regarding the construction of a proposed new road at St. Ives. This was to run "from the corner of Mr. Anthony's Cellar upon the Beach, & so through the Warren, & through the Ground beyond the new Stamping Hill so as to come out into the present Road at a small distance to the Northward of Wheal Margery Mine."[1] The mine would actually appear to have been put to work in the 1770's, for the *Mining Journal* of September 1 1849 stated that it had been "partially worked" about 80 years before with a small pressure engine, and made a profit of between £70-80,000.

It seems likely that operations were at first restricted to the land, and not extended under sea. Clear evidence for this view may be found in an advertisement for the sale of the mine's materials in 1817, which stated that

MINE MATERIALS.

◆

TO be SOLD by AUCTION, on MONDAY, the 22d inst. at Ten o'clock in the Forenoon, at WHEAL MARGERY, in the Parish of *St. Ives*,

ALL THE

MATERIALS

ON THAT MINE;

Consisting of 47 9-feet, 4-inch Pumps, with lead rings and flanch bolts suitable thereto ;
　　One 4 feet 3-inch Clackpiece ;
　　One 4 feet 3 inch Windbore ;
　　One...... 3-inch H. Plunger piece and
　　　　　　Windbores ;
　　One 9 feet 3-inch Plunger pole ;
　　One 10 feet 6¼-inch ditto ;
　　One 9 feet 7 inch Plunger case, with stuff-
　　　　　ing box to suit the 6¼-inch
　　　　　pole ;
　　One 9 feet 3-inch Working Barrel ;
　　One 6 feet Plunger case and Stuffing box
　　　　　to suit the 3-inch pole;
　　Several cast iron Air Pipes ;
　　About 19 fathom of faggoted Iron Rods,
　　　　　1-inch square;
　　About 13 fathom ditto 1½-inch ;
　　About 18 fathom ditto ¾ ditto ;
　　A Pressure Engine complete, with 6¼-inch
　　　　　pole ;
　　A good Oak Bob, with Guagen, Plummer
　　　　　blocks and Brasses ;
　　Duck and Drake Bobs complete ;
　　Three good Whims, (11 feet Cage)
　　Three Whim Ropes, and two Iron Kibbles;
A great quantity of Timber and Plank, great part of which is nearly equal to new, for Mining or Building.
Also a quantity of Oak Timber, Hutches, Barrows, Kieves, Streakes, Chests, &c. &c.
A good Smith's Bellows, 30-inch; Anvil 1 cwt. 2 qr. Vice 35 lbs. A good screwing Stocks ; Tinners' and Smiths' Tools, &c. &c.

The whole of the above Pumps are equal to new, having been in use but a short time, and the water in the Mine being pure.

Dated Dec. 8, 1817.

Advertisement detailing the sale of mine materials at Wheal Margery, December 1817
(Noall Collection)

17

the pumps were equal to new, having been in use but a short time, "and the water in the Mine being pure" — *i.e.*, uncontaminated by salt, which would have corroded them. It is a well known fact that the submarine workings of Wheal Margery, unlike those of the St. Just mines, were subject to considerable percolation from the sea bed. Other items offered in the sale included cast iron air pipes, about 19 fms. of faggoted iron rods, one inch square; a pressure engine complete with 6¼" pole; a good oak bob "with Guagen, Plummer blocks and Brasses;" duck and drake bobs; three good horse whims (11' cage); three whim ropes and two iron kibbles; timber; and tools.[2]

Following this suspension, Wheal Margery appears to have remained idle for about eleven years; but in November 1828 it was announced that "two mines, one tin, the other copper, called Wheal Margery and Wheal Folly, both in the parish of St. Ives," were to be set to work immediately.[3] Margery, it should perhaps be pointed out, was the copper mine. Some curious details regarding this working were extracted some years ago by the late Dr. A.K. Hamilton Jenkin from the mine's cost book, once in the possession of Sir Edward Hain, but now lost. They include the following: October 1828: "Fixing a set of Roolers (rollers) in whim shaft." February 1829: "Wheal Penwith adventurers for a Chest, 7s." "Stephen Major & Co. 12 days assisting about the Engine at New Quay and St. Ives at 2/6 per day." "For expenses ordered the Masons at sundry times and on laying the foundation stone of the Engine House." (Drink money allowances!) "St. Ives Harbour dues on the Engine, £2." Among the working expenses, 1828-30, may be mentioned: "Quils (500—1,000 a month) at 6d. a 100." (These were used in blasting.) "Powder 8d. a lb." This working came to an end in 1831, and among the materials sold on 13-14 April were air pipes and poppet heads, the buyers including Wheal Elizabeth and Wheal Adelaide adventurers.

In September 1849, when Trelyon Consols (*q.v.*) was launched, its promoters purchased the sett of Wheal Margery with the object of bringing the latter's deep adit under the Wheal Venture part of Trelyon Consols in order to drain five E.—W. and two N.—S. tin and copper lodes. It seems doubtful whether this was ever done; and when Wheal Margery re-started in 1853 its sett was sold back to the adventurers in that concern for £200. During May of that year it was announced that engines were to be erected forthwith on Margery and the enterprise carried on with spirit, ensuring a considerable demand for labour.[4]

In May 1856 it was reported that the mine had made good progress during the previous twelve months, giving the possibility of a dividend at the next account, but it was thought more prudent, with so much ore being broken, to use any profits to increase their crushing and stamping power.[5] Unfortunately this encouraging performance was not maintained; and in December 1857, with the cost book showing a four months' loss of £1,621.15s.10d., a call of £2 per 1024th share was made.[6] With results continuing poor, dues were suspended by favour of the Earl of Mornington, the lord, in October 1859.[7] The May account for 1860, however, showed a quarter's profit of £538, enabling a dividend of 10s. to be paid.[8] By October, dues were again being remitted to the lord, although the accounts had slipped back into the red. A guinea was paid to Mr. S. Higgs, jun., for the use of his patent right for precipitating copper.[9] During 1861 some adventurers began relinquishing shares.

At a meeting held on February 4 1863 attention was called to a pamphlet recently circulated by Mr. Henry Viner among the "distant" — non-Cornish — shareholders reflecting on the conduct of the purser and management generally. The meeting resolved that, believing Viner's pamphlet and letters to be written in a malicious spirit, they wished to record their full confidence in Mr. Higgs' conduct of the mine, adding that "from his well known integrity and high commercial position, it would be quite unnecessary to pass this resolution, but for the satisfaction of the distant shareholders to whom Mr. Higgs cannot be personally known."

However, resolutions could not make dividends, and the cost book showed another adverse balance, of £694. The agents reported the 122 fm. level extended 13 fms. 3 ft. E. of the American shaft, the lode for the last 3 fms. and in the end worth £7 per fm. America shaft lay near the cliff; and according to Henwood the 120 (sic) level was eventually driven 121 fms. under the sea. The 110 fm. level E. was not producing sufficient ore to value, but in No. 1 winze, 3 fms. 2 ft. below the level, the ground was worth £8 per fm., sinking at £6.10s. per fm. Four fms. further E. they were stoping in the bottom, the lode worth £14 per fm. The western end of the 110 was unproductive, but in one place three men were stoping the bottom above where the lode was worth £15 per fm. A trial rise put up in the back of the 40 E. of the American shaft was 8 fms. above the level; the lode for nearly the whole height was poor, but had recently improved, now worth £7 per fm. They were employing 24 men on tutwork, and also had 12 pitches with 32 men on tributes varying from 6s.8d. to 13s. in the £. Generally, the points had slightly improved, but all speculative operations had been curtailed, activity being confined to the more promising places.[10]

By January 1865 the underground labour force had increased to 124—58 on tutwork and 66 on tribute. Two months' sale of copper ore had about met cost for that period. They proposed extending the 142 level E. and W. under some good ore ground which had been driven through in the level above, in expectation of opening up further good tribute ground.[11]

A call of 10s. per 960th share was imposed in May 1865. The agents (Richard James and William Rogers) reported Wellesley Engine shaft sunk 7' below the 122 fm. level, the lode 3' wide and of healthy appearance, yielding a large quantity of mundic, with some copper ore. There was little doubt of having a course of ore under this bed of mundic, as this was almost invariably the case. The 122 level was communicated with this shaft from the American, through which they intended to let the water flow, and so do away with 50 fms. of pitwork in the American, considerably relieving the engine. The American Flat Rod shaft had been set to sink by 9 men from the 142 level to the 152; these workers had also contracted to cut ground for barrow road, winze plot, bearers and cistern, and put in a drawing lift and penthouse for £230. the 132 E. had been driven more than 40 fms. into ore ground. A rise was being put up in bavk of the 132 to hole a winze partly sunk in the bottom of the 122. In the 100 E. the lode was "hove" by a cross-course, and six men were cross-cutting S. to find it. "This, in our opinion, is a point of great importance, as this is the only place (where) we have seen this cross-course below surface; therefore the lode has not been seen to the E. of it anywhere. This is a new feature in the mine, and, if found good at this level, can be easily cut at all the other levels; therefore we should have a new mine laid open for 140 fms. high. We need not remind you that these cross-courses often improve the lode, and make it very valuable."[12]

Results, as opposed to expectations, continued disappointing. In June it was claimed that the loss on working was mainly due to the very low produce of the ore raised.[13] During that year Spargo gave the depth of adit at Engine shaft as 35 fms., and depth under 140 fms. The labour force comprised 112 men, 31 females and 10 boys. The mine possessed a 30″ pumping engine and a 25″ stamping and winding engine.

The account for four months ending June 1866 (reported in November) showed a debit of £797.4s.9d., leading to a call of £1 per 715th share. The American shaft had been sunk to the 155 fm. level, the last 2½ fms. yielding 2½ tons of black tin. The 155 W. was worth £12 per fm. and the back of the 155 E. £15 per fm. They had 25 tributers working on copper at an average of 12s.6d. in the £, a total of 60 men being employed underground. Mr. S. Higgs, the purser, stated that over £97,000 had been spent in calls paid in and money received for ores sold in developing the mine, with as yet no profit accruing to the adventurers. He tried to comfort them by referring to neighbouring Providence, where £102,000 had been spent in 16 years before any dividends were distributed, since when she had paid more than £90,000; it was equally probable that with a little further patience Margery might participate in similar satisfactory results. But how could this be, with the shadow of the coming mining depression already falling across the land?[14]

In January 1867, with calls of £1 still being made each quarter, the Crown relinquished its dues in respect of the submarine section, and Earl Cowley was expected to do the same in regard to his rights. "The fact is, mineral owners who do not give up dues in calling mines simply cut the throats of the geese who lay golden eggs for them." The agents had been greatly disappointed in that a change from copper to tin in the bottom of the mine, where they were nearing the granite, had not been maintained, as they had hoped to have a good tin mine there. The lode in the 155 E. had fallen in value, and the tin in the 155 W. had changed again to copper, while at the shaft bottom the lode was not nearly so good, but still maintained its size, being 6′ wide.[15]

A slight improvement occurred in August. In the American shaft, 9 fms. below the 155, there were mixed patches of lode and killas more than 5' wide, the leading part, 2½" wide, being clearly defined with an improving appearance, worth £20 per fm. for tin for length of shaft, 12'; the granite had not yet been reached. In the 155 E. of the American shaft the lode was worth £12 per fm. for copper ore. 27 men were working on tribute at 12s.6d. in the £. These improvements led Mr. Higgs to adjourn a special meeting called to decide the future of the mine, to a later date, their hopes being pinned on a favourable change when the granite was reached. Hope was certainly needed at that time, for the call had been fixed at £1.10s. per 702nd share, defaulting shareholders owed £443 and the mine was heavily in debt to the bankers (Messrs. Bolithos).[16]

Disaster struck the mine on August 15 1868, when a boiler explosion resulted in the death of Abraham Craze, one of the engine-men. The boiler in question belonged to the pumping engine installed when Wheal Margery was re-started in 1853; damaged in an earlier, non-fatal explosion around the year 1860, it had been repaired but its condition, particularly that of the tube, was regarded by some as suspect. The engine was looked after by three engine-men, each working an eight-hour shift. The three were John Vivian, of St. Erth; Abraham Craze, jun., of St. Ives; and Digory Penhall, of Phillack. On Sundays, however, the normal eight-hour routine was not observed; and on the day of the explosion — a Sunday — John Vivian, who came on duty at eight a.m., was not relieved by Craze until 9.30 p.m. Thirteen and a half hours is a very long spell to put in at so monotonous and yet exacting a job as engine-minding; and by reducing Vivian's efficiency and watchfulness probably contributed to the accident.

At the inquest on Craze evidence was adduced to prove that Vivian had tested the "feed" (water supply) to the boiler a few minutes before handing over to Craze, yet expert examination of the wreckage seemed to show that the tube had become overheated through lack of water. There being consequently some doubt as to what had actually happened, the jury returned a verdict that "Abraham Craze was killed by boiling water and steam which was accidentally thrown over him by the bursting of a boiler; but whether such bursting and explosion of the said boiler were the result of negligence or otherwise, there is not sufficient evidence to show." Some idea of the primitive conditions prevailing on this old mine is given by the fact that Abraham Craze, fatally scalded under the arms, over the back and around the neck, was obliged to walk back to him home at St. Ives — nearly a mile distant — before receiving any medical care. He died about ten the following morning, convinced that the accident was the result of his comrade's failure to ensure that the "feed" had been properly maintained.

This disastrous explosion sealed the fate of Wheal Margery. The adventurers, already wearied by incessant calls, decided to call it a day; and on September 4 offered the setts, leases and materials for sale in one lot.

Included were the 45″ cylinder pumping engine; a 20″ winding, stamping and crushing engine; and about 120 tons of pitwork.[17] The mine was soon after dismantled, one of the engines being purchased by Providence Mines to operate their new man-engine. At the final winding-up of the company in June 1873 the adventurers divided 12s. per share, derived from the sale of materials.[18]

For many years thereafter the mine dumps provided useful road metal for the St. Ives Borough Council. Then, in 1891, Mr. (later Sir) Edward Hain, the shipowner, built Treloyhan Manor on its site as his private residence, making a thorough clearance of the last surface remains when laying out the grounds, so that virtually nothing is to be seen today of this interesting old bal save the adit in the cliff at Leigh Cove.

Wheal Margery lay in metamorphosed killas, overlying granite. The principal lode coursed about E.35 deg. N. underlying 26 deg. S.E., copper being found in the higher levels and tin in the lower. The shafts were known as High Burrow, Flat Rod and America. Dines gives the output from 1854 to 1870 as 16,400 tons of 5% copper ore, 100 tons of black tin and 35 tons of pyrite. The mine may have raised much larger amounts of metal during earlier periods, but no records of these survive.

1. Matthews, J.H., *History of St. Ives* (1892) p.489
2. *Royal Cornwall Gazette* December 1817
3. *Royal Cornwall Gazette* November 22 1828
4. *Cornish Telegraph* May 25 1853
5. *Cornish Telegraph* May 28 1856
6. *Cornish Telegraph* December 16 1857
7. *Royal Cornwall Gazette* October 21 1859
8. *Cornish Telegraph* May 30 1860
9. *Cornish Telegraph* October 10 1860
10. *Royal Cornwall Gazette* February 13 1863
11. *Cornish Telegraph* February 1 1865
12. *Cornish Telegraph* May 31 1865
13. *Royal Cornwall Gazette* June 6 1865
14. *Cornish Telegraph* November 7 1866
15. *Cornish Telegraph* January 30 1867
16. *Cornish Telegraph* August 14 1867
17. *Cornish Telegraph* August, and October 7 1868
18. *Cornish Telegraph* June 25 1873

MURRISH'S, NANKERVIS'S, HELLESVEOR, NANJIVEY AND TREGENNA STAMPS

The Stennack River, which rises in Bussow Moors and flows eastwards through the Stennack Valley to emerge on the beach below St. Ives churchyard wall was made to drive a number of water stamps and grist mills on its way to the sea. Two sets of stamps, Murrish's and Nankervis's, were sited near the present St. Ives reservoir, with a third set just below in Hellesveor Moor and a fourth further down the valley at Nanjivey.

In notes for a talk to the St. Ives Old Cornwall Society in 1926, Dr. Hamilton Jenkin stated that stamps were working "about 50 years ago" (c. 1876) "where Lady Hain's garage now stands." These were known as Tregenna Stamps, and presumably stamped stuff from Wheal Margery.[1] He gave no indication as to how they were powered.

1. Dr. A.K. Hamilton Jenkin's Notebook, I, pp. 27, 39, CR0, Truro; MS, p. 23, in the Hamilton Jenkin collection, Redruth Public Library; *Mines and Miners of Cornwall*, Vol. I, 1961

PEDNOLVER MINE (NORTH WHEAL PROVIDENCE)

In photographs of St. Ives taken during the 19th and early 20th centuries the engine house of a mine standing on the blue-black rocks of Pednolver Point, between the harbour and Porthminster beach, appears as a striking feature, its presence in this situation, almost cheek-by-jowl with the fishing luggers, aptly illustrating the two industrial axes on which the town's prosperity then revolved. The house, like the luggers, has long since gone, but its internal stone staircase, cut into the rock of the headland, has been incorporated in the Pednolva Hotel which now occupies its site.

The mine itself is an ancient one. On June 30 1860 the Truro correspondent of the *Mining Journal* stated that it had been worked "far beyond the memory of men," when an adit was driven westwards under St. Ives from a rocky carn called Penolva, which formed the south part of St. Ives harbour. About 1822 or 1823 the driving of the adit was resumed until it was 95 fms. long. A shaft was sunk on to the adit 66 fms. from its mouth, and 18 fms. deep, which could still be seen, covered with a grating in the back yard of a small house in the town. Several winzes were sunk, one 12 fms. from the mouth, to a 10 fm. level.

In October 1859 a cost book company styled the North Wheal Providence Mining Company was formed to work the property, which they held for 21 years at 1-18th dues from the Earl of Mornington. It comprised Old Trenwith (evidently the eastern part of Wheal Trenwith) at the west and Penolver Mine at the east. The sett was about 800 fms. square, and at the time of its re-opening correspondents claimed that the mine embraced "the whole borough of St. Ives" and was "in the very town of St. Ives, the lodes running directly under the houses."

By December 1859 men had been set to work clearing the adit level, which had been driven 95 fms. by the former company on what was believed to be one of the St. Ives Consols lodes. Elsewhere a cross-cut was started towards Wheal Trenwith lode.

Thomas Spargo was secretary and purser of the company, Capt. Richard Hall the manager and George Henwood agent and consulting engineer. 5,000 shares were offered for sale in February 1860 at a price of £2, the terms being subsequently modified as buyers were slow in coming forward. By March 1860 about a ton and a quarter of "peacock" copper ore had been raised, and so many visitors came to obtain specimens that the adit entrance had to be secured with a lock and a shed was built to hold the ore.

During the summer of 1860, by which time the adit had been driven a further eight fathoms, difficulties arose over the disposal of the mine waste. It having been decided by the Lords of the Admiralty and the Harbour Commissioners that there was nothing to prevent the company from tipping its waste into the sea, John Uren the younger was acquitted at the Petty Sessions in August of a charge of throwing mine waste into the sea. Nevertheless, the company decided to erect a wall to keep the waste back, and the committee were authorised to apply to the Admiralty for authority to build it. At the same time blocks of granite for the purpose were brought to the cliff, while elsewhere preparation were made to sink an engine shaft.

North Wheal Providence, otherwise Pednolver (or Pedn Olva), circa 1870
(Courtesy Royal Institution of Cornwall)

Spargo called for claims in January 1861, and tender for building a boiler house and other buildings was accepted. By March the engine shaft had been sunk 20 fms. below adit and 3 fms. in greenstone, and many fathoms of levels had been driven. The committee was authorised to buy a cottage for not more than £200, but this does not appear to have been done, since the company was short of funds and a number of shares were forfeited. Work ceased soon afterwards, when the adit had been driven about 15 fms. and the cross-cut an unspecified distance towards the Wheal Trenwith lode. In May 1861 liabilities exceeded assets by £1,273.16s.8d.

Attempts made in the summer of 1861 to raise fresh capital were unsuccessful, and a meeting held in August authorised Spargo to wind up the company, as the creditors were pressing, and despite the fact that the workings had been carried to within about 5 fms. of what was believed would be one of the most valuable lodes in the district.

North Wheal Providence engine-house in the 1880's Note the broad-gauge railway stock in the left foreground
(Noall Collection)

In the cause of Harvey and others v. Hall, the Vice-Warden's Court ordered the sale of 130 fms. of 12″ capstan rope in December 1861 and called for debts. The shares were listed in the *Mining Journal* from October 1859 to November 1861; in January 1862 a limited company was formed to work the property, possibly as a reorganisation of the present company.

In the cause of Harvey and others v. Spargo, tenders were invited for a 36″ steam engine, still at Halamanning Mine, in February 1862. In February 1863 William Harvey of Hayle successfully petitioned the Vice Warden's Court to wind up the company, and debts were called for in March and July. The list of 40 contributories to 3,680 shares was settled early in 1864 and calls were made in April 1864 and November 1867. The liquidation was completed by March 1873; a later source gives the date as 24th December 1873.

Another cause heard at the Vice-Warden's Court whilst the affairs of this

IN THE COURT OF THE VICE-WARDEN OF THE STANNARIES.

STANNARIES OF *Cornwall*

Between

George Henwood   Plaintiff.

and

John Dale   Defendant.

To the Vice-Warden of the Stannaries.

The Petition of *George Henwood of Lochwinnoch near Glasgow Mine Agent* sheweth to his Honor

1.   That a Mine called *North Providence* situate in *the parish of Saint Ives* in the Stannaries of *Cornwall* has been worked and carried on for *three years* last past and upwards, and still is so worked and carried on by a Company of Adventurers.

2.   That the Defendant is the *principal Agent* of the said Company, and is sued by the Plaintiff as such *principal agent* according to custom.

3.   That there is now due to the Plaintiff from the said Company, the sum of *Thirty three pounds and twelve Shillings for the services of the Plaintiff performed in for and about the said Mine and the works thereupon as Manager or Agent and for monies laid out and expended by him thereon at the request of the said adventurers between the first day of August 1859 and the thirty first day of December 1860 —*

which sum, although the same has been, before the filing of this Petition, demanded by the Plaintiff of the Adventurers, and of the Defendant as such *principal agent* still remains unpaid.

The Petition to the Vice-Warden of the Stannaries in the case of Henwood v. Dale regarding North Wheal Providence
(Noall Collection)

unfortunate enterprise were being settled consisted of an action brought by George Henwood, of Lochwinnock, near Glasgow (plaintiff) against John Dale (defendant) for payment of £33.12s. due to him as wages and money he had laid out as manager and agent of "a Mine called North Providence situate in the parish of Saint Ives in the Stannaries of Cornwall" between August 1st 1859 and December 31st 1860." The mine itself was said to have been "worked and carried on for three years last past and upwards and still is so worked and carried on by a Company of Adventurers" — although by the date of the hearing — August 6 1861 — all activity had ceased and the company was about to be wound up. Dale had been chosen as defendant in this cause, by reason of his being the company's principal agent, this being the usual custom.

The North Wheal Providence Tin and Copper Mining Company, Ltd., registered in January 1862 apparently for the purpose of reworking the mine, had seven signatories, among them, Thomas Spargo, who put their names down for 1,250 shares. A notice of the dissolution of the company was lodged in March 1862. In July 1863 the secretary entered a plea in the Court of Chancery to wind up the company, stating that it professed to be a mining company but had never possessed any lands; had never carried on any business; had made no calls; had contracted debts; and was now hopelessly insolvent. However, Thomas Turner, one of the signatories, having been discharged by the Bankruptcy Court in November 1862, was regarded by the Chancery Court as having no *locus standi*, and the petition was dismissed. The company was finally dissolved by notice in the London Gazette in March 1882.

When the working of Wheal Trenwith was resumed by St. Ives Consolidated Mines early this century, the Pednolver adit was explored for a distance of 542 ft., but no other development took place there.

References:
North Wheal Providence Mining Company:
MJ 1859 (22.10, 17.12), 1860 (11.2, 3.3, 7.4, 23.6, 30.6, 11.8, 18.8, 25.8, 10.11), 1861 (12.1, 30.3, 1.6, 8.6, 27.7, 10.8, 14.12), 1862 (1.2), 1863 (14.2, 28.2, 14.3, 18.7), 1864 (30.4), 1867 (0.11) SCR, C.R.O., Truro (1971)
North Wheal Providence Tin and Copper Mining Company, Ltd.:
MJ 1863 (25.7)
PP 1864
AHKJ. 1961 i p.24
DT.31.606/2539, P.R.O. (A) (1971). The BT.31 series is liquidators' files at the Public Record Office, Kew, The (A) reference indicates that it was inspected when the organisation was in Ashridge, near Berkhampstead, Hertfordshire. (Per Justin Brooke)

WHEAL QUEEN: WHEAL ST. AUBYN AND TREGENNA

The north-eastern side of Steeple Lane, which ascends from Trelyon to the summit of Worvas Hill, is bordered by a croft and a plantation within which are to be seen plain evidences of early mining activity. In the N.E. corner of the croft a small hole in the ground, looking rather like the opening of a badger's sett, is actually the approach to a very narrow tunnel which, entered backwards on hands and knees, leads into a large, high chamber where an extensive ore body must have been stoped away by the ancient miners. The roof of this cavern was excavated almost to grass, as may be seen by the roots of trees which penetrate through; whilst several passages leading off from the sides — some filled with water — show where veins of ore were followed into the surrounding country. The name of this very strange and primitive working has not been recorded.

Near the centre of the croft a footpath passed directly over a shaft's mouth sollared by granite slabs. Exploration showed that this shaft — a fairly narrow one — after descending vertically for some distance opened on to a sloping tunnel where further progress was soon blocked by water. An iron bucket encountered here crumbled away on being touched. It is thought that this working may have been part of a mine known as Wheal St. Aubyn and Tregenna. Within the past few years the shaft has been filled in, for safety reasons.

The little wood west of the croft extends to the covered reservoir near the top of Cock Hill, as the NW side of Worvas Hill is locally called. One of the earliest references to mining in this piece of ground occurs in a deed relating to Wheal Queen, dating from 1836. In it, the sett is described as "situate in Cock Hill in St. Ives... in the tenement of Hendra." Cock Hill tin bounds were then owned by Thomas Richards, of St. Ives, innkeeper, who granted the sett to Henry Penrose and Robert Quick, blacksmith, of the same place, on July 25 1836, at one-fifteenth toll to the lords and bounder, "Provided...the one-fifteenth part...be brought to grass well spalled and made fit for Stamping free and clear of all Cost and charges." The adventurers were also to pay all parish rates and assessments levied on the lords' dues. The grant was for one year, after which a renewal could be applied for. The grant itself cost 10s.6d., whilst the sett, "if any," was valued at £2.2s. A condition was that the lessees should work the bounds effectually, failing which there would be no renewal.

Having obtained the grant, Penrose and Quick formed a little company on the cost book system on October 7 1836, with a modest capital of £200 in £1 shares, the first call being of 5s. However, as only 27 shareholders could be found, subscribing between them (on the first call) a paltry £7 — and some of these failed to pay up! the venture fizzled out like a damp squib.[1]

The earliest known reference to Wheal St. Aubyn and Tregenna is continued in a notice published in the *Penzance Gazette* of September 9 1846. This stated that, in conformity with a previous advertisement dated July 15 1845, certain tin dues would be paid at the King's Arms Inn, St. Ives, on October 10 1846, to the lord and bounders of the mine, which was situated in Little Tregenna Estate. The representatives of the late Sir John St. Aubyn of Clowance and St. Michael's Mount, and the representatives of the late

Francis St. Aubyn of Trengwainten, Esq., would each receive a third part; and the owners of the remaining third were invited to appear and prove their title to Mr. Henry St. Aubyn, purser of the mine, on or before that date.

It appears that Wheal St. Aubyn and Tregenna had only recently been started by Henry St. Aubyn, and it was described a few weeks later as "one of the most promising tin mines that has been discovered in Cornwall for many years...The tin is of a very superior quality — the course is from East to West, and there is another lode nearly parallel congenial for copper. The workings are at present from seven to eight fathoms from grass."[2] In January 1847 a valuable find was made when driving the adit level west, 10 fms. from grass, a tin counter lode 1' big, underlying west, cut there, producing stuff worth £6.5s. per barrow. It lay within two fms. of the standard (main) lode.[3] Despite these favourable appearances, the mine seems to have had but a very short career.

1. Old deed of Wheal Queen, courtesy of A.W. Guthrie, Trowan Vean, St. Ives
2. *Penzance Gazette* October 28 1846
3. *Penzance Gazette* February 3 1847

WHEAL RACER

From the lay-by at Buttermilk Hill on the St. Ives-Zennor road an old mine track runs up in an easterly direction to the shafts of Wheal Racer on the 700' contour line. This mine exploited two parallel lodes up to 3' wide and dipping towards each other, which were the westward continuation of some of the Goole Pellas lodes. In 1906 an investigation of the mine's possibilities was carried out by Capt. Hearne, formerly underground agent on the Glencarn Mining Reef in the Transvaal. It was said that although "Wheal Racer had not been raced for about fifty years, the prospects of the mine were most encouraging and hopeful." Some fine bunches of tinstuff had been discovered, and realised excellent results.[1]

A local board of directors was thereupon set up, comprising a varied assortment of well-known personalities; and in January 1907 they issued the prospectus of "Wheal Racer, Ltd." with offices at St. Ives, and a capital of £10,000 in £1 shares. This document stated that the company had been formed to acquire and work a large tin mining area, the eastern part of which had formerly been known as Wheal Racer Sett, held under licence from Edward Hain and R.W.G. Tyringham (the lords.) The licences carried the right to a joint lease for 42 years at a minimum rent of £25 per annum, merging into a royalty of 1/25th when black tin was worth £80 per ton or more, and 1/30th when it was below that price. The property had an extent of about 300 acres, and the lodes in it ran approximately parallel with the supposed western continuation of the St. Ives Consols Standard lode, known locally as Wheal Gwyn or Wheal Winze. The old Wheal Racer sett covered only thirty acres of the present sett, and was situated on the extreme east of it, leaving about three quarters of a mile of virgin ground on the run of the lodes to the west. The old mine had been closed down because of the low price of tin, but since then the burrows had been re-worked at a profit.[2]

Advertisement detailing the Prospectus of Wheal Racer, January 1907   (Noall Collection)

By June some machinery had been erected, and pumping had begun. Two tons of tin were returned at the Redruth ticketing on 16 December, realising £76.10s. per ton, compared with the average price of £72.4s.9d., showing that it was of excellent quality. Although great things were still being promised in respect of this mine, its ''race'' was soon run, and early in 1908 the company went into liquidation. A year later (January 1909) when a cash balance of £404 was distributed to merchants at the rate of 4s.4d. in the £, the following particulars were given of its history.

The company was formed in February 1907 with a nominal capital of £10,000, of which £5,000 was issued and fully paid. After spending over £6,000, an appeal was made to the public with an issue of 2,500 shares (priority) of £1 each. The response was anything but satisfactory, and liquidation then became inevitable. Liabilities to merchants and bankers amounted to £1,852. Sales (presumably of tin) realised £103 and plant sold fetched £572. Against these, wages, rents, law costs and fencing cost £259, and liquidator's expenses

£12, leaving the balance of £404 for distribution, as stated above. The balance sheet showed that during the first year of operation £2,102 was spent on machinery (including erection); merchants' bills amounted to £2,047, and wages and salaries to £2,099.[4]

An old miner told the writer that Wheal Racer was a good mine, the ore being of excellent quality and the workings comparatively dry. However, she failed to prosper because her promoters were very ignorant of mining matters, their chief interest being to sell materials to the undertaking. They failed to allow for the underlie of the lodes when sinking their shaft. There were three lodes, which underlay at such angles as to indicate a convergence at a point 60 fms. from surface. The shaft was sunk at the wrong place to meet the junction; whilst the stamps were set up in an old quarry at an inconvenient distance from the mine, whereas had they been better sited the stuff might have been trammed to them through a drift. Wheal Racer consequently came to grief, though in more capable hands it could have made a fine little mine. So highly did this miner think of the property that he himself sought permission to reopen it, but the mineral lord would not give his consent.

1. *St. Ives Weekly Summary* November 178 1906
2. *Western Echo* January 26 1907
3. *Western Echo* June 8 1907
4. *Western Echo* January 23 1909

ST. IVES CONSOLS

This was one of the really great mines of the St. Ives district, and exhibited many unusual characteristics which makes a study of its history particularly rewarding. St. Ives Consols lies to the west of the town in the upper part of the Stennack Valley, its setts being bounded on the west by Rosewall Hill and Ransom United, and on the east by Wheal Trenwith, the same E.-W. lode system coursing through all three mines. Its most important lode is the Standard, or, as it has sometimes been called, the Virgin, with a strike of E. 30 deg. N., and nearly vertical, but with a slight southerly underlie. In Consols it runs on the northern side of the valley, whose floor it crosses at Nanjivey, to pass through Trenwith on its southern side. In Consols it was worked to a depth of 177 fms. from grass, or a total depth from surface of nearly 200 fms. Salmon (1863) describes the lode in the bottom level as hard and unproductive, which led to the bottoms being abandoned around the middle of last century.

The Standard was intersected by two principal cross-courses, or *trawns*, as they were locally termed, both underlying W. and composed mainly of decomposed granite. They crossed the lode about 120 fms. apart, the western trawn bearing S. 40 deg. E. and the eastern S. 5 deg. W., with an angle, therefore of 45 deg. between them, so that they converged rapidly going S. The Standard lode varied in width from 6″ to 8′, and was composed mainly of quartz, peach (a form of chlorite) and a large amount of schorl. It was rich in cassiterite, with occasional bunches of copper. The great trawn heaved this lode about four fms.

The most remarkable features of St. Ives Consols were its *carbonas*, the extraordinary deposits of tin found only here and in a few other neighbouring mines. One of these, which lay near Penbeagle, was of such an immense size, that after some of the ore had been extracted, a waggon and long team of horses might have been turned around in it anywhere. (Needless to say, they never were.) These caverns, when being worked, bore a truly magnificent and unforgettable appearance. A visitor who inspected one of the largest, described how the scattered lights, the great number of miners in their soiled and torn working clothes, the pillars and beams of wood supporting the roof and walls, and the rock lining the vast cavern, all dimly discerned, at intervals, by flickering and uncertain gleams, produced a most striking effect.[1]

The carbonas have been described as analogous to the "pipe-veins" and "flats" of the limestone lead districts. One, called Lawry's carbona, branched off the Standard lode, at the 57 fm. level opposite Duke's shaft, dipping rapidly to the south, and forming stanniferous flats of varying size which were worked in a series of irregular caverns completely different from ordinary Cornish mine workings. Another — the most famous — known as the "Great Carbona," went off at the 77. About 40 fms. S. of the Standard lode, the level, here driven on the western trawn, intersected Kemp's lode, bearing nearly N.-S., which appeared to be a carbona branch. The lode was driven on for some distance until it met Noal's lode and the pipes and flats coming down from Lawry's carbona; at their junction the whole opened out into one of the most remarkable deposits of tin ever known in Cornwall, the workings consisting of huge caverns ten or twelve fathoms high and equally wide. All these great carbona deposits were formed about the western trawn, whose soft material was easily excavated when driving cross-cuts through which the tin stuff was brought back to the working shafts on the Standard lode. All these carbonas lay to the S. of the Standard, but as they neared it were gradually small. They seem to have been developed by the contact of a series of approximately E.-W. lodes ranging about 80 fms. S. of the Standard, with the converging cross-courses.

A similar phenomenon was seen in regard to Daniel's lode, about the eastern cross-course. The beginning of a carbona had been found in a level driving S.E. at the 67, about 12 fms. in from the Standard. A pipe in the end, surrounded completely by granite, consisted principally of schorl, with sufficient tin to make the stuff worth six shillings per barrow. The presence of large quantities of schorl was an indication of high productivity in these carbonas.

Following the destruction by fire of the Great Carbona in 1844, activity was concentrated principally on Daniel's lode. This bore about E. 5 deg. S. and lay 80 fms. S. of the Standard at the 127, being on the same run as Noal's lode and the branches that seem to have developed the Great Carbona to its

St. Ives Consols; said to be circa 1863

largest extent. The workings here often attained an immense width — up to 40' — although when unproductive the lode could scarcely be seen. In 1863 Daniel's lode was producing about half the tin raised in the mine. It was worked by cross-cuts from the Standard driven on the eastern cross-course. Because of the lode's variability the conditions here were continually changing; but as much as 24 tons of tin had been raised from the pitches in a month; and at the back of the 127 one pare of men worked continuously in the same pitch for nearly four years.

Three lodes had been intersected north of the Standard — the Perran, North branch, and North lode. The last had been cross-cut on the great cross-course from the Standard at the 87 and 107 and by intermediate levels at the 77 and 97. It was described as promising. The Caunter lode branched off from the Standard at Stamps Plat shaft at the 107, with a bearing of E. 25 deg. S.[2]

Apart from the carbonas, Consols possessed another great natural curiosity, some particulars of which were given by Mr. J.N.E. Millett in the *Journal of the Royal Institution of Cornwall*, in 1842. About the middle of the previous January a miner working in the 137 fm. level in a carbona, broke into a *vug* (sometimes spelt *vugh*) or hollow in the lode, measuring about 2' wide, 3' high and 8' long. The roof was of country granite, the other walls of the vug being formed by the lode, composed of quartz, caple, fluorspar, tin and blistered copper, producing about two tons of tin per hundred barrows. On the roof

33

were masses of crystallised quartz. The sides, which inclined about 50 deg., were also composed of crystals, whilst from the floor also rose formations of the same material. Another vug of this nature was discovered in 1874.

The principal shafts (from E. to W.) are Cornish, Stamps Plat (Plot), Old Sump, East Virgin, West Virgin, Ransom and Wheal Mary. Consols is connected by adit both with Trenwith, on the E., and Rosewall Hill and Ransom United, on the W.

As its name implies, St. Ives Consols consists of an amalgamation of several small mines. According to that invaluable but now forgotten compilation, *St. Ives by the Sea*, one of these was named Wheal Cogar, its count house being at the entrance to Hellesvean. St. Ives Consols was started in 1818 by the notorious borough-monger, Sir Christopher Hawkins of Trewithen, as a means of strengthening his political influence in the town. He put in as the first manager Mr. James Rowe, father of the James Rowe who ran the celebrated St. Ives Academy where many St. Ives sea captains of the last century received their education.

Hawkins probably expected the mine to last no longer than suited his electioneering purposes; but it soon became evident that, purely by chance, he had discovered a very rich property, and the mine was prosecuted with ever increasing vigour. A curious tradition has been handed down regarding the first boiler installed at St. Ives Consols about the year 1820. This was conveyed from Redruth by Mr. James Sandow, a St. Ives carrier, after whom Sandow's Lane in the Stennack is named. On descending Redruth Hill, the drug chain round the waggon wheel broke, placing the horses in imminent danger. With great presence of mind he stood on the shafts and whipped up the horses, his whip lashing from side to side "like a rainbow" until the ascent on the other side of the valley allowed them to be safely halted. Had the heavily laden waggon overtaken the horses, or had one of them fallen, the consequences would have been disastrous. Reaching St. Ives he drove through Back Talland (Albert Road), which then formed the entrance to the town, but on reaching the bridge which crossed the Stennack River near the present Western Hotel (West Bridge) the weight of the boiler caused the capstone to fall. This was possibly the first engine boiler ever to pass through St. Ives.

In the very early days there was a set of primitive-looking stamps on the mine worked by a waterwheel, known as the "Tangye Stamps. Mr. George Tangye, a member of the well known engineering family of that name, from Illogan, saw in this proof of the fact that his ancestors had originated at St. Ives. He claimed that, in his youth, these stamps had already been working for a hundred years, which would make them much older than St. Ives Consols itself.

A glimpse of St. Ives Consols in 1824 is afforded by an advertisement inserted in the *Royal Cornwall Gazette* during April by William Trenery, mine broker, Redruth, offering for sale one 74th share by private contract. "This mine is leaving a monthly profit and has the most flattering appearances, and there is no doubt it will make a great and lasting mine."

Consols was eventually taken over by Mr. James Halse, the St. Ives solicitor, who, like Sir "Kit," had great political ambitions. Both of them were elected to represent the borough in Parliament in 1826; Hawkins retired in 1828; and in 1830 Halse lost his seat to two Whig opponents, Wellesley and Morrison. Halse determined to regain his political ascendancy by creating the garden village of Halsetown to house his own miners, each of whom thereby obtained the vote under the "scot and lot" principle. There being no secret ballot, these men were obliged to vote for him, sometimes against their convictions. Halse dealt severely with any recalcitrants. In 1832 two miners named Thomas Rosewall and Richard Curnow, who had switched their allegiance from Halse to his political opponent, Winthrop Mackworth Praed (the poet) were each committed to Bodmin gaol for a month on the pretext of having broken their contracts to work in his mines. Halse also openly practised the "truck" system. A notice issued at Consols mine threatened every employee with immediate expulsion and forfeiture of wages if they patronised any publicans, shopkeepers or tradesmen not connected with the Halse interest. As a result, Richard Major and William Thomas, two carriers, lost their contract for carriage in Consols mine.[4] By such measures Hales regained his seat in 1832 and retained it until his death in 1838, and this despite the 1832 Reform Bill, which reduced the representation of St. Ives from two members to one.

Consols suffered a fair number of accidents in its early years. In 1826 Capt. H. Bennetts fell to his death down a deep shaft; and in 1830 a miner called Richards was killed when a stone fell from surface and fractured his skull. William Renoden died in February 1838 when an old covered shaft suddenly opened and precipitated him seventy fathoms; his son, in trying to save him, narrowly escaped the same fate.[5] In March 1842 two fatal accidents occurred on successive days. In the first, a lad named Moorshead had a leg smashed by the crank of a fly wheel; in the second another young miner named Stevens was crushed by a heavy piece of timber.[6] Walter Callaway was killed in a level by falling ground in March 1844.

The most spectacular accident which occurred around this time, however, happily without injury or loss of life, was the destruction by fire of the Great Carbona. Under the date of April 20 1843, in the printed version of Capt. John Tregerthen Short's diary, appears this entry: "Consols Mine took fire on Friday, the 12th inst., and is still burning. It is conjectured that some of the miners must have placed lighted candles against the woodwork." The date "1843" here is probably a publishing error, the event being dated by Salmon, in his very authoritative account of St. Ives Consols, to April 1844. The present writer collected some traditions of the fire from old miners in the 1930's. They stated that the workmen shored up the entrance to the Great Carbona with timber, but a lighted candle stuck to the woodwork to show they way in burned down and set light to it. The flames rapidly spread into the excavation whose

35

sides and roof were supported by an enormous stull made of extremely large bulk timber which, because of the restricted air supply, smouldered for six weeks. The whole area was left in such a dangerous state that it had to be abandoned; but some years after the mine itself had closed, a band of tributers who had formerly worked in Consols attempted to reach the Great Carbona by sinking a shaft above it from the northern slope of Penbeagle Hill. As usual in such cases, their efforts failed through lack of funds. In 1961 Mr. Nankervis, of Wicca Farm, showed the writer two specimens of ore recovered from the Great Carbona by an ancestor immediately after the fire. These appear to consist principally of tin. The sides affected by the fire were smelted by the heat, and have a bright, gleaming brassy appearance. To handle such relics as these is to reach across the years and make contact wth the very stuff of mining history. Some years ago Mr. Jim Hodge, then of the South West Water Authority, examined the workings below Penbeagle, and saw some of the charred timbers of the Great Carbona. The area has, however, now been sealed off.

The loss of so valuable and productive a section as this would have crippled and probably closed any lesser mine; and it is a measure of the greatness of St. Ives Consols that it was able to survive this disaster without any loss of output or reduction in dividends.

In 1845 Brunton's round frames for tin dressing were introduced. Two serious accidents occurred the following year. When the brothers John and William Richards were tamping a hole in January the powder prematurely exploded; William had a leg and arm broken and was feared blinded in both eyes, but John escaped with bruises. In August, James Magor, aged 15, fell from the 40 to the 47 fm. level and was killed.

Steady progress continued to be made throughout the 1840's and '50's, with dividends being distributed every year except 1847, 1849, 1854 and 1855. Then, at the meeting held in August 1958 Capt. Bawden reported that they had communicated Wheal Trenwith deep adit with the 20 E. in Consols; this would discharge one-fifth of the water which now had to be drained to surface, effecting a saving of 25% in coal.[7] In January 1859, it was said that in seven days of the last weeks of December, three men and two boys had broken and sent to grass the enormous quantity of 12 tons of tin (£800 worth) by which they earned over £200, and the pitch had since been let to six hands for a month at sevenpence in the £ — a tribute at which they could still realise good wages.[8]

A remarkable incident occurred on October 4 1859. One of the agents sitting in the account house heard a noise like a heavy train passing, and noticed that a tumbler of water on the table was in agitation. Two men working underground, 130 fms. from surface, heard a rumbling noise and experienced a trembling sensation, whilst at the 75 fm. level in Providence (nearly 125 fms. from surface) miners heard a sound as if a kibble had fallen in a shaft or a stull had given way. This earthquake shock was not observed in any other mines of the Land's End district, though at surface it was widely felt in almost every locality.[9]

In the autumn of 1861 the Rev. William Booth (later General Booth, founder of the Salvation Army) conducted a revivalist campaign at St. Ives, a detailed account of which was published in pamphlet form the following year by C. Taylor Stephens, the "postman poet" who delivered the mail between St. Ives and Zennor. In this it is stated that "on Tuesday 19th (of November) a meeting for prayer was held in the bowels of the earth, 110 fathoms below the surface, at the St. Ives Consols mine. There were penitents there. One of the company informed us that the glory of God filled the place." It must have been a truly remarkable scene. One visualises the level feebly lit by guttering candles struck in convenient niches around the walls, the pale, bearded face of the preacher, the dense throng of miners gathered round him in their rough, work-stained working clothes. The great revival choruses, sung with that curious Cornish blend of vigour and sweetness, reverberate through the labyrinthine workings of the mine. In the background, the splash of water from the roof and the distant sigh and rattle of the pumping rod provide an unusual accompaniment to the music.[10]

In December one of the agents, Mr. R. Kernick, aged 78, was presented with the sum of £16 on his retirement after holding this position for 38 years, a record of service which must be almost unique in Cornish mining.

On August 2 1862 Capt. John Nancarrow, manager of St. Ives Consols, gave evidence before Lord Kinnaird's Commissioners enquiring into the condition of mines. He began by stating that he also managed East Treskerby, near Chacewater. Consols produced tin but only a little copper. The lowest level was 187 fms. from surface — they called it the 200. The men ascended and descended by ladders. There were 182 men and boys working underground, with 360 men, women and girls at surface. The lowest levels then working were the 167 and 177; they were also working in every level up to the 97, at the 87, and up to the 67 and 47. They had no ends in which a candle would not burn. No artificial means of ventilation were required, except putting a sollar in the bottom of one level, the 170, which was "warm." Blasting smoke hung about in that level for an hour or two, but they only worked it by two cores out of four, so that it was completely cleared when the next came. He knew of no one in the mine who suffered from miners' disease.

The men were allowed two pounds of candles per week, including those in the "warm" end, who only worked six hours a core. They generally worked eight hour shifts, six days one week and five the next. The miners contributed sixpence each month to the club and sixpence for the doctor, but there was no barber. The women did not have to contribute, neither did the agents, but the doctor did not attend the latter. The women worked under cover, and had places attached to each of the dressing floors where they could take their meals. Capt. Nancarrow knew of no boiler explosion on the mine in a period of 45 years. "The water is easy in this neighbourhood, and our engines are not forced; I mean we have a small quantity to pump."

Henry Curwen Salmon wrote a very detailed account of St. Ives Consols in 1863, from which some particulars have already been given. He noted that the mine had originally been in 47 shares, which were successively increased to 94, 470 and 940. It lay in granite, which in some of the eastern shafts was overlain by hornblendic schists and greenstone. As usual in almost all granite mines, the water was only trifling. In Old Sump shaft there was a 30″ pumping engine which had been at work for 45 years and still possessed a wooden beam — one of the very few then left in the county. This raised water from the 177 to the 107 by three 6½″ lifts. At the 107 the water went back to Ransom shaft, on which there was a 50″ engine. This raised the water by three 8″ lifts to adit, and also raised a still larger column to surface for condensing and other purposes by a 12″ pole from the adit.

There were two whim engines, a 22″ and a 20″. Half the tin stuff was drawn by kibbles through Stamps Plat shaft, a quarter from East Virgin, and the remainder from Old Sump, West Virgin and Ransom shafts, but principally Old Sump. A 26″ stamping engine worked 48 heads, and 30 other heads were worked by four waterwheels. The heads varied from 3 to 3½ cwt., and all stamped with grates. The average monthly return of tin was about 23 tons, produced from about 4,600 barrows of work — 200 barrows of work yielding on average one ton of tin. The "barrow" by which all tin stuff was estimated in the districts equalled 22 gallons "old ale measure." The weight of work contained in a barrow varied with its nature — the richer the work, the greater being the specific gravity; but as a rough average, six barrows weighed a ton, which gave the approximate weight of the barrow as 3 cwt. 1½ qrs. The assay of a sack was made on half a noggin, "old wine measure," and, taking tin at a standard of £40, each grain produced from this half noggin showed tin to the value of a penny in the barrow, and consequently one pennyweight of tin to the value of 2s. "Of course, a mode of calculation such as this is barbarous in the extreme, but tributers are so accustomed to it, and are so suspicious about the introduction of the system of trying by weight, with which they are unfamiliar, that it is very difficult to alter." As tin was always estimated at £40 a ton under this system, the barrow was really worth at current prices of black tin (£60 a ton) one half more than its nominal value. Thus, work priced at 6s. per barrow was really worth 9s.; and as six barrows made a ton, the work would be worth 54s. per ton. From these facts, Salmon deduced that, as 200 barrows of work yielded on average one ton of black tin, the true value of the stuff was 36s. per ton — a high average, fully a third if not nearly a half greater than that of the county. The quality of the tin was "superior common."

The mine was managed in succession by Capts Richard Hodge, John Gluyas, Holman, George Davey, Nicholas Tredinnick (later of East Crofty), Thomas Treweeke (later of Wheal Margaret) who held the post for twenty years, Edward Bawden and John Nancarrow. Capts. Martin George and Richard Martin were the underground agents, the dressing agent being Capt.

38

Wilkins. Mr. Robert Bennett was the first purser, followed by Edwin Ley, J.N.R. Millett, Edwin Ley (a second time), William Darke, and Capt. Phillip Aplin. The accountant, John Vivian, had held that post for 38 years.

The mine began to distribute profits in 1827, since when there had been 104 dividends, totalling £107,418.10s. The early records of returns had been lost, but from March 1835 to December 1862 the value of tin raised amounted to £478,030.15s.

The surface of the mine was divided into a remarkable number of small enclosures belonging to many different owners. This meant that there were over twenty lords — "and that a mine can be worked at all under such circumstances shows the excellent system of mutual conciliation which is so characteristic of Cornish landlords in the granting of mining setts." Salmon does not identify these lords; but in 1904 George Treweeks (son of Thomas Treweeke, the former manager) stated that the Great Carbona *only* was in the hands of Messrs. Bolitho and Williams, and Mrs. Harris of Penbeagle; whilst taking the owners of the setts from east to west, they were Praed, of Trevetho, Lord Cowley, the Bolton estate (later purchased by Sir Edward Hain), Mr. Richards of Venwyn, Mrs. R. Harris of Penbeagle, the Bolitho family, Mr. Williams of Caerhays Castle, Lord St. Levan, and Messrs. W. Pearce, W.H. Trevorrow, T.J. Chellew, and Dr. G.B. Rosewall. The principal shareholders for over forty years were the Earl of Lauderdale, Sir Anthony Maitland, and the father and grandfather of A.J. Balfour, the then Prime Minister.[11] Before leaving Salmon's account, it is interesting to note his statement that in Consols, as in the extreme western (St. Just) districts the men bored single-handed, with hammers weighing from five to six pounds. This is not confirmed by any other authority, all surviving evidence indicating that St. Ives miners bored double-handed.

Spargo (1865) gives a glowing account of St. Ives Consols, observing that "it has held its course for nearly half a century, through evil and good report, never deceiving old or new investors, and is now the favourite mine, both far and near, as a security for money." By September 1866, however, the picture had somewhat altered, a debit balance of £1167.15s.6d. on the cost book having to be partially cleared by a £1 call, estimated to produce £940. 84 tons of tin had been sold during that quarter at prices varying from £44.7s.6d. to £47.10s., realising £3803.14s.1d., whilst 22 tons held in stock were valued at £980. The agents reported the 167 E. on Caunter lode worth £10 per fm., whilst the Great Carbona; cut at the 97 level, was worth £11 per fm. The 147 E. on Daniel's lode was worth £20 per fm., four or five pitches there being valued at £14 to £22 per fm. A total of 156 hands was employed underground, 100 on tribute at an average of 12s.6d. in the £. The purser stated that the round buddles were now complete and would considerably reduce the cost of dressing tin.

In March 1868 the deficit amounted to £2,179, but this was reduced to £281 by December; and in May 1869 Consols again entered the dividend list with a payment of 10s. per 940th share. At the latter meeting the lords of the Bolton estate, Mr. J.A. Stephens, Dr. Rosewall, and others, were thanked for having resigned dues during the recent difficult period. The labour force had increased to 205 underground, 121 of these on tribute at 8s. in the £ — this being an average figure, one assumes. In the November quarter £300 was charged on account of a new 60″ engine then being erected.[12]

In January 1870 when Matthew Richards was re-charging a hole in the 150 fm. level on Daniel's lode, using an untipped iron tamping bar, the powder ignited, driving the bar against his forehead his skull was fearfully shattered, and death must have been instantaneous.[13] The new 60″ pumping engine commenced work that same month; but whilst it was being installed some of the best pitches became flooded, causing a fall of production which was reflected in a loss of £480 at the February account.[14] In August 1871 prospects appeared a little better, but only 155 men were now working underground, 72 of these on tribute. A report on the mine by Peter Watson, published in December, stated that altogether £10.15s. had been paid on each of the 940 shares, or £10,105, in return for which shareholders had received £491 per share in dividends, totalling £461,540. He thought the shares, now changing hands at around £10, greatly undervalued, as the prospect of resuming dividends seemed good.[15]

In May 1872 the agents expressed the hope that they would soon cut the rich Ransom lode, worth £60 per fm., which Rosewall Hill adventurers had driven to the limits of their sett in the 100 fm. level, at its junction with the cross-course at the 107 in Consols. Later that month the lode in the bottom of the 177, on the Caunter, suddenly widened to 7′, worth £100 per fm. Then, in July, miners searching for the rich western lode in the 107 made contact with a great flow of water which drained all levels below the 110 in Rosewall Hill. How glad they must have been to have their new 60″ engine working to cope with the inflow! The Rosewall Hill lode was duly found, being described as a "remarkable discovery;" but this did not prevent the mine recording a loss of £1,162 in the August quarter.[16]

However, the cutting of Ransom lode, with further important discoveries on Daniel's lode and on the Caunter, caused the shares to strengthen from £11 to £17 in February 1873. The Rosewall Hill adventurers had meanwhile accused Consols of trespassing on their property. The matter was referred to the lords for arbitration; and P.H. Aplin, the Consols purser, announced in May that an amicable settlement had been reached. The lords had decided the boundary in favour of Consols, but the latter would have to pay Rosewall Hill £165.2s.6d. for their encroachment. There were 16 pitches working on the new Ransom lode at 9s.6d. in the £, two on Daniel's and seven on Lawry's. A month later, the stope in the bottom of the 107 E. of slide on Ransom lode was valued at £50 per fm.

Soon after this, the very promising nature of some new discoveries made in the eastern part of the mine induced the adventurer to agree to the placing of an underground engine on the Caunter lode 200 fms. from surface. By December, it had been installed, and was working most satisfactorily, without injuriously affecting any of the other workings. This would enable them to sink below the 180 level on a lode worth £30 per fm. Already the 180 level, driving S.E., was valued at £50 per fm. and a stope in its bottom at £25. The engine itself appears to have been a 6″ horizontal type with vertical multitubular boiler and 8 fms. of 4″ working lift attached. Notwithstanding the officially inspired statement to the contrary, the smoke which it generated must have been very unpleasant for miners in the adjacent stopes. It was an interesting innovation, comparable in some ways with the submarine steam winder installed in Levant in 1876 (See the author's *Levant, The Mine Beneath The Sea*, 1970). However, whilst in Levant, this expedient was amply justified by the impossibility of sinking a shaft in the sea, no such consideration applied in the case of Consols; and the decision to instal an underground engine there represented a fundamental and — as events showed — a fatal misconception of the manner in which the mine should have been worked.

This was made abundantly clear by Mr. George Treweeke when reviewing the history and prospects of the mine in 1904. He stated that the Caunter lode at the furthest point east being worked, near Trenwith House, had a S.E. bearing, whilst Daniel's lode, one of the main trunks of the Great Carbona, had a bearing E.5 deg. S.; it could therefore be predicted that the intersection of these lodes would occur in the southern part of the Trenwith Estate, or at Bahavella. Such lode intersections were usually associated with great deposits of mineral; in this instance it was reasonable to suppose that copper as well as tin would be found, as small quantities of copper had already been raised at the old Bahavella mine (*q.v.*) Thomas Treweeke (when manager of Consols) had recommended the adventurers to sink a shaft near Trenwith which would have enabled the vast amount of unexplored rich mineral ground to the east of Consols workings to be properly developed, and to follow up the valuable Caunter lode, the stuff from which was so rich that they carried it in sacks. But his advice went unregarded; and the stuff continued to be taken from near Trenwith back to Consols, which prevented the possibility of opening up any new ground, "and was so expensive as to mean giving twenty shillings for a sovereign." So they picked the eyes out of the mine for the sale of a little ready money, and eventually it was knocked.[17]

In April 1874 a call of 30s. was made, and the shares subsequently slumped to 25s. each. However, the shareholders were cheered the following month on learning that a lode of rich grey copper ore had been found in driving the 170 fm. level on Daniel's lode, "such as was never seen before at the depth in this district." In two days, hundreds of pounds' worth were broken and brought to grass without firing a hole, the ground opening out and revealing a large deposit of similar quality. This lode was observed to have a northerly inclination, similar to what it had displayed at the 120 and 150 levels directly above, and where it was so rich that dividends of £3 a share — or £2,280

41

— were made for many quarters in succession. In the level above the 170, and 20 fms. in advance, an immense "vugh" recently discovered was being cleared out, and a tin lode was already in view 14′ wide, worth from 7s. to 9s. per barrow. The Caunter and Ransom lodes had never looked better, and the prospects of the mine were never brighter.[18]

However, these favourable prognostications were soon belied by events. At a meeting in April 1875 a quarter's loss of £700 was disclosed, leading to a call of £1 per share. Expenses throughout the mine were curtailed, beginning with the management, which it was hoped would save £100 a month. "The meeting was thinly attended, and presented a great contrast to the stormy one of last December, when the election contest was at its height." This was presumably a reference to the notorious Parliamentary contest in which Charles Praed, after defeating Sir Francis Lycett, was afterwards unseated for bribery. The mine's position continued to deteriorate during that summer. At an adjourned special meeting held in October at the account house, it was proposed by Mr. Michell and seconded by Mr. Wellington that the machinery and materials be disposed of by public auction, the motion being carried by 657 votes (shares) to 30. Mr. W. Husband afterwards proposed and Mr. D.F. Stevens seconded that "the committee be empowered to sell and liquidate the property of the mine," and this was carried *nem con*. Mr. P.H. Aplin, the Purser, occupied the chair during this historic meeting.

The decline of this great mine now proceeded steadily towards its inevitable conclusion, aided by the current mining depression; and in October the setts, plant and machinery were offered for sale by auction, as a going concern. Among the items listed were the 60″ pumping engine with two 10 ton boilers; 26″ stamping engine with two large fly wheels, wrought iron axle and sweep rod; one 16-heads axle and three 12-heads axles, together 52 heads, with lifters, &c., complete; 22″ winding engine with cage and 8 tons boiler; 20″ winding engine with cage and 10 tons boiler; 6″ horizontal engine; 800 fms. of underground railroad, with tram waggons; all the tin floors, with their excellent and lofty sheds; 21 large centre-head buddles; six square buddles; 124 self-acting and other tin frames; Brunton's patent calciner, 12′ bed, with water wheel and driving gear; three plunger lifts for pumping slime; four water wheels for driving dressing machinery; and a large number of tin kieves. Also offered were the "rich Tin Leavings throughout the Mine, being the accumulation of many years, during the greater part of which this has been one of the largest tin-producing mines in the county. The setts are held upon favourable terms, are large in area, and comprise rich and productive mineral ground. The water charges are easy, and the mine is favourably situated for the supply of material. St. Ives Consols has paid, in profits to the adventurers, about £140,000; and coupling this with the fact that a large proportion of the ground included in the setts remains unexplored, a rare opportunity is now offered to an enterprising Company for mining investment."

The auction took place on October 27; but the times were not propitious for mining investment, and the reserve price of £5,000 was not reached. Capt. Josiah Thomas, the famous manager of Dolcoath, had been asked to give an independent valuation of the property, his figures being:

Machinery		£2,905
Tin leavings at surface and on the various dressing floors		5,280
Deducted cost of returning the same	£2,040	
Deducted allowance for waste of tin in dressing	240	−2,280
Net value of tin leavings		3,000
Total value of the mine as a going concern		5,905

Capt. Thomas stated he did not think the figures for the tin leavings at all too high. "If all the dressing floors were to be cleaned up to bottom, and all the dressing machinery removed, it is not unlikely that more tin than I have calculated might be returned from the leavings throughout the mine." The mine was again offered for sale on November 10, but the highest offer fell £1,000 below the reserve. Mr. P.S. Bolitho was anxious to continue the mine, and offered to take a hundred shares in a further venture; but the Lauderdale trustees, who held the largest interest, were determined to pull out. In December it was rumoured that St. Ives Consols had been bought by Mr. George Treweeke, supposedly acting for Messrs. Bolitho and Williams.[19] Apparently an effort was made to save the mine. A report in January 1876 said that it had gone to work again, and that there was no doubt, from the capital to be expended, that the enterprise would be prosecuted with vigour, affording occupation for a large number of men. But these hopes proved false; and in July a writer noted that "the mines of Cornwall are fast passing away into mournful ruins. St. Ives Consols is gone, and Providence is going, and there is no sign that they will be revived in this generation, and so the miners are emigrating."

The collapse of St. Ives Consols, which had employed half a thousand people and been one of the mainstays of the district for generations, was an appalling tragedy. Its passing was thus described some years afterwards in *St. Ives By The Sea*:

"When St. Ives Consols was working, St. Ives was in her palmy days. The 300 underground men, besides surface and stamps hands, made pleasant days for the shopkeepers 'down-town.' The 'stampses,' with their at least 200 hands, literally lined the Stennack Valley from the mine to Bal-floors, opposite the Board Schools. A great number of the men, women and children working in Consols came from the town, as well as from Halsetown and the neighbouring villages; and the road leading up the Stennack Valley to the mine was 'black with people' going and coming from work, mornings and evenings, and echoed to the whistle, song, shout and laughter of the merry stamps — boys and girls, who were so sleek and jolly, and confident and happy in their work that, as the saying goes, they 'would have mobbed a showman.' Ah, those were good old days then! The continual string of carts and waggons, that sometimes one could scarcely pass, which went creaking and rolling up the high road, the cracking of the whips and the shouts of the drivers, the babel of the voices of the miners going or coming from their cores — and of the stamps pares, with the rattle and roar of the machinery, filled the whole neighbourhood with bustle and happy life. When the last engine or fire-stamps stopped...such a sudden quiet caused the people of the neighbourhood to be oppressed with the solemn stillness, and they went about with downcast looks and drooping spirits as if they had lost a relative or dear friend. For some time after Consols had stopped, this valley was filled with the dying remains of the mine, whose gigantic frame showed here and there some little quiverings and convulsions of life, until at last nothing was left but a bleaching skeleton.''

Indeed, the ''corpse'' of St. Ives Consols provided rich pickings for a good many years for tributers and others, who obtained from the burrows and higher levels tin enough to keep the fire stamps working and pay the promoters for their enterprise. It was during this period that a spectacular fire took place at surface. About 2 a.m. on December 21 1881, whilst a terrible storm was raging, people living in the higher part of the town and particularly in the Stennack, heard a series of detonations, like minute guns. It was first thought these were distress signals from a vessel, but the sound did not come from the direction of the sea. It was afterwards learned that the ''dry'' at Consols had taken fire by some means unknown, and there being no assistance at hand was burnt to the ground. Several dynamite caps were stored in the building, and it was their detonation which had alarmed the district.

Very little of the old mine may be seen above ground today. All the engine houses have gone; but just opposite the entrance to Hellesvean a high wall fronts the main road braced by two iron rails. It is said that whilst tramming

Sump Shaft headgear, St. Ives Consolidated Mines   (Noall Collection)

on a high bridge fixed over the road here a miner fell over with his waggon full of ore, and was crushed to death in the road with the waggon on top of him. The former count house is now the farm house of Consols Farm. Nothing survives of the stamps that lined the Stennack Valley, and even the stream which once drove them is gradually disappearing underground to provide a wider road to serve St. Ives' principal modern industry — tourism.

J.H. Collins, writing in the *Records* of the London and Westcountry Chamber of Mines (1907) gives the following statistics regarding Consols. Before 1827 tin and copper production was worth £200,000. Between 1827-92 tin production amounted to 16,460 tons, valued at £819,467, copper and sundries (1827-71) £5,000; making the total recorded returns £1,024,467. These figures include 850 tons of tin valued at £40,000 recovered from dumps, etc., between 1876-92.

In 1907 St. Ives Consols was taken over by a company known as St. Ives Consolidated Mines, Ltd., who proposed to work it with Trenwith, Rosewall Hill and Ransom United, Giew and Georgia, in a large combined undertaking. The first directors were Horace Barrett (chairman), Sir Francis Fox, Sigismund Moritz, Lieut.-Col. Thomas, John T. Chellew, Lieut. Francis Berkley Henderson, and Edmund Schiff. Archibald Finlay Maclaren joined the board a little later. This was one of a number of mining enterprises set on foot in Cornwall at this time as part of the so-called "electric pump boom," and was associated with some of the most progressive elements in the industry.

In connection with this new venture, Mr. James White gave a review of the past history of Consols. According to his account, the depth of Ransom shaft was 105 fms., Sump shaft 175 fms. and Millett's shaft 40 fms. Regarding the last, he stated it had originally been commenced to facilitate the working of the Caunter lode, which it would have intersected at the 60 fm. level. Following the retirement of Capt. Richard White, who was the resident manager and the principal in the execution of this work, the sinking was abandoned, to the great detriment of the mine. The Caunter lode, coursing S.E. from the E.-W. Standard lode, was discovered at Stamps Plat shaft against the large cross-course at the 105 fm. level. It proved very rich at this point, and was opened on most successfully in depth and length. Daniel's lode lay 127 fms. E. of Stamps Plat shaft, and had an E.-W. strike. "I am informed," said White, "that its junction with the Caunter lode had been reached, and was of a very rich character. In consequence of its immense distance from the Old Sump, requiring years of great expense to bring up levels to enable deeper points to be reached, sinking and working were accomplished by internal arrangements which soon got out of hand, and the mine closed down." The "internal arrangements" would, of course, have included the curious little underground engine installed in December 1873. James White's article strikingly confirms Mr. George Treweeke's statement regarding the eastern workings, save for the fact that the latter did not believe that the junction between Daniel's and the Caunter had been reached. White thought that the carbonas, with their branches, lying south of East and West Virgin shafts were exhausted, and that recourse should be had to deeper sinking in that section.[21]

The new company encountered some considerable difficulties in putting the mines to work, due to the fact that water from Consols was being fed into the town's supply. The problem was solved by the company paying substantial compensation to the Council, who then constructed a new surface reservoir at Bussow (as described in the section on Wheal Trenwith.) The company's first report, issued in January 1910, stated that the shafts and levels down to adit had been cleared, whilst the central power station for supplying electricity to pumps in Trenwith, Ransom United and Giew was nearing completion. Their authorised capital was £220,000, of which £184,607 had been subscribed and issued.[22]

The Smith Shop, St. Ives Consolidated Mines (Noall Collection)

By April, the adit had been cleared for a distance of 6,615', disclosing standing ground which assayed up to 336.5 lbs. of tin per ton. According to a miner who worked in St. Ives Consols at this period, the mine was drained by two adits — the upper, or "shoal" (shallow) adit, whose entrance may still be seen in the wall in front of Nanjivey Terrace, and the lower adit at Trenwith Place. Water was conveyed underground on high launders through Consols and discharged through the shoal adit to reduce the amount of pumping required at Trenwith.

46

An unfortunate accident occurred during September, when a carpenter was killed by falling down a shaft. Another sad fatality took place on February 21 1911 when William George, a stationary engine driver in the power house, came into contact with a three ton flywheel and was knocked into the pit. It was believed he had been attempting to adjust the generator guard, which was thrown up and pushed him against the wheel.

A report issued by Mr. Charles M. Rolker on June 19 1912 stated that in Wheal Mary — i.e., St. Ives Wheal Allen — section a short stretch of ground above adit had sampled 75.7 lbs. of metallic tin per ton over a 60' length of drive with a computed vein width of 2.42'. Pay ore had been left standing in portions where the ore was hard; he believed further unworked portions of such ground existed on the Standard lode, both E. and W. The parallel Daniel's and Noal's lodes, together with the Caunter, Williams', and Kemp's lodes, also offered good prospects.[23]

The Power House, St. Ives Consolidated Mines   (Noall Collection)

On July 18 the St. Ives Consolidated Mines were visited by members of various mining and engineering societies. They made a tour of the properties under the guidance of Messrs. T.J. Chellow and E. Schiff (directors), F.C. Cann (manager) and other officials. Reporting this occasion, the *Mining World* spoke in glowing terms of the "splendid establishment" of these mines, adding that the power house alone was worth a journey from London to see. They had already spent £140,000, cleared 4½ miles of adits, and stripped and enlarged five shafts to take double skip roads to water level. The power house (of which a description was given in the booklet issued in connection with the societies' visit) consisted of four Diesel oil engines of the four cylinder vertical type, direct coupled to 135 kilowatt three-phase alternators. Three 250 kW transformers transformed the current from 650 vols to 6,000 volts for transmission purposes. This power house was sited at the rear of the present Leach pottery, in the upper part of the Stennack. As well as the power house, the central offices, and stores for the entire group of mines were also sited on St. Ives Consols, farm buildings being used for the purpose.

By September, Sump shaft was reported timbered to the back of the 117 and clear below this point. East Virgin was also timbered to the back of the 117, and the sinking pump in this shaft working at the 107, being fed by the air lift. As soon as the 117 level was unwatered the pump would be lowered to that point, thus reducing the head of the air lift 60', doubling its capacity. The 107 fm. level W. could then be cleared towards Ransom shaft, enabling the values of the virgin ground there to be ascertained.[24] The pumps used at Consols and in other sections of the group were of the vertical three-throw type, with Guttermuth valves.

Progress continued to be made in 1913. During May they were stoping above the 107 and 47 fm. levels. Over a four week period 125 tons of ore, assaying 29.24 lbs. of black tin per ton, and 185 tons, assaying 23 lbs., had been broken and sent to Giew mill. The water was being held below the 127

The Power House switch-board, St. Ives Consolidated Mines   (Noall Collection)

in June, in Sump shaft sections; whilst in East Virgin the lode in the stope above the 107 fm. level W. had improved in value, assaying over 30 lbs. of black tin per ton. By November, however, stoping was only being carried on above the 25 fm. level W. of East Virgin shaft, though the pumps were still running.

Inside the Power House, St. Ives Consolidated Mines   (Noall Collection)

Soon after the outbreak of the Great War St. Ives Consolidated Mines, Ltd., ran into serious financial difficulties; and in 1915 a petition was brought against it in the Companies Winding Up Court by the Anglo-American Oil Co., Ltd. The official receiver's report stated that St. Ives Consolidated Mines, Ltd., had been formed in June 1908 with a nominal capital of £220,000 in 80,000 preference and 140,000 ordinary shares of £1 each; its liabilities amounted to £138,582, and assets were expected to produce £18,704. The company had been promoted by the National Mineral Corporation, Ltd., registered on November 30 1907, and acquired the latter's mining properties and rights at St. Ives for £140,000 fully paid shares. The corporation bought these properties from Cornish Proprietary Mines, Ltd., in November 1907 for £14,990. Cornish Proprietary Mines was registered on December 20 1906 and acquired the same properties for £5,570 in cash. In December 1908 St. Ives Consolidated Mines promoted the British Radium Corporation to work Wheal Trenwith for pitchblende, uranium and radium. The Radium Corporation

49

was for a time very successful, but subsequently failed for reasons given in the section dealing with Trenwith. This in turn precipitated the collapse of St. Ives Consolidated Mines, Ltd., whose directors also blamed want of sufficient working capital to complete the exploitation of their various enterprises on which so much capital had been spent. They honestly admitted that "it might have been a wiser policy to have tackled one property at a time instead of spending so much money on so many properties."[25] A contributory factor to their failure (not, however, admitted by them) was undoubtedly their failure to develop the promising eastern section of the mine, towards Bahavella and Trenwith, spoken of so highly by George Treweeke and James White. Whether this omission was due to lack of capital or an inability to appreciate the great and still untested potential of this section must remain a moot point.

The St. Ives Consols and Wheal Trenwith sections of the company's St. Ives mines were thereupon abandoned. In February 1917 the Thermo-Electric Ore Reduction Corporation took over their assets from a receivership, and continued production at Giew, but announced that the valuable power plant at Consols would be dismantled and shipped to Australia. The corporation was developing an important tungsten mine at Wolfram Camp in Queensland, whose output was regarded as essential to the war effort. It would have taken at least two years under prevailing conditions before a suitable power plant could have been built for this venture, but the Consols equipment was ready to hand to fill this need. Mr. Cann, the manager at St. Ives, was instructed to proceed to Queensland with his staff to supervise the erection of the plant there. Accounts published at the time indicate that this operation was successfully accomplished; but local tradition nevertheless insisted that the ship carrying the engines and generators was sunk at sea by a German submarine. The closing of St. Ives Consols power house robbed Giew of its electrical supply, this loss being made good, on a temporary basis, by the installation of a suction gas plant on that mine. In the latter part of 1917 this gas plant was dismantled and sent to the Mount Carbine Mines, in North Queensland, which also belonged to the Thermo-Electric Corporation. Giew was then supplied with power by the Cornwall Electric Power Company from their generating station at Hayle.[27]

1. Trans. Roy. Geol. Soc. of Cornwall, v, 22.
2. Salmon, H.C., The St. Ives and Lelant Tin Mining District, Cornwall (*Mining and Smelting Magazine*, March, 1863.)
3. *St. Ives Times* October 15 1920 (quoting *Western Morning News*.)
4. Praed, Winthrop Mackworth, *Trash* (1833); Noall, Cyril, *Beloved St. Ives*, (1957.)
5. *Falmouth Packet* February 24 1838.
6. *Penzance Gazette* February 16 1842.
7. *Cornish Telegraph* August 25 1858.
8. *Royal Cornwall Gazette* January 21 1859.
9. Edmonds, Richard, *The Land's End District*, (1862.)
10. *The Revival at St. Ives, Cornwall...Conducted by the Rev. Wm. and Mrs. Booth*, (1862.)
11. *St. Ives by the Sea* (1904.)
12. *Cornish Telegraph* May 26 and November 24 1869.

13. *Cornish Telegraph* January 12 1870.
14. *Cornish Telegraph* February 23 1870.
15. *Cornish Telegraph* December 20 1871.
16. *Cornish Telegraph* May 8 and 22; July 10; and August 28 1872.
17. *Cornish Telegraph* May 22; June 25; and December 10 1873.
18. *Cornish Telegraph* May 12 1874.
19. *Cornish Telegraph* April 21; October 27; November 3 and 11; and December 15 1875.
20. *Cornish Telegraph* January and July 1876.
21. *Western Echo June 8 1907 (quoting Cornishman.)*
22. *St. Ives Weekly Summary* January 29 1910.
23. *St. Ives Times* June 21 1912.
24. *St. Ives Times* September 13 1912.
25. *St. Ives Times* September 3 1915.
26. *St. Ives Times* February 23 and December 7 1917.
27. The account given here of the torpedoing of the ship carrying the Consols power plant to Australia cannot be confirmed from any documentary source. The story is, however, very well known at St. Ives; and in 1973 the late Mr. Phillip Chellew (a son of one of the original directors of the mine) assured the writer that it was true. In view of the curious conflict of evidence on this point, the article in the *St. Ives Times* for December 7 1917 (copied from the *Western Morning News*) may be quoted at some length. After describing the urgent need to provide tungsten and molybdenum for the war effort, it continued: "For this purpose the Thermo-Electric Power Corporation purchased the St. Ives group of mines in Cornwall and with the aid of special facilities from the Ministry of Munitions, was able to remove to Queensland the power station of the mines in question, comprising four Diesel oil engines and complete electrical plant. The success of its operation was contributed to by the Cornwall Electric Power Co., which replaced with power drawn from the Hayle Works that previously supplied by the St. Ives station. Pending this installation, the Corporation was able to keep the Giew Mines running by the utilisation of a suction gas plant there set up. This plant, in turn, is now being dismantled for the purpose of re-erection on the Mount Carbine Mines in North Queensland, which are also the property of Thermo-Electric. It will be of exceptional interest to Cornishmen to know that in carrying out these operations the Corporation derived much assistance from the Manager of the St. Ives Mines; Mr. F.C. Cann, who is now busily engaged in reorganising the group of mines in Queensland known as Wolfram Camp." From this, it would seem that the Consols power plant, or at least a section of it, did arrive safely in Australia. Possibly it was the Giew suction gas plant which was sunk at sea, as this was sent out later in 1917, at the height of the German U-boat campaign. Local opinion, however, is definite that it was the Consols plant which was lost.

    In connection with his researches into the history of the Cornish electric power industry, Mr. E.W.A. Edmonds, of Perranwell Station, made enquiries in 1981-2 of the Queensland Department of Mines concerning the fate of the generating plant sent from St. Ives Consols and Giew to Wolfram Camp. In reply, Mr. G.V. Sandercock, Senior Inspector, stated he was unable to give details of machinery installed there, but quoted from the Under Secretary's Annual Report for 1918, which stated: "Several causes delayed completion of the new and extensive reduction and concentration works being erected by the Thermo Electric Ore Reduction Corporation at Wolfram. Among these was loss of machinery by acts of war." This seems to confirm that some of the machinery was lost at sea.

    The Report for 1918 by the Warden for the area referred to the near completion of the machinery, including "central power plants," but the suction gas plant ex-Giew was never mentioned as actually erected.

ST. IVES HARBOUR BEACH WORK

The Stennack River was used for centuries by miners and tin streamers for dressing their tinstuff, the residues from Rosewall Hill, St. Ives Consols, Trenwith and other mines being carried down by the stream and deposited on the harbour beach at its outfall under the churchyard wall. These tailings still contained an appreciable proportion of tin, which by the action of the tides became highly concentrated in certain parts of the beach. In 1887 an enterprising local blacksmith called John Carter Tregear, appreciating the value of this material, obtained a licence from the Duchy of Cornwall, the owners of the foreshore, to stream the sand for tin. Six years previously Tregear had obtained the St. Ives Corporation's consent to erect a water wheel near the Western Hotel to process waste material from the mines; and the beach sand was carted there and treated in buddles fed by the Stennack River.

In December 1887 Tregear complained to the Duchy office that ship masters were ballasting their vessels with tin-bearing sand taken from the harbour within the limits covered by his licence. The Duchy thereupon wrote to the Corporation (the harbour authority) requesting that they should put a stop to this practice, and require ships to take their ballast from another part of the harbour. The Council did not take very kindly to this demand. It was pointed out that ships removing ballast were performing a valuable service as the harbour, throughout its history, had always had a tendency to be choked with sand; moreover, vessels had a traditional right to take ballast from the port. Dark hints were also thrown out that Tregear, by sending his refuse down the stream, was blocking the water course, and that he should be careful what he was about! After considering the matter at a special meeting, the Council decided to refer the matter back.

This version of the story has been pieced together from old newspaper reports. An old St. Ives resident gave the following slightly different version of it: "When they were digging along the Wharf to lay a sewer, the men came across a wooden leat, which went right out to the adit under the Harbour Office; and as they were shovelling the sand, they could hardly lift it, it was so heavy. It consisted, in fact, of a deposit of tin from the mines, and Mr. Carter Tregear took it away to the beach under the Church wall and fixed up a buddle which was fed by the Stennack River. It proved to be almost pure tin."

The wooden leat and adit referred to here formed part of the old scheme devised by John Smeaton in 1766 and carried out in 1798 to rid the harbour of sand; see under Wheal Dream. It may be thought surprising that Tregear was able to operate a buddle under the churchyard wall. This would, indeed, be quite impossible today, as the sea comes right up to Pednolva Walk at high tide. However, in his day, before the building of the West Pier, the beach level was much higher, being up to the lifeboat house door, so that the scheme might then have been quite a practical one.

SOUTH ST. IVES

In June 1864 James Lane, a London sharebroker, reported that a company was in course of formation to work ground south of St. Ives Consols, and a week later a prospectus was issued. Although described as a limited company, this concern, the South Saint Ives Tin and Copper Mining Company, Limited, does not appear to have been registered.

The prospectus stated that the property lay between the Providence Mines and Rosewall and Ransom, south of and adjoining St. Ives Consols in granite and near the greenstone junction. It measured 450 fms. from E. to W. and 500 fms. from N. to S., and had three E.-W. lodes and two cross lodes running into St. Ives Consols. Earlier operations were said to have been stopped by water, from which description it appears that part of the property, which lay on both sides of the St. Ives — Towednack parish boundary, may at one time have been worked as Wheal Gift, *q.v.*

The purchase consideration was £5,000, of which £3,000 was in cash and £2,000 in shares credited as paid. The mine was held for 21 years at 1-21st dues. Work began on the mine in the autumn of 1864. Its shares were listed in the *Mining Journal*, 5s. paid, from July to August 1864 and from November 1864 to February 1865. No production is recorded. The secretary's name in 1864 was given as Henry Chapman and that of the manager as Capt. John Nancarrow.[1]

1. MJ 1864 (25.6, 2.7, 29.10)
   MSM 1864 (Aug.) p.96
   Prospectus, 1864 (June), LSE (1965). This is a Stock Exchange prospectus, in a huge bound volume, at the Guildhall Library, London. (Per Justin Brooke)
   Jenkin, Dr. A.K.H. *Mines and Miners of Cornwall*, i, p.34

WEST ST. IVES MINE

In December 1866 a cost-book company was formed to work West St. Ives Mine. This was bounded on the south by St. Ives Consols and Providence mines, and on the west by Rosewall Hill and Ransom United, and should not be confused with West St. Ives Consolidated which was formed in 1868 to work Trevessa and Brea.

The property was held at 1/18th dues from the Duke of Cleveland and the Earl of Mornington, and was said to be kindly for tin and copper. Work began at the end of 1866, and in January 1867 the manager reported that the lode in the end was still continuing its large size and yielding good stones of copper ore. A branch coming out of the footwall to the north was expected to fall in with the lode. In November a meeting was held at which an encouraging report was produced. In May 1868 a shareholder wrote a long puff on the mine, quoting inspection reports. He noted that the mine lay on the coast close to the granite-killas junction, and that an adit had been driven

30 fathoms from sea-level, giving backs of 50 fathoms. The main workings were on an east-west tin lode, and there was another lode to the south of it. A skip-road had been completed. Spargo (1868) added that there were only four men driving the adit from the sea, and that no sales had been made.

The number of employees rose to 15 in 1870, and the workings were said to be 25 fms. deep. A year later Spargo commented that the company had better do one of two things, either abandon the sett or work it more effectually. In July 1871 the lode in the adit end driving west was looking better, improving in size and producing more tin, and was expected to improve further. In September the lode, designated No. 1, was reported to be improving and getting bigger, producing occasional good stones of tin and copper. Soon after, however, the mine ceased operations. Its shares were listed in the *Mining Journal* from December 1866 to April 1872. The secretary of this London-based company from 1867-70 was G. Still; purser (1870) Christopher Stephens; and agent (1867-70) Capt. T. Uren.[1]

West St. Ives Mine is conjecturally identified with the working known locally as Hor Bal, *q.v.*

1. *Mining Journal* January 5 and November 2 1867; April 11, May 30, October 31 1868; January 1 1870; July 29, October 16 1871; Spargo 1868, p.241; 1871 p.57. Williams 1870 p.13.

WHEAL TAVAS

To the north of the Standard lode which courses through the Stennack Valley, and on which the important mines of St. Ives Consols and Trenwith were situated, lay the North lode, exploited by Wheal Ayr in the clay slate, and by Wheal Tavas, and Rosewall Hill and Ransom United mines in the granite. Dines (p.118) quoting Cann, completely misunderstands the latter's statements regarding Wheal Tavas, and so wrongly identifies it with Wheal Applin, on the Bahavella lode, coursing to the south of the Standard lode. "Tavas" is the Cornish language word signifying "tongue" or "language."

TRELYON CONSOLS

The early history of this ancient mine is lost in obscurity; but it appears to have been formed by an amalgamation of several small bals bearing such names as Trelyon Downs, Wheal Venture and Wheal Widden. The sett, sandwiched between Wheal Margery to the N.W. and Wheal Providence on the S.E., lay in the moors on the eastern flank of Worvas Hill, with drainage rights to the cliffs N. of Porthrepta (Carbis Bay) Beach.

"Trelyon Consolidated Mines" was established in 1849 to develop Wheal Venture — 34 fms. deep, and worked by horse power — by bringing up Wheal Margery adit, then 150 fms. distant, under it, to unwater several tin and copper lodes. To this end, Trelyon Consols adventurers bought Wheal Margery sett and added it to their own. However, in the event, this mode of working does not seem to have been adopted, the mine being drained instead by a steam engine which also supplied power for stamping and winding.

In February 1851 the tin lode in the 32 fm. level was reported very good, 2' wide and worth £40 per fm. The shaft was sunk 9 fms. below this level and the lode found to hold good. The copper lode in the 60 also looked well, and they expected to cut the same run of ore in the 30. Returns were more than paying cost.[1]

In February 1853 the mine was reported much improved. The 32 fm. level E. was worth £20 per fm. for copper and tin, and other levels were producing tinstuff of excellent quality.[2] The six months' account ending March 31 1853 showed a credit of £544.2s.7d., enabling a dividend of 15s. to be paid. On the credit side of the cost book was an item of £200 "by Wheal Margery Sett."[3] This sale was effected to enable Wheal Margery, *q.v.*, to be re-started by a new company.

On June 1 as William Allen was tamping a hole in the 40 fm. level a spark ignited the charge, which exploded and killed him on the spot, his son also being seriously injured.[4] Capts. Richard James and John Trevorrow reported in March 1857 that their prospects were most cheering, the machinery in good working order, and the engine performing the whole work — pumping all the water and winding and stamping all the stuff.[5]

In August 1858 proposals were made for working Trelyon Downs bounds conjointly with Providence during the term of their respective setts, each mine bearing an equal proportion of profit and loss. Trelyon Consols would receive £10 per annum for the use of their pumping engine.[6] This new venture was managed by a joint committee under the name of "Providence and Trelyon United."

The February account for 1860 was a most favourable one, a profit of £768.12s.6d. being achieved, and a dividend of £1 per 572nd share paid. Providence Mines contributed £15, half of three months' water charge, whilst Trelyon Lower Mine (Providence and Trelyon United) contributed £75.8s.7d. as its proportion of general operating costs. The 30 fm. level was driving W. of Parry's shaft by 6 men at £10 per fm., lode worth £15. No. 4 stope, working in the back by 4 men at £6 per fm., worth £20, was the nearest stope to the end. No. 1 stope in the bottom, driving by 6 men at £5 per fm., was worth £40. At this point there was a branch of rich tin running nearly at right angles to the lode, worth £25 per fm.; they had opened 5 ft. on it, its course being a little E. of N. The 10 fm. level driving W. was still improving, but not producing sufficient tin to pay for opening the ground. In Trelyon Lower Mine the 16 fm. level was driving E. of Flat Rod shaft by 6 men at £11 per fm., lode worth £8. Two men were working the backs on tribute at 8s.6d. in the £, and earning good wages.[7]

In the December quarter 12 tons 17 cwt. of tin were sold for £984.2s.8d., but only a small profit (£78.14s.9d.) was made. In the 30 W. of Parry's shaft the lode had been poor throughout the period but had improved within the last 4 days and was now worth £12 per fm., driving at £7.10s. In the 20 W. of Parry's the lode had also been of little value, driving at £9 per fm. The stope on the carbona branch in bottom of the 20, running N.E. of the Standard lode, was worth £15 per fm., working at £6. The New shaft was sunk and complete to 4 fms. below the 10 fm. level; they expected another month would put it to the 20, whilst in 4 months it should be complete to the 30. Below that point it would be the sump at about the centre fo the tin ground. While this was being done they would sink below the 30 as far as the water allowed; they had already sunk 6 ft. below this level where the lode was worth £15 per fm. 54 men would be engaged on this operation. In Trelyon Lower Mine the 16 fm. level E. of Flat Rod shaft had passed through the junction of granite and killas and driven 8 fms. into the latter, which was much softer for opening the price being consequently reduced from £14 per fm. to £3.10s., the lode worth £15. Two tributers working in the back of the 16 fm. level 40 fms. behind the end in granite, were making good wages at 9s. in the £ tribute.

The agents, commenting on their choice of site for the New shaft, stated: "After carefully considering the matter, we fixed upon one of the shafts worked many years since, which is about 50 fms. E. of the present one. This we have cleared 9 fms. below the surface, and have 6 fms. more to reach the bottom and then about 8 fms. to sink to communicate with the 16 fm. level. This will be in the heart of the tin ground now being laid open, and is much required for ventilation, and also to afford facilities for cheap and advantageous stoping."[8]

Messrs. Higgs and Son, the pursers, stated in March 1863 that the mine could be considered as a more permanent concern than at any former period. The North lode, which had been opened on in the past few months, appeared as productive as the lode which had hitherto made the profit. "Providence and Trelyon United Mine (on which we have expended about £1,000) will now meet its own cost and when more developed leave a profit, so we do not anticipate any further call."[9] In June 70 men were employed on tutwork and 8 on tribute.[10] The pursers' optimistic predictions were not fulfilled; and the account for February 1865 showed a quarter's loss of £178 and a total debit of £566, resulting in a call of 10s. per 572nd share. Eighteen tons of tin had been sold for £996. It was wistfully recalled that three years since a dividend of £1 per share was regularly declared upon the same quantity of returns.[11] They were then working at a loss on the Lower Mine, whilst the North lode would not pay at the current price for tin. However, the stopes over and under the 50 were looking remarkably well and should help to pay the cost of the mine, apart from the North lode and Lower Mine.[12]

The April account for that year included an item of £423.14s.2d. for "Merchants, boiler and fittings, coals, &c." Mr. R.H. Bamfield was instructed to take proceedings against shareholders in arrear of calls. There were several good points in the mine, and should they turn out as expected, it was hoped to raise 20 tons of tin in the coming quarter.[13] Spargo commented at about this time that the adventurers' perseverance deserved better results. He gave the depth of adit as 20 fms., with another 70 fms. below. The mine possessed a 24″ (double) pumping, stamping and winding engine, the stamps having 16 heads.

The agents' report for March 1866 showed the 70 fm. level on Engine lode driving E. of New shaft by 2 men at £6 per fm., the lode producing low quality tinstuff. The 50 N. and S. on North South lode, with various stopes, was also being worked. In the 30 N. on this lode the lode was small, but an improvement was anticipated, as a good lode had been found in the level above (the 20.) Altogether, there were 11 pitches working by 51 men at from 7s. to 15s. in the £. In Providence and Trelyon United the 40 E. of Lawry's shaft was driving by 4 men at £10 per fm., the lode disorganised by a cross-course. They had a total of 86 men employed underground.[14] This number fell to 70 by December. Although a call of 10s. was then made, the purser gave the actual loss on the three months as only about £50, and prospects appeared excellent, so that a return to the average price of tin for the past 15 years would leave a very satisfactory profit.[15]

By 1867 Trelyon Consols was again meeting costs, but the low price of tin mitigated against dividends. In the six months ending in June 40 tons of tin were raised.[16] The half yearly account presented in July 1868 showed that 43 tons 19 cwt. of tin had been sold for £2,316.15s.4d., at an average price of £54.6s. per ton; only a nominal loss was made. The cross-cut at the 70 fm.. level E. of New shaft on Engine lode was extended 9 fms. 3 ft. N. of lode, and they had only 2 fms. 3 ft. more to drive to reach the North lode; this was one of their best points, as a large quantity of tin had been raised on this lode at shallower levels. It had not been worked below the 50; therefore, when intersected in the cross-cut in two months' time, there would be 20 fms. of backs standing whole for great length. Four men were driving the level at £10.10s. per fm. In the 70 W. of New shaft the lode was producing tin stuff of low quality. This was also a point of importance, as they expected to cut the North South lode after driving a further 3 fms. 24 men were engaged on tutwork, with 30 pitches working on tribute by 66 men at an average tribute of 13s.4d. in the £.[17]

During 1870 uranium was supposedly discovered in the ores, but a sample submitted to a London firm for analysis proved to be of little value.[18] The six monthly account held in June that year showed £1,700 spent on labour, £403 on materials, and £191 on coal; whilst 28 tons 13 cwt. of tin (sold at an average of £71.10s. per ton) realised £2,053, copper £4.5s. and sundries £13. Although the lords had "handsomely given up dues during pleasure," a loss of £223 had been made, the total debit balance being £2567, which necessitated a 15s. call. The agents reported six tribute pitches working in back and bottom of the 60 S. at 10s. in the £. In one pitch the lode was of unusual character, producing mineral of strange appearance, some of it resembling uranium, "but from a trial made it does not produce any of that rich material." The tin found here was, however, of excellent quality, not only in the lode, but also in the granite six feet away. It was these deposits in the granite which often led to carbonas in that neighbourhood. At the beginning of the period they were paying costs, but two pitches had since declined in value, which led to their returns being less than during the previous half year. Nearly all their loss, however, had been caused by the expense of adding a boiler to the engine and changing the stamps, which were now in very good order.[19] The mine was then 86 fms. deep and employing 100 people.

A circular issued to shareholders on March 4 1871 announced an important discovery of tin in the 60 fm. level three weeks previously, the lode now yielding a ton of tin per fathom as far as seen.[20] This lode — the South lode — continued highly productive during the following months, but this did not restore the mine to a state of profitability. In June one stope was reported worth £30 a fm. and two others £25. There were eleven tutwork operations in progress, and 14 pitches working by 30 men at an average tribute of 12s. in the £.[21] A summary of the results achieved since operations commenced in 1849, published in December, showed that in that time the adventurers had paid £81,544.7s.6d. in wages, £2,361.8s.8d. in dues, and £4,004 in dividends, a total of £89,909.16s.2d. Of this sum, £10,203.17s. had been supplied by calls, £75,733.5s.3d. by the sale of 1,197 tons 8 cwts. 3 qrs. 10 lbs. of tin, at an average of £63.5s. per ton, £1,785.8s.7d. from the sale of 261 tons 18 cwts. 2 qrs. of copper at an average of £61.16s. per ton, and £1,038.6s.9d. from sundries, total £88,760.17s.7d., leaving a current debit balance of £148.18s.7d.[22]

Trelyon Consols shares rose from £4 to £9.10s. in May 1872 "in anticipation of cutting the lode running through Richards's ground." The agents reported in June that about 4 fms. further driving in the 70 E. of New shaft would intersect the North lode, and several promising points were being explored. In the 50 E. of Lawry's shaft, in Providence and Trelyon United, there was a lode 2' wide worth £30 per fm. Complaints were made about the cost of coal, which had increased from 11s.11d. per ton in November to 15s.9d. in April. Tin raised in the six months' period amounted to 24 tons 4 qrs., representing a slight decrease.[23] In August, when driving the 60 fm. level N. of New shaft, the North lode was cut; it was 9" wide and worth £15 per fm.

The agents' report for May 1873 is very interesting, in that it makes mention for the first time of the Hendra section, where £400 had been spent on development, producing tin worth only £40. Hendra Farm lies on the N.W. side of Cock Hill, and these workings were probably somewhere near its summit. They had spent about £50 in altering and repairing the engine, which was now in good working order; this had effected a twenty per cent saving in fuel consumption. These outlays had resulted in a rather heavy loss being made. Capt. Richard James spoke confidently of Providence and Trelyon United, which would increase their tin output as operations deepened and extended eastward. "There is something strong and healthy in the appearance of the lode which warrants this favourable opinion." The mine was in a fair state of working, well ventilated; the footways were good, and tramroads had been laid down in two of the principal levels. Should the North lode be found of value in the 60 cross-cut N. of New Engine shaft, and the 70 reach the tin ground S. of cross-course, the mine would reach a paying state; meanwhile, they must continue to make a loss of around £80 a month.[24]

A loss of £522 was recorded in December, and a call of £1 imposed. The lords continued to remit dues, and had also consented to the adventurers working the Cock Hill lode, on which no development had been carried out for about 40 years, as permission could not be obtained from the former Lords. The lode was considered to be of great importance to the mine. It appears to have been located in the Hendra sett, and may have been within the limits of Wheal Queen (q.v.)[25]

Unfortunately, falling tin prices now undermined the plucky and long-suffering shareholders' efforts to bring the mine to a profitable state; and in April 1874 Trelyon Consols was put up for auction as a going concern, but failed to reach the reserve price of £750.[26] As a result, the machinery and materials were offered by auction on June 30. They included a 24″ pumping and stamping engine with 11 tons boiler, whim cage and a 16 head stamps axle; two iron and one wood tram waggons; three whim kibbles; 40 9″ iron air pipes; 15 cwt. of steel borers; two bells; wood rods and iron work from Lawry's shaft to Engine shaft; a superior miner's dial; burning house; and the account house furniture.[27]

The shafts of Trelyon Consols, though fenced, remain open and potentially dangerous among the rhododendrons and bracken on the slope of Worvas Hill near Steeple Lane. They are known as New (150 yards N.E. of Knill's monument), Parry's Lawry's, Flat Rod, Daniel's and Whip, whilst the principal lodes were East-West, North and North-South. The principal adit, known as Chyangweal adit, at one time supplied water via the Hain Walk to the reservoir at Albert Place. This has now been discontinued, but the 100 years' old main still remains in use.

One of the great personalities connected with Trelyon Consols was Capt. Perry, of Chyangweal. Beginning his career as a stamps' boy, he rose by diligence and application to being miner, agent and finally manager of the mine. He became very wealthy, and claimed that the secret of his prosperity was that, however small his income might be, he always managed to live within it, spending no more when a mine agent at £100 per annum than when an ordinary miner at £40. The money thus saved, he adventured in the palmy days of mining, and made large profits. He was equally successful as a tin streamer. Thus the one-time stamps'-boy died in 1878 worth about £20,000 — say, half-a-million in modern currency. He was a great philanthropist, and distributed much of his wealth among the poor and to good causes, including the temperance movement and Methodism.[28] "Parry's" shaft, at Trelyon Consols, was probably named, but misspelt, after him.

1. *Cornish Telegraph* February 14 1851
2. *Cornish Telegraph* February 9 1853
3. *Cornish Telegraph* June 1 1853
4. *Cornish Telegraph* June 8 1853
5. *Cornish Telegraph* March 25 1857
6. *Cornish Telegraph* August 25 1858
7. *Cornish Telegraph* March 14 1860
8. *Cornish Telegraph* December 12 1860
9. *Royal Cornwall Gazette* March 20 1863
10. *Royal Cornwall Gazette* June 19 1863
11. *Royal Cornwall Gazette* February 3 1865
12. *Cornish Telegraph* March 8 1865
13. *Cornish Telegraph* June 14 1865
14. *Cornish Telegraph* March 14 1866
15. *Cornish Telegraph* December 26 1866
16. *Royal Cornwall Gazette* June 20 1867
17. *Cornish Telegraph* July 8 1868
18. *Cornish Telegraph* May 18 1870
19. *Cornish Telegraph* June 28 1870
20. *Cornish Telegraph* March 8 1871
21. *Cornish Telegraph* June 28 1871
22. *Cornish Telegraph* December 20 1871
23. *Cornish Telegraph* June 19 1872
24. *Cornish Telegraph* May 21 1873
25. *Cornish Telegraph* December 3 1873
26. *Cornish Telegraph* May 6 1874
27. *Cornish Telegraph* June 24 1874
28. *Cornish Telegraph* July 23 1878

WHEAL TRENWïTH

Wheal Trenwith is a mine which enjoys a reputation altogether disproportionate to its size, and rightly so, for its history is a romantic one, particularly in regard to its association with Madame Curie, the discoverer of radium. The sett lies on the southern side of the Stennack Valley, the principal shafts being located near the little hamlet of Trenwith Square, overlooking the valley's narrow, steep-sided "waist." Indeed, the escarpment just below these houses consists largely of old mine refuse, whilst part way down the slope may still be seen the concrete bed of some of the old dressing machinery.

Trenwith Main lode is actually the N.E. extension of the Standard lode of St. Ives Consols; it courses E. 25 deg. N., underlying N. South lode runs parallel to it 20 fms. to the S. The shallow parts of the mine are in metamorphosed killas and greenstone, the deeper workings being in granite. The shafts, from W. to E., are Wills' (120 yards E. by N. of Nanjivey cross roads), Victory (a little W. of Trenwith Square), Berriman's (adjoining the

N.W. corner of the Trenwith car park), Old Sump (at the top of Trenwith Burrows Hill) and Dale's (at the western end of Trenwith Place, by the steps leading to Parc-an-Roper coach park.) On March 3 1922 the *St. Ives Times* reported that, following heavy rain, the surface sollar of an old shaft had subsided in a pathway between Trenwith Place and Parc Avenue, revealing a chasm 10 yards across and 20 yards deep. The cavity was filled in by St. Ives Mines, Ltd., who owned the property, 100 loads of stuff being required for the purpose, the adit at its bottom being first covered with a thick layer of concrete. Adit level in Trenwith is linked with St. Ives Consols on the W.; it terminates near Royal Square, water issuing therefrom forming part of the town's supply. (See Appendix.)

The mine's origins are lost in the mists of time, but it was clearly one of the earliest to be set to work in the borough. In May 1812 "tin Twelfth Dole or Dish (being the Lord's dues) of that valuable Tin and Copper Mine, called Wheal Trenwith, situate in the Borough of St. Ives, and comprehending in the Sett the whole of the Manor and Barton of Trenwith" was offered for sale privately for a term of three, five, or seven years by William Lander, the proprietor.[1]

It would appear from this advertisement that in its early years Trenwith produced tin and copper in proportionate amounts, but as the workings were extended the tin seems to have largely disappeared, and it became principally a copper producer. The mine was prosecuted vigorously for this metal from 1825 onwards. In May 12 1826 a cargo of copper ore raised there was loaded into the schooner *Polmanter* at St. Ives pier, and on the 16th another cargo on board the *Betsey*. These were the first shipments of their kind ever remembered to have been made from that port.[2] Copper ore had, in fact, been sent from St. Ives by sea as early as 1585; see under Western Worke.

In October 1828 a young miner named Woolcock was fatally injured in a blasting accident. A few years after it would seem that the mine was temporarily "knocked." This may be inferred by an agreement made on October 1 1832 between St. Ives Corporation and John and William Chellew, the text of which is to be found in the second volume of the old St. Ives Borough Accounts. It shows that the Chellews granted the Corporation permission to lay water pipes or aqueducts through a part of their property comprising a stable, grist mill and mill leat, part of the barton of Trenwith, and an adjoining garden "formerly the Plot of a Tin Stamping Mill...for conveying and supplying the Water from the Mouth or Entrance of the Deep Adit or Water Level belonging to Wheal Trenwith Tin and Copper Mine in the Barton or Estate of Trenwith...for the only proper use and benefit of all the Inhabitants of the...Borough." The Corporation undertook to pay each of the Chellews 2s.6d. annually by way of acknowledgement, the agreement to cease if and when the pipes were removed. The grist mill mentioned in the document stood at the eastern end of Trenwith Place by the steps leading from Royal Square to Parc Avenue. The Stennack Valley at that period contained a number of water mills and stamps, all powered by the Stennack River, which finds its way to the sea below St. Ives churchyard wall. Trenwith adit at that period terminated at Dale's shaft, its water then running in a leat to the "Fountain" behind Royal Square. The fact that the adit stream was taken over for supplying drinking water in 1832 shows that Wheal Trenwith must then have been idle, as the discharge for a working mine would have been quite unsuitable for this purpose.

The suspension of the mine at this time must have been very short lived. Statistics show that between 1825 and 1856 13,080 tons of copper ore, yielding 1,450 tons of refined copper and 20 tons of black tin were produced, the total value of this metal being £114,000. The miners also raised large quantities of a black substance which they mistakenly took to be black copper ore, and accordingly despatched as such, admixed with genuine copper, to the refiners. The resulting product, however, proved of very inferior quality, and realised prices which greatly disappointed both miners and smelters. In 1843 the geologist Henwood noted that a specimen of this unsatisfactory copper was examined by Mr. Michell of Calenick smelting house and found to be alloyed with "titanium" — *uranium* may have been intended here — in a metallic state. The ores were then inspected, and pitchblende being discovered amongst them, its prejudicial effect on the copper ores was explained to the workmen, who thereafter rejected it. "Was there ever an instance in which an acquaintance with mineralogy and chemistry would have been more useful" concluded Henwood with unconscious irony; for the great potentialities of pitchblende were then quite unknown, uranium itself being regarded as little more that a metallurgical curiosity, whilst radium, which always occurs with it, had not even been discovered. So, huge quantities of this now extremely valuable ore were thrown away heedlessly by the miners on the burrows of Wheal Trenwith, much of it being later broken down by the "spallers" or stone breakers with their hammers, and used for repairing the streets of the borough! It used to be said that that streets of London were, metaphorically speaking, paved with gold; but the streets of St. Ives are, in a quite literal sense, paved with uranium — another metal of great value, and today eagerly sought after in all parts of the world.

Wheal Trenwith's fortunes fluctuated greatly over the years, and it does not appear ever to have enjoyed a long period of continuous operations. Its cessation around the year 1832 has already been noted, and the mine was again suspended in 1849. It was set to work again for the last time as a copper producer in 1853. The *Cornish Telegraph* reported on May 25 that three companies had been formed for working Carrack Dhu United Mines, Wheal Trenwith and Wheal Margery, all in the parish of St. Ives, and close to the town. Engines were to be erected on all three forthwith, "and from the strength of the parties concerned, there is reason to expect that they will be carried on with spirit, so that the demand for labour in this neighbourhood is likely to be very great."

One of those who found employment at Trenwith unfortunately soon afterwards met with a fatal accident. On June 5 1854 as Richard Stevens was standing on a stage timbering an old shaft, the chain holding the stage slipped, causing a sudden jerk. He lost his balance, fell 20 fms. and was instantly killed, leaving a widow and four small children to lament his loss.

The optimism felt at the restarting of Trenwith in 1853 proved to be misplaced, for it ceased work again in 1856, the machinery and materials being advertised to be sold by auction on February 23 1857. Included were an excellent 40″ cylinder steam pumping engine, 8′ stroke with 9 tons boiler; capstan shears; 150 fms. 9″ capstan rope; balance and angle bob; 150 fms. of 8″ and 9″ flat rods; 240 fms. of iron stave ladders; machine and horse whim kibbles; two horse whims; strips, buddles, trunks and frames; kieves, etc., on the stamps floors; hutches and dressing tools on the copper dressing floors; and the account house furniture. Enquiries should be made of Capt. Hollow, on the mine, Mr. Bamfield, solicitor, St. Ives, or George Sealy, auctioneer, Marazion.[4]

Following this closure, no further attempt to revive the mine was made for half-a-century; but during this period of quiescence (January 1874) what was described as "the adit-shaft of Wheal Trenwith Mine in a field to the West of the old engine-house on the hill" was found to be in an open and dangerous condition, and instruction were accordingly given for it to be properly secured, the contract being awarded to Mr. Robert Roach, stonemason, who had had previous experience of this kind of work. He employed two miners, John and William Berriman, brothers, to assist him. These men laid granite slabs across the shaft with a hold in the soil about 3 fms. from the top of the burrow by which it was surrounded. The gaps between these slabs were filled in and some rubbish thrown over all, preparatory to levelling in from above, when the entire sollar gave way, carrying with it into the shaft William Berriman and his brother's 13 year old son. John Berriman descended the shaft by the windlass rope, and extricating the boy from the rubble with which he was partly covered, brought him safely to grass. William was not so fortunate, having been killed by one of the granite slabs which fell upon him. His body was recovered the following day by a party of about 20 miners, volunteers, led by John Curnow, timberman at St. Ives Consols, the work being attended with great danger. The dead man was carried in a very mournful procession to his home at Chyangweal, near the Providence Mines, where he had been employed. It was thought the accident had been caused by the covering stones not being of sufficient length to obtain a firm hold in the ground. The shaft, previously known as Adit shaft, was re-named Berriman's shaft in commemoration of this tragic mishap.

During the mine's period of idleness following the 1856 closure the adit outfall was once more pressed into service as a water supply. In 1887 Mr. E. Noy unsuccessfully sought permission from the Council to work a sett near the Trenwith water course, promising not to pollute the stream if they agreed. He had already carried out some unauthorised work there, and one of the

63

councillors stopped these activities until the Council had been consulted. A Mr. Bamfield claimed to hold the sett, which had been granted in 1811 "for ever more." Bamfield had offered it to the Corporation in 1885 for a nominal sum, but this had not been accepted. He was, however, still willing to let the Council have it, and they thereupon agreed to purchase the sole rights for £10.

Victory Shaft headgear, Trenwith Mine (St. Ives Consolidated)   (Noall Collection)

With the subsequent growth of the town the value of the Trenwith adit water supply increased enormously. When, therefore, proposals were issued in 1906-7 for re-working Trenwith mine, together with St. Ives Consols, Rosewall Hill and Giew by a new company, St. Ives Corporation were faced with the necessity of finding an alternative source. Not unnaturally, in the circumstances, the Council looked to the mining company to provide compensation to help meet the cost of the new scheme; but their attitude evoked some acid comment in the *Mining Journal* in May 1907. After noting that Messrs. Edmund and Arthur Schiff and their friends had taken up the mine setts, the paper continued: "Just when one is about to congratulate Messrs. Schiff on their perspicacity, up bob certain members of St. Ives Town Council and oppose the working of the said mines unless a heavy premium is paid, on the score that the drinking water for St. Ives and Carbis Bay comes through and will be rendered undrinkable if the said mines are worked. Consequently the Schiff group is asked to find a large part of the cash to provide a new drinking water supply for the increasingly fashionable resorts of St. Ives and Carbis Bay. Possibly Messrs. Schiff have never heard of the 'Pirates of Penzance,' or they would not have generously offered £1,000 towards a scheme in which they are not interested to the value of one penny, and towards which they are now asked (or, rather, 'morally pressed,') to contribute £5,000. The St. Ives district is a good one for mining ventures; but if the men who are bringing their own and their friends' money there are to be met with 'stand and deliver,' they will be well advised to go to other equally promising districts where tribute is levied in less rude fashion.'' The ''tribute'' was, however, duly paid; this money being used to construct a surface reservoir at Bussow Moor, the waterworks there being opened on Easter Monday, 1910.

The company formed to develop Wheal Trenwith in 1908 was known as the St. Ives Consolidated Mines, Ltd., reference to which has already been made under St. Ives Consols. Their object, as far as Trenwith was concerned, was to purchase radium. This element had only recently been isolated by Mme. Curie, but a great demand had already arisen for it, both for medical and commercial purposes. The person who first appreciated the value of the Trenwith pitchblende deposits seems to have been Edmund Schiff, an American of mixed Jewish and Welsh parentage, who came to Cornwall as a child and became one of the outstanding mining engineers in the country. He got in touch with Mme. Curie, and raised money from American friends with which the equipment was brought for her to carry out her first experiments. As a result, she produced the first sample of radium ever to be isolated. This was sold to Sir Julius Wernher, a cancer sufferer, for £60,000. After his death the radium was given to Hampstead Cancer Research Hospital, the first they had ever had. Schiff was also associated with the development of the pitchblende deposits at the Terrace Mine, St. Austell. He evolved an ambition scheme to pump water from radioactive springs in Wheal Trenwith to Tregenna Castle Hotel, which it was proposed to turn into a "radium spa." The harmful effects of exposure to radiation were then little appreciated, so it was perhaps just as well that this particular venture had to be abandoned owing to the death of his partner, a wealthy American. Schiff was himself relatively prosperous at this time, but died a pauper at Gunnislake in 1952 at the age of 92.[6]

Sir Francis Fox was also associated with the development work at Trenwith. In his book *Sixty Years of Engineering* he recalled that, having heard in 1908 that boxes of rich radium ore were being forwarded to Mme. Curie in Paris from Cornwall at a price of £200 for 150 lbs. weight, he went to Trenwith and spent several days digging among the burrows. Several lumps of very heavy ore were found and submitted to the great chemist Sir William Ramsay for analysis. They proved to be pitchblende of a very high quality, worth £3,380 a ton, each ton containing 192 milligrammes of radium. Ramsay extracted eight milligrammes of radium from these ores, this being exhibited at Burlington House on May 12 1909, the first sample or radium ever produced in this country from British ores. He was quoted at the time as saying that the ores were equal in productiveness for radioactive materials and uranium compounds to any pitchblende which had come under his notice from any part of the world.

Headgear and tramroad, Trenwith Mine (St. Ives Consolidated)   (Noall Collection)

The extraction of radium from pitchblende is a difficult and complex process; and in December 1908 a subsidiary company, called the British Radium Corporation, Ltd., with a nominal capital of £40,000 in 5s. shares, was formed for refining this substance from the concentrates, with an under-lease and licence to work Trenwith for pitchblende, uranium and radium. The purchase price payable to the parent company was £35,000, to be satisfied by £5,000 in cash and £30,000 in fully paid shares. St. Ives Consolidated had a call upon all unissued capital and subscribed for 20,000 shares for cash. Sir Francis Fox and Sigismund Moritz were appointed on the board to represent the company. A firm at Frankfurt undertook to purchase the Radium Corporation's entire output; this German connection was later to have most unfortunate consequences.

Operations began by processing dump material rejected by the old copper miners, this being picked by hand, there being no mill available; but the objective was to recover the mine, and in January 1910 it was reported that electric pumping plant had been installed, enabling the workings to be re-opened rapidly with gratifying results.[7] Power for these pumps was derived from the central generating station at St. Ives Consols. By April, the water was down to the 5th level below adit, and exceptionally high grade pitchblende was being mined in addition to fair quantities of good grade ore sorted from the stulls. The total stock was valued at £30,000 for uranium and radium. The first consignment of five tons of high grade pitchblende had been sent to the

66

Corporation's works at Limehouse for treatment.[8] During May, four tiny heaps of crystals, which together would barely cover a shilling representing 295 milligrammes of pure radium bromide, were displayed at their London offices, its value being about £6,000. In a circular dated June 19 the shareholders of St. Ives Consolidated, Ltd., were informed that a crushing plant, with a capacity of 24 tons per day for treating the large quantities of milling ore at surface — sufficient, it was said, to keep the plant fully occupied for a number of years — was being erected. Meanwhile, Limehouse continued to be supplied with hand-picked pitchblende.[9]

Despatching pitchblende from Trenwith Mine, circa 1910   (Noall Collection)

On July 18 members of various mining and engineering societies in Cornwall, under the presidency of Lord St. Levan, visited the mine and examined the surface equipment. Mr. Schiff showed them some interesting experiments with 50 milligrammes of radium bromide obtained from Trenwith ore. The Radium Corporation at this time was proving very successful, having recently paid a 20% dividend. It was virtually the only radium manufacturer in Britain, and Trenwith the only producer of pitchblende.[10] The erection of the ball mill in the Stennack Valley — it stood on the site of Rosewall Cottages — was completed by September. Good indication had been found in the mine of a new eastern pitchblende zone between No's 3 and 5 levels about 130' E. of Berriman's shaft.

Early in 1913 it was announced that 85 tons of copper had been recovered.

Profitable tin ground had also been found in No's 9 and 10 levels W. of Victory shaft, and W. of the copper and uranium zone. In May, the lode above the 100 fm. level near the cross-course in Victory shaft section had greatly improved in value and width. A six ton parcel of ore broken over a stoping width of 3' had assayed 30 lbs. of black tin per ton. The July report stated that the stoping of pitchblende ore above No. 3 level W. of Victory shaft had been commenced with very satisfactory results, and good values were anticipated in this western section both in the shallow and deeper levels. Radium worth £11,134 had been sold in a four weeks' period by the Radium Corporation. Their radium bromide had recently been independently tested and pronounced of the greatest purity and excellence. Deliveries had been made to hospitals and other institutions in Berlin, Frankfurt-on-Main, London, Liverpool and Glasgow as well as to physicians in America and South Africa.[11]

Speaking at St. Ives Consolidated's annual meeting in December the Chairman stated that the Radium Corporation's new works at Elmer's End, when in full operation, would give the parent company profits from some 4,000 milligrammes of radium bromide at £20 per milligramme. Most unfortunately, the two companies soon afterwards ran into serious financial difficulties. The outbreak of the Great War in August 1914 resulted in a severance of relations between the British Radium Corporation and its German opposite number, leaving the former virtually without a purchaser for its product. Faced with this predicament, an appeal was made to the Government for assistance, the company undertaking in return to supply them with all the radium required for the luminous dials of watches, compasses and clocks. Regrettably, this was refused, though Government did purchase what was described as £250,000 worth of inferior radium from America. The Trenwith radium mine had been the only profitable section of St. Ives Consolidated's various interests, and its collapse inevitably followed. The Anglo-American Oil Company petitioned, as a creditor, for its winding-up in February 1915, but the company at first resisted, claiming that if a compulsory order was made about 4-500 men would be thrown out of work. After five postponements in the Companies Winding-Up Court, the order was finally granted in March.[12] Arrangements were subsequently made for production to be continued at Giew, but Trenwith and St. Ives Consols were abandoned.

Apart from its dumps, which have since been largely overlaid by material excavated during the construction of the Parc-an-Roper coach park, the most interesting reminder of this old mine today is the little group of houses at Trenwith Square, between Victory and Berriman's shafts. The mine captain's dwelling, facing east, is substantially built of granite. Its iron gate posts were once decorated with cleverly wrought figures of a cock and hen. Adjoining at the N.E. corner of the square is the old count house, or office. Along the eastern side of this building formerly ran an iron stairway or ladder leading to a raised platform, upon which an agent would stand to auction the pitches to the tributers assembled below. One other curious relic of this mine, the "buckstone," on which the bal maidens used to break or "buck" the copper ore into small fragments with their hammers, was destroyed some years ago during road widening operations. It stood at the eastern end of Rosewall Terrace, beside the road leading to the coach park.

1. *Royal Cornwall Gazette* May 1812
2. Capt. J.T. Short's *Diary*; *Royal Cornwall Gazette* May 20 1826
3. Second volume, St. Ives Borough Accounts
4. *Cornish Telegraph* February 11 1857
5. *Cornish Telegraph* February 17 1887
6. *Western Echo* June 28 1952
7. *St. Ives Weekly Summary* January 29 1910
8. *St. Ives Weekly Summary* April 30 1910
9. *St. Ives Times* June 21 1912
10. *St. Ives Times* July 26 1912
11. *St. Ives Times* August 29 1913

TREVALGAN

Trevalgan Hill lies to the north of Buttermilk Hill (the western extension of Rosewall Hill), with Trevalgan Farm running northwards from it to the sea. In May 1813 "1-4th in a Pair of Bounds, called Trevalgin, alias Trallegan Bounds" in St. Ives was offered for sale, this being again in the market two years later under the name of "Trevalgin, alias Trullegan Bounds."

TROWAN CONSOLS

A printed circular issued to the adventurers in "Trowan Consols Mine" in 1846 showed that this enterprise had sustained a loss of £1,038 in the December quarter, necessitating a call of £10 per share.[1] It appears then to have been in the development stage, for only £81 worth of tin had been sold. In the corresponding quarter of 1847 the accounts showed a profit of £136, and Capt. Penberthy hoped for a still better result at the next account.[2] The mine had by then attained a depth of 25 fms. This "Capt. Penberthy" was probably the uncle of Sir Henry Irving, with whom the great Victorian actor-manager spent his boyhood years at Halsetown. Trowan Consols had a fairly short career; work was suspended in 1851, but the materials were not sold until May 1854. They included a 26" steam engine, boiler, 24 heads stamps, 200 fms. flat rods, pumps, three horse whims and 100 fms. of ladders.[3] A legal action took place in October 1849 (Kernick v. Hobson and others) concerning the sale of shares of defaulting shareholders in this mine.

The location of Trowan Consols is not known with certainty, but it may have been identical either with Wheal Racer or (more probably) Goole Pellas, both situated on the northern flank of Rosewall Hill. Trowan Farm formerly

Mine Materials for Sale.

TO BE SOLD BY AUCTION, on Wednesday, the 10th of May next, to commence precisely at 11 o'clock in the forenoon, at

TROWAN CONSOLS

MINE (NEAR ST. IVES.)

The following valuable

MINE MATERIALS,

VIZ:

A very good 26 inch cylinder

STEAM ENGINE

(9 feet Stroke in, and 8 feet out,)

With a 7 Tons Boiler, 1 Fly-wheel and Connections complete ; 24 Heads of Stamps, Iron Axles; Frames, &c., complete ; 3 Balance Bobs, and 1 V Bob Sheaves, 200 fathoms of one and a half and 1¼ inch Flat Rods.

8 fathoms of 7 inch Plunger Lift, with 8 inch Pole complete,

18	do. of 6 inch	do.	with 5 inch do.
53	do. of 5 inch	do.	with 4½ inch do.
14	do. of 4 inch Drawing Lift,		

2 9 feet, 5¼ inch Working Barrels,
1 9 feet, 6 inch Windbore,
1 9 feet, 5¼ inch   do.
1 3 feet, 5 inch Door Piece,
3 9 feet, 4¼ inch Working Barrel,
2 9 feet, 5 inch Windbore,
35 fathoms of 1 inch Bucket Rods,
60   do.   of 5 inch Wood Rods, with Plates, &c., complete,
3 Horse Whims, Shears,
Smith's Bellows, Anvil and Vice.
Smith's and Miner's Tools,
Bolts and Burs, Flanch Rings,
Screwing Stock and Gear,
Scales, Beams, and Weights,
A quantity of new and old Iron and Steel.

200 fathoms of Whim Chain, Whim and Winze, Kibbles, Water Barrels, 100 fathoms of Ladders Winch and Chain, Triangles, &c. of Flat Rods, Cisterns, Buckets, Prongs, Brasses from 3¼ to 5¼ inches, Staples and Glands, Blocks, Ropes, Chests, Barrows, Buddles, Kieves, Frames, Sheds, Launders, a quantity of new Timber, Pulleys, Air-pipes, Grinding-stone, a large quantity of Plank and other Timber,

A Good Dial, and all the

COUNTING HOUSE FURNITURE

and a variety of other articles.

For further particulars apply to Capt. Joshua Daniel, the Agent ; Mr. Henry Noell, Mining Offices, Hayle ; or to the auctioneer,

MR. JAMES PERMEWAN,

Dated 20th April, 1854.   Penzance.

Advertisement detailing the sale of mine materials at Trowan Consols, April 1854
(Noall Collection)

included a piece of land on this hill known as Trowan Downs, but this was later exchanged for a portion of cliff owned by the adjoining farm of Anjue Green. In September 1886 Mr. Eustice, C.E., of Hayle, having reported to the St. Ives Water Committee that the stream of "Trowan Down" was running at four gallons per minute, it was decided to instal a syphon in the adjoining shaft, and lay pipes, to augment the town's supply.[4]

Some mining activity appears to have been carried out elsewhere at Trowan. On December 31 1804 1/12th of one pair of tin bounds "in Trowan Lane End, in the parish of St. Ives," was put up for auction at the Union Hotel, Penzance.[5] Again, according to an old tradition, a tunnel connected Trowan hamlet with the cliff, which used to be employed for smuggling. Some years ago the farmer, Mr. Arthur Berriman, related this story to the St. Ives Senior Scouts, who explored Trowan Cliff, and there found the entrance to this old passage, which was probably a mine adit. They were able to explore it for a distance of fity yards, but beyond this point the tunnel was blocked by debris.

1. At St. Ives Museum
2. *Penzance Journal*, December 1 1847
3. *Cornish Telegraph*, May 3 1854
4. St. Ives Water Committee Minute Book
5. *Royal Cornwall Gazette*, December 15 1894
   VJ 1847 (27.11, 4.12); 1849 (11.8, 20.10); 1850 (7.12); 1854 (29.4)

WHEAL WELLESLEY

Shares in Wheal Wellesley, St. Ives, were offered for sale in August and September 1836 by local share-dealers. The mine was one of a number mentioned in an article in the *Plymouth and Devonport Journal* which was criticised by the *Mining Journal* in October 1836 as being "misleading." The mine adjoined St. Ives Consols, of which it later became a part. Collins (1912, p.610) states that Wheal Wellesley was raising tin in 1836, probably on the strength of the *Mining Journal* reference.[1] The mine was presumably named after Pole Tylney Long Wellesley, elected one of the two M.P.s for St. Ives in 1830.

1. *Mining Journal*, 21 August, 3 September and 1 October 1836; Dines (1956, p.114)

WESTERN WORKE

The earliest mine at St. Ives of which any detailed record has survived was the "western worke" mentioned in a letter written at St. Ives on October 27 1585 by John Otes to Mr. William Carnsewe, of Bokelly, in Cornwall, Quarter-Master to the then Lord Lieutenant of that county, Sir Walter Raleigh. Successful attempts were then being made by the Company of Mines Royal to establish a copper smelting industry at Neath, in South Wales, using the expertise of German specialists in this field. Copper ore raised in Cornwall was sent by sea to Wales to be refined. Ulricke Frosse, for example, was overseer of "mineral woorkes" at "Perin Sands," whilst there were other copper works at St. Just, ores from the latter being brought overland to St. Ives for shipment.

Concerning the St. Ives mine, John Otes stated: "More to certyfye your W'rshipp for the western worke at St. Ives. There was 2 men of o'rs wroght one whole weeke, and wrought 2 feathem from the place. Mr. Denham did appoynt forth right in the load and found nothing, but at the place they began: more, the clyff is so lose that it falls, so y't the men wold not work but one week, soe it is gyven over tyll Mr. Denham's return."

In another letter written by Ulricke Frosse from Neath to Robert Denham on July 4 1585, reference was made to the ores of St. Ives and St. Just: "Yo'r owre of St. dives is very harte to melte it, hopinge we will over com it, what St. Ust owrs will do, we longe to se it."[1]

It is interesting to speculate just where the Western Worke was situated. One conjecture is that it may have been Wheal Providence, which borders Carbis Bay beach; and this identification may perhaps be strengthened by Norden's reference to a mine at "Carbisse" in St. Ives in 1584; but this was a tin-work, and the Western Worke was a copper producer. Perhaps a more likely candidate is Wheal Margery, just south of Porthminster Point, an ancient bal where copper, as well as tin, was raised in appreciable quantities.

1. Grant-Francis, Col., *The Smelting of Copper in the Swansea District of South Wales from the Time of Elizabeth to the Present Day*, 1881. (Per Justin Brooke.)

SECOND SECTION
TOWEDNACK DISTRICT

AMALVEOR MINE (JOBY'S MINE)
BAL-GUY
WHEAL BASKET AND WHEAL BAYEW
BILLIA
WHEAL CONQUER
WHEAL DIPPER
DRYSACK AND MANUEL'S POOLS
DURLO
GEORGIA CONSOLS
GIEW (SOUTH PROVIDENCE)
LADY DOWNS
WHEAL MONTAGU (GREAT CLEVELAND)
WHEAL MUSIC AND WHEAL SANDWICH (TRENDRINE HILL)
WEST PROVIDENCE
WHEAL RANSOM
REETH CONSOLS
NORTH WHEAL REETH
WEST WHEAL REETH
NEW WEST WHEAL REETH (BALDHU)
ROSEWALL HILL AND RANSOM UNITED: GOOLE PELLAS
WHEAL RUBY
OLD TINCROFT CONSOLS (NEW TINCROFT UNITED)
WEST WHEAL TIN-CROFT
TOWEDNACK BOUNDS
TREVEGA BAL (TREVESSA AND BREA: WEST ST. IVES
    CONSOLIDATED: BREA CONSOLS)
WHEAL TYRINGHAM CONSOLS (WHEAL BUSSAR, BUZZA,
    BESOW, BUSSOW, OR BOSSOM: WEST WHEAL PROVIDENCE)
WHEAL UNION (WHEAL WENS)

AMALVEOR MINE (JOBY'S MINE)

On Amalveor moors may be seen a series of mine dumps, shafts and an adit. These are the remains of Amalveor Mine, and form the source of the water supply at Beagle Rose which is connected to the covered reservoir on Worvas Hill. At the eastern end of these workings is a small mine which was still being worked single handed by a man called Joby in the 1920's, hence called Joby's Mine. He would go down the shaft, fill the bucket with ore, then ascend to surface and haul it up by the windlass. After this he would take a long rest and a smoke and was "as happy as the day was long."[1]

1. Per Mr. E.T. Berryman, Beagletodn, Towednack

BAL-GUY

On July 25 1839 7-12ths of Wheal Guy Bounds, in Towednack, were renewed for Sir Christopher Hawkins; the bounder would receive 1-12th dues and the lord 1-15th. The bounds, which had four corners, covered 50-60 acres. A Mr. Mitchell claimed 5s.6d. per year due to him for 14 years past for renewing the bounds, this amount having been last paid by Robert Bennett. The mine was expected to go to work soon. On April 18 1848 Thomas Mitchell of St. Ives said Sir Christopher Hawkins had 4-12ths of "Bal Guy in Towednack in Hammel Veor and other estates, part common, part enclosed." He thought the bounds were nearly three miles round, the freehold belonging to Grylls, Berryman and Rosewall.[1]

The mine itself appears to have had at least two periods of operation. The *Penzance Gazette* of June 16 1847 announced the forthcoming auction of a mine in Towednack called Bal-Guy, with all its materials. It was described as a "very promising tin mine," and the equipment comprised a horse whim, pumps, about 300' of Norway balk in plank, and other materials, all quite new and in good working order. The mine had only been worked by the present adventurers for a few months; they had spent about £140 in clearing up and collaring the shafts of the old workings; and the only reason why it was now offered for sale was the failure by several of them to pay up their back calls. Most of the remaining adventurers would co-operate with any respectable Company in the continued prosecution of the enterprise. Further information could be obtained from Capt. William Roach or Mr. Peter Thomas, both resident near the mine.

1. DD.J. 1339, CRO, Truro

WHEAL BASKET AND WHEAL RAYEW

On December 7 1807 a tin sett was granted "in all those two fields called the Towednacks in the parish of Towednack on a lode called Wheal Basket, with liberty to drive an adit called Wheal Bayew adit through part of the tenement of Amalveor."[1] "Bayew" is apparently an alternative spelling of Behu; see under Billia, Durlo and Giew. "Basket" is not otherwise known.

1. Sett Book, Praed Coll., C.R.O., Truro

BILLIA

The Billia is an ancient mine lying immediately to the W. of Giew. Its early history cannot easily be disentangled from those of its neighbours, Giew, Behu and Durlo, as it was at various times worked with them under different names. At the sale of the effects of R. Gyles, a St. Ives bankrupt, advertised to take place at the Star Inn, St. Ives, on August 18 1812, one of the lots consisted of a twentieth part of "Wheal Billiard and Gue Tin Mine," in the parish of Towednack.[1]

During the mid-19th century the mine formed part of Giew Consolidated, but following the collapse of that venture it enjoyed a brief independent existence as Billia Consols between 1865-67. In April 1867 it was reported that about twelve months previously some 20 miners had had a hairsbreadth escape when working in the 30 fm. level of Billia Consols. The immense range of suspended workings, nearly half a mile in length, of Reeth Consols, closely adjoined the place where they were clearing away some old ground supposed to have been last worked some seventy years previously. The enormous body of water pent up in Reeth Consols unexpectedly burst in upon them, and only the comparatively shallow depth at which they were employed saved them from the vast flood which followed.[2]

Billia Consols was suspended in 1867; and following two unsuccessful attempts in that year and in 1869 to restart the whole complex of mines of which it had been a part, the machinery and materials of the "Billia, late the Durlo Mine," were advertised for sale in February 1870. On offer were the 36" pumping engine, 9' stroke in cylinder and 8' in shaft, with 10 tons boiler; a 22" winding engine, 8' x 7' stroke, with whim cage and boiler; a 27" stamping engine, with boiler and 36 heads of stamps; various pumps, including 30 fms. of 10" in the Billia shaft and 30 fms. of 7" above adit in Robinson's shaft; 150 fms. of 9/16" whim chain; 500 fms. horizontal iron rods; 56 fms. 9" main rods; 150 fms. of old ladders; four tram wagons; 300 fms. bell wire; two horse whims; 100 fms. of 3" air pipes; 100 fms. iron stave ladders; and a brass bell.[3] This advertisement appeared on several occasions; but in the meantime Thomas Treweeke, jun., of Lelant, published a statement to the effect that he had purchased the mine, with all its setts and materials, together with adjoining setts necessary for its proper development.[4] However, in April it was announced that the mine had been bought in at the sale for £1,400 and placed in the hands of Capt. Arundel Anthony for the purpose of forming a

75

BILLIA (LATE DURLO) MINE, TOWEDNACK,
WEST CORNWALL.

IMPORTANT MINE SALE.

TO BE SOLD, by auction, by Mr. JOHN PER-
MEWAN, auctioneer, on Billia, late the Durlo,
mine, Towednack, on Tuesday, the 15th day of March,
1870, at 11 o'clock, a.m., the following machinery and
materials :—

1 36-in. cylinder pumping engine, 9 ft. stroke in cylinder
   by 8 ft. in shaft, with 10 tons' boiler and fittings.
1 22-in. cylinder winding engine 8 ft. and 7 ft. stroke,
   with whim-cage, boiler, and fittings complete.
1 27-in. cylinder stamping-engine, with boiler and fittings, and 36 heads of stamps attached.
39 10 inch 9-feet pumps.
27 8 ,,   do.
10 7 ,,   do.
20 6 ,,   do.
10 5 ,,   do.
 1 10 ,, H. piece.
 1 10 ,, door piece.
 1 10 ,, 9 feet windbore.
 1 8 ,,   do.
 1 6 ,,   do.
 1 9 ,,   do.
 1 8 ,, door piece.
 2 6 ,,   do.
 1 5 ,,   do.
 1 6 ,, working barrel.
 1 4 ,,   do.
 1 9 ,, top door-pieces.
 3 8 ,, top door-pieces.
 4 10 ,, pumps.
30 fms. 10-in. pumps in the Billia shaft.
30 ,, 7   ,,   above the adit in Robinson's shaft.
 1 11 inch pump.
 1 9 ,, H piece.
 1 4 ,, door piece.
150 fms. of 9-16 inch whim-chain.
500 ,, of 2 horizontal iron rods.
 7 pairs of strapping-plates.
 1 pair of main-caps.
 2 pairs do. with side plates.
 1 pair do.
 2 pairs of strapping-plates.
13 sets   do.
Iron work for balance-bob.
56 fms. of 9-inch main rods.
42 ,, 8 ,,   do.
150 ,, ladders (old.)
 4 tram-waggons.
250 fms. of 9-16 in. whim chain.
300 ,, bell-wire.
20 ,, ladders.
 2 balance-bobs complete.
 1 horse-whim, with shaft-tackle complete.
 1 piece of 8-inch main rod.
120 fms. of ½-inch chain.
 2 pairs of caps.
 1 balance-bob.
 1 horse-whim complete.
33 2 ft. shieves.
A triangular shears, blocks and chain.
100 fms. 3-inch air pipes.
100 ,, ½-inch chain.
100 ,, iron stave ladders.
Brass bell.
 4 kibbles.
 3 skips and 1 catch.
Screw stocks.
Stamps' floors, materials on do.
   do.   carpenter's shop and saw house
Account-house furniture, &c., &c.

The above, with the adventurers' interests in the setts,
will first be offered in one lot, subject to the conditions
of sale, and, if not so sold, will be offered in convenient
lots.

Particulars can be obtained, and the machinery inspected, on application to Mr. JOHN MICHELL, of
Nancledrea, near the mine ; or to the AUCTIONEER ;
or to Mr. Rn. WELLINGTON, Chyandour ; Mr. J. B.
COULSON, Penzance ; or to the undersigned,
            RODD and CORNISH,
                Solicitors, Penzance.

Dated 14th Feb., 1870.

Advertisement detailing the sale of mine materials at Billia Mine, February 1870
(Noall Collection)

company.[5] At about this time the adjacent Giew mine was taken up by a London-based company who operated it under the name of South Providence. (See under Giew.)

"Billia Consols" is reputed to have sold 145 tons of black tin between 1865-7.

1. *Royal Cornwall Gazette* August 1812
2. *Cornish Telegraph* April 10 1867
3. *Cornish Telegraph* February 16 1870
4. *Cornish Telegraph* March 2 1870
5. *Cornish Telegraph* April 6 1870

WHEAL CONQUER

This mine is situated on Conquer Downs, about a mile and a half S.W. of Towednack church. A somewhat ambitious attempt at developing it in the 1820's quickly came to grief; and in 1824 its materials were offered for sale. "Wheal Conquer Mine" was said to lie in the parishes of Gulval and Towednack, near Penzance, its most valuable piece of equipment being "a Steam-Engine, on the principle of Bolton and Watts (*sic*), 19½" inch Cylinder, double, 6 feet 3 inch Stroke, with a Balance Bob, complete." In addition, there were pumps ranging from 8" to 6", 30 fms. of ladders, whim, capstan and shears, 80 fms. of capstan rope, two shaft tackles for whim, "winz tackle" — a winz was a primitive winding appliance, not to be confused with a *winze*, or underground shaft — tools, wheelbarrows, and other items, all nearly new. Enquirers were referred to Capt. Bawden, on the mine.[1] In 1836 the mine was reworked as Lady Downs and Conquer, in 1857 as Wheal Conquer Consols, and in 1859 under its old name of Wheal Conquer. (See also under Lady Downs.)

1. *Royal Cornwall Gazette* July 23 1824.

WHEAL DIPPER

A contributor signing himself "Den a Gernow" gave the following copy of an 18th century mine account to the "Notes and Queries" column conducted by Dr. J. Hambley Rowe in the 1920's and '30's for the *Western Morning News* (No. 199 of the series):

"Wheal Dipper account made up from October 28, 1757, to the end of May, 1758:-
"The Wheal Bussey adventurers for a whim, £14.19s.; Henry Davies, for a Lawnder, 3s.; Michael Baragwanha, for his bargain in the shaft, £6; Mrs. Maugham and Grenfell, for timber as per bill, £2.15s.5½d.; David Martins, for smith cost, as per bill, £3.4s.; Marten

77

Davey, for smith cost as per bill, £1.1s.4d.; Captain Thomas Uren, as per bill, £3.5s.; Henry Oliver, as per bill, 12s.; Nicholas Barens, for fixing the whim and timber, £1.5s.; Martin Trewheela, for carriage of timber, 1s.; Samuel Botterall, for carriage of timber, 2s.3d.; Paul Curnow, for 27 stems labour and drawing timber, £1.8s.3½d.; Richard James, for 3½ stems labour and drawing timber, 8s.0d.; Michael Baragwanha, 27 stems labour at 24 per month, £1.1s.6½d.; Gabriel James, for ditto, £1.1s.6½d.; Gabriel James, for a book, 2s.; expences publishing surveys and bringing up the cage, 9s.3d.; Henry Davies and Co., at St. Erth, as per bill, 11s.7d.; expences making up this account, 3s.5d.; keeping the book and collecting the cost, 5s.; the whole cost is £38.19s.5d.; to be deducted for a whim sold, £20; remains to be divided, £18.19s.5d.; a tenth part of £18.19s.5d. is £1.17s.11½d. A twentieth part, 18s.11¾d.''

"An abstract of the separate costs of the foregoing account, adventurers' names, shares, and separate costs: Mr. John Stephens, 1-10th, £1.17s.11½d.; Henry Davies 9-20th, £8.10s.9¾d.; Richard James, 1-10th, £1.17s.11½d.; Gabriel James, 1-10th, £1.17s.11½d.; Michael Baragwana, 1-10th, £1.17s.11½d.; Thomas Curnow, 1-20th, 18s.11¾d.; Paul Curnow, 1-20th, 18s.11¾d.; Wm. Harry, 1-20th, 18s.11¾d.''

"Account of the cost and charges in Wheal Dippa from February 2, 1759, to March following: To Richard James, for 15 stems, 12s.6d.; Michl. Baragwanna, for 15 stems, 12s.6d.; Paul Curnow, for 15 stems, 12s.6d.; Gabriel James, for 15 stems, 12s.6d.; Richd. James, for ½ doz. candles, 3s.6d.; expenses publishing surveys, 1s.; Martin Trewhela, for carriage of timber, 1s.; Michl. Bargwannah, for oil, 2s.6d.; Rich. James, for his trouble to Marizion, 1s.6d.; expence and collecting the cost, 5s.6d.; £3.5s.; to a former acctt., £38.19s.5d. — £42.4s.5d.; to be deducted for materials sold, £24.10s.; remains to be divided, £17.14s.5d.''

"Den a Gernow" stated that Wheal Dipper's exact location was unknown to him, but he thought it probably lay in Ludgvan, Lelant or Towednack. Some of the personal names mentioned in the old document are certainly well known in that area; but perhaps a better clue to its location is provided by the name of the mine itself; for in 1832 one of the many lodes passing through the setts of West Wheal Reeth, in Towednack, (q.v.) which had produced immense quantities of tin, was listed as the "Dippa."

Henry Davies, mentioned in Wheal Dippa account, was the uncle of Davies Gilbert, FRS, and owned cellars at St. Erth in which timber, lime, coal and similar commodities were sold. Maugham and Grenfell had a similar establishment at Marazion, to the successful management of which the Grenfells, later represented by Lord Desborough, owed much of their early financial success. In public competition with each other, bands of miners through their "cappens" offered to open up so much ground at so many pounds per fathom, and the lowest offer was usually accepted. These public tenders, generally held on the mine, were called "surveys." A "stem" was a job or piece of work not paid by time. At Wheal Dipper it was apparently worth 10d. Seven shillings a dozen for miners' candles shows that these necessary articles were comparatively expensive.

DRYSACK AND MANUEL'S POOLS

In Bussow Moor are two pools left by tinners, one being called Drysack, Cornish for "bramble brake". The other is known as Manuel's Pool, after Emanuel Martyn, who owned stamps nearby and was drowned there.[1]

1. Dr. A.K. Hamilton Jenkin's Notebook, II, 1924-25, p.58, CRO, Truro

DURLO

Durlo (or Durloe) lay on the west side of the St. Ives-Penzance road at Cripple's Ease. Although included in the sett of Wheal Reeth, it was at an early period worked independently of that mine. On October 22 1825 the following interesting advertisement appeared in the *Royal Cornwall Gazette*: "For Sale by Private Contract, Durlo Tin Mine, with all the Materials and Buildings thereto belonging, in the parish of Towednack, comprising the most extensive Sets in the neighbourhood, having all the lodes of Great Wheal Reeth, Wheal Margaret, Georgia, and the principal lode in Wheal Gew Tin Mines, leading through them, and including the Mines of Tin Croft, Croft Wheal Reeth, Chylason Adit, and the Beyow" (Behu). "Several other Lodes are in these Sets, on which no trial has been made. The Mine is in a regular course of working, with a Fire-Engine of 30 inches cylinder, and a Water-Wheel of 30 feet diameter and 3 feet wide on the breast for drawing the water; a Fire Whim of 16 inches cylinder, working double, with brass condensing work, together with all requisite Materials and Erections for working the Mine in the most advantageous manner." A further sale — of materials only — was advertised in May 1827; the 30" engine was not then mentioned; the 16" was described as being complete with cost iron boiler, and brass air pumps. There were also 34 fms. of 8" and 14 fms. of 6" pumps, one horse whim, and a large water engine bob.[1]

At various times Durlo was worked with other adjacent mines under such titles as Reeth Consols and Giew Consols, but in 1859 it was again operating independently and making a profit. Between then and 1864 462 tons of black tin were sold, this being the only known record output.

1. *Royal Cornwall Gazette* May 5 1827

GEORGIA CONSOLS

This mine lies about a mile south of Towednack Church, in the valley to the west of Nancledra. According to Dines, the property contains twelve lodes, only two of which have been worked — Coles, coursing E. 12 deg. N., underlying steeply S., and Lane, striking parallel with it and 15 fms. S. at the 22 fm. level, but underlying 20 deg. N. The adit opens near the stream 380 yards N.E. of Little Amalebrea Farm; and the shafts are known as High Burrow, Flat Rod, Engine, East Whim and Noon West. The country rock is whitstone (a fine-grained granite) underlain by granite.

In a sale of tin bounds advertised during January 1815 3/32nds shares in "Great George and Little Georga," Towednack, were offered. Other Towednack bounds mentioned at the same time included "One 4th in the Ba-O-Bounds, in Camelwidden," *i.e.*, Amalwhidden, lying to the north of Georgia.[1]

Said to have been formerly worked by hand and horse labour to a depth of about 25 fms., the sett of the "Georgia Tin Mines" was acquired in 1847 "by an influential party in London," who intended conducting it with spirit on the cost-book system. The sett measured nearly a mile square, or at least 700 fms. on the run of the lodes, and equally so in a N.-S. direction. The mine was divided into 2,048 shares; but the management committee would have no power to make calls or incur expense beyond what was approved by the shareholders. By reason of the mine's contiguity to Rosewall Hill, St. Ives Consols, Balnoon, Reeth Consols and Ding Dong, great and lasting profits were anticipated.[2] In March 1848 the "North, South and West Georgia Mines" were acquired by Cornwall New Mining Company.

Between 1852 and 1855 the mine produced 170 tons of black tin. A new 21 year sett of the property was granted in 1872; but three years later the Georgia Tin and Copper Mining Company went into liquidation, when the 45" pumping engine, three new horse-whims and 200 fms. of new ladders were offered for sale.[3] In the early years of this century Georgia mine was acquired by the St. Ives Consolidated Mines, Ltd., who, in their first report issued in January 1910 stated that it had formerly been worked in a spasmodic manner on a comparatively small scale. The mine was again investigated in 1929, but found too poor to warrant development.

1. *Royal Cornwall Gazette* January 1815
2. *Penzance Gazette* March 10 1847
3. *Royal Cornwall Gazette* August 7 1875

GIEW (SOUTH PROVIDENCE)

On the western side of Trink Hill, and adjoining the St. Ives-Nancledra road, stands the fine engine-house of the old Giew mine; sited at Frank's shaft, if is one of the most striking memorials in the district to its now defunct mining industry. Across the road and lower down the hill may be seen a square calciner stack, machinery beds and other remains on the site of the old Billia mine, which, with several other small concerns, was at one time worked with it under the name of Giew Consolidated; eventually the whole group was given the name of Giew.

An early mention of the mine occurs in 1819, when the materials of "Wheal Gue Mine, in the parish of Towednack," were offered for sale by private contract. The items comprised a 20" cylinder engine, double, "on the best construction, and compleat;" a quantity of 10", 7" and 6" pumps; a large assortment of iron pump rods; 8" and 4" plungers, with cases; water engine plate rods; balance bobs; whim ropes; and chains. Capt. John Berryman or Capt. William Trewhella, near the mine, would treat for the sale of any of these articles.[1]

The ruined engine-house of Giew Mine   (Noall Collection)

The first great success of this mine came in the latter half of 1840, when tin was £46 a ton. Output increased steadily, reaching 200 tons per annum in 1843 and 260 in 1850. Giew was regularly yielding £10,000 to £14,000 a year when, most unfortunately, a "run" took place in one of the shafts, cutting off access to a part of the mine. "In an ill-fated moment, the shareholders, who had drawn their thousands in profits, were seized with a fit of economy, and thought they would retrench their fortunes by working the Durlo part of the mine, and withdrawing expenditure from the main works.'' This was a mistaken decision. Nevertheless, Durlo gave from March 1859 to January 1865 no less than 513 tons of tin, averaging around £71.10s. per ton; but the fall in tin standards which then set in caused the mine to be suspended. Billia Consols, the third constituent of Giew Consolidated, survived until the winter of 1867, when it too collapsed in another mining depression.

The decision to abandon the enterprise had not been unanimous, however, and in August 1867 an unsuccessful effort was made to salvage it, but the price asked for setts and materials — £3,900 — could not be raised. The name chosen for this abortive venture was ''The Billia, Durloe, Western Durloe, Behu, Giew, and Reeth Consolidated,'' with the additional right to work a piece of virgin ground to the E., called Trink Hill. The machinery included a new 36″ cylinder steam pumping engine; a 27″ cylinder steam stamps with 32 heads; nearly 200 fms. of pitwork; ''and every other article belonging to a mine in complete working order.''

The promoters asserted that the late proprietors had directed operations to the western part of the mine called the Billia, and although working to a very limited extent — a few fathoms deep and long only — returns of nearly £7,000 had been made. In addition to prosecuting this section, the new owners intended to place an engine on Frank's shaft, which had been sunk to 142 fms. only in order to work the virgin ground to the E., which was expected to yield more tin than any other mine in the district.

The reason assigned for the stopping of the group, which had raised £191,449.14s.10d. worth of tin during a continuous working from 1838 to 1858, was this: Robinson's Engine shaft had been sunk into a hole or pit, from which the levels could be extended for only a short distance, owing to the foulness of the air caused by imperfect ventilation, in fact, the miners were nearly choked and incapacitated from performing barely half their proper duty. Additionally, the pumping engine (a 40″ only) was a weak and miserable machine consuming much time and expense in repairs. Finally, the sides of the Engine shaft gave way, burying a great depth of pitwork in the debris. This made a thorough reconstruction necessary, or else a cessation of operations; the latter course was decided on and took place in 1858 — a time when, above all others, the mine should have been more vigorously prosecuted, as the price of tin averaged £12.11s. per ton more during the following eight years than in the period when it worked. The tin dressing plant had also been conducted in such a slovenly fashion that an immense quantity of tin was allowed to escape to the river.

It was now proposed to erect a powerful engine on Frank's shaft, which would allow a communication to be made with Robinson's at all levels, so obtaining the necessary ventilation and discharge and permitting the economical working of the rich ore-ground, dipping E., standing between the two shafts. Economies in working would be made by introducing the skip and wire rope for drawing, and improving the dressing floors.

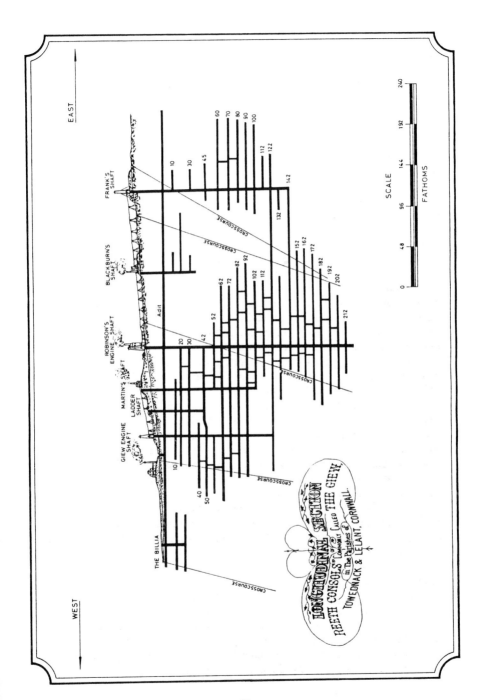

WEST

EAST

THE BILLIA

GIEW ENGINE SHAFT
LADDER SHAFT
MARTIN'S SHAFT
ROBINSON'S ENGINE SHAFT
BLACKBURN'S SHAFT
FRANK'S SHAFT

Adit

CROSSCOURSE
CROSSCOURSE
CROSSCOURSE
CROSSCOURSE
CROSSCOURSE
CROSSCOURSE

LONGITUDINAL SECTION
REETH CONSOLS COMMONLY CALLED THE GIEW.
In The Parishes of
TOWEDNACK & LELANT, CORNWALL.

SCALE

FATHOMS

0   48   96   144   192   240

83

A very large quantity of broken lode lying in the backs, over the levels, not worth returning when tin was only £40 a ton, would now add materially to the sales. The mines were estimated to yield 25 tons of tin monthly, worth £1,250, whilst the cost should not exceed £800, so that a profit of £450 per month could be anticipated.

Despite the failure of this flotation, another attempt to resuscitate these mines was made in 1869 by Thomas Treweeke, of Lelant, who bought the property for £1,400 in cash and £1,000 in paid-up shares. He also secured the sett of the unexplored ground E. of Giew Consols and Reeth Consols in Trink Hill extending half-a-mile E. on the run of the lodes, and of the same width. The lords of the whole of this property were the Hon. Mrs. Gilbert, J.A. Stephens, the Duke of Cleveland, the Countess Dowager Sandwich, W.B. Tyringham, the Champernowne family, Sir William Williams, Messrs. Rodd and Tremayne, H.H.C. Phillips, T. Woolcombe, and others.

In a report dated October 7 Capt. Peter Eddy stated he believed hundreds of men could be employed in the mine even before it was in fork. The new virgin ground E. of Frank's shaft was believed to contain a run of tin ground quite distinct from the old shoot. Nearly all the ends driving in that direction from the 45 to the 122 fm. levels were opening out profitable ground when they were suspended. He recommended erecting an engine on the largest and best shaft — Giew Engine — and clear to the 122 level. This would command the top water of the mine to the 60, and a 4″ lift below that would keep her dry. Frank's shaft could be adapted to skips to discharge the stuff from the eastern ground.

Capt. William Hollow thought highly of the speculation, whilst Capt. Richard Martin spoke in glowing terms of the tin ground in the Billia, the north lodes, the promising ground at the bottom of Frank's shaft, and the new eastern ground. Capt. John Daw described the North lode as one of the champion lodes of the district. The enlarged sett now measured 1,200 fms. long by about 400 fms. wide, and lay in one of the best localities in the county for tin. Capt. Thomas Julian, of Great Wheal Vor, thought that the fact of so much wealth having been raised from the lodes which ran through this and adjoining mines a good augury for success.

Capt. Arundel Anthony said he had made enquiries of men who had worked many years in these mines, and all had confirmed the value of the unwrought ground in the mine. There was also tin in the levels and stulls worth thousands of pounds. Capt. John Nancarrow, of St. Ives Consols, believed that up to 20 tons a month of tin might be raised as soon as the water was cleared. There were three engines on the mines, and a variety of valuable pitwork. Capt. Thomas Michell estimated the total value of the machinery, "the substantial and workman-like adit," and tin on the floors and burrows at quite £5,000. Frank's shaft being completed to the 142 level under adit would enable thirteen levels to be driven eastward into the newly acquired virgin ground, which added at least another £8,000 to the value of the property. "During my agency in

St. Ives Consols dividends exceeding £100,000 were paid the adventurers, and were I twenty years younger I would guarantee to do that amount or more for the adventurers in Giew Consols, as the prospects are better than they were in St. Ives Consols when I was there.''

Capt. Treweeke arranged a meeting at the White Hart Hotel, Hayle, which decided that a company with a capital of £12,000 in 48 shares would effectively test the property. Shares were taken up by Mr. Magniac, M.P. for St. Ives, T.S. Bolitho and Sons, Major Bickford and Messrs. Harvey & Co. Other adventurers came in soon after.[2] Eventually 39-48ths of the required sum was subscribed, but one of the party who was refused the management of the concern withdrew his support, and the scheme collapsed like a pack of cards.

Local initiative having failed, a London based company then took over the mine, and operating it under the somewhat confusing name of ''South Providence'' drained it to the bottom, but a Chancery suit followed, and little further was done.

South Providence was 10 fms. deep and employed 12 people in the spring of 1870, presumably only the shallow workings being active. G. Still was then the secretary, Christopher Stephens purser, Capt. James Evans manager and Capt. Thomas Uren agent. In 1871 it sold 1 ton 12 cwt. 1 qr. 16 lbs. of black tin for £119.2s.4d. No sales were made in 1870 or 1872. A new company, also with London offices, took over the property around 1873 and operated it until 1889. The pursers during this period included William Pascoe (1873-4), Edward Pascoe (1875); managers, Capt. James Craze (1873-4), Capt. William Brabyn (1875), Capt. J.W. Craze (1877-8), Capt. William Pascoe (1880-1); and agents, Capt. William Brabyn (1873-4) and Capt. William Pascoe (1877-8). The committee (1877-81) consisted of S. Bewely and Co.

In December 1874 a correspondent, under the heading of ''Gew (or South Providence)'' reported that the mine's 50" steam engine was not working properly and that attempts to speed it up had led to breakages in the pitwork. The prospects for draining the mine that winter were almost hopeless. Underground workings were suspended in 1877 and the whole mine was idle in June 1878, though in 1880 it was being worked above adit and the dumps were being turned over, four persons being employed.

With Reeth Consols, the property was put up for sale by private treaty in June 1885 and again in May 1889, owing to Chancery proceedings between the former owners. The sett was described as being over a mile long. It had a good account house, smithy, engine house, carpenters' shop, changing house, and 50" and 36" steam engines, as well as 11" pitwork and other machinery, plant and appliances. Production included 12 tons of black tin sold in 1875, 37 tons 15 cwt. 1 qr. 23 lbs. in 1877-8, and 15 cwt. in 1881. Collins gives the output as 80 tons of black tin sold between 1855 and 1882.

The letters in the inscription ''S.P. 1871'' on the bob wall of the old engine house at Giew are believed to stand for ''South Providence.'' It is actually more than a little puzzling to understand why that name was bestowed on the mine, particularly since it had previously, and more logically, been appropriated to South Wheal Providence (South Wheal Speed), which does actually lie near to and S. of the Providence Mines at Carbis Bay. Dines (p.128) in fact refused to believe that the O.S. map was correct in calling Giew, South Providence; but in this he was himself mistaken.

Thomas Treweeke — a persistent man, if ever there was one — secured in the option on Giew again in 1893; and he "swore he would float it or die in the attempt," for "the property is an El Dorado." His prospectus for "Wheal Reeth & the Gew" was issued in January 1894, but met with no success.

In 1908 Giew was taken over by St. Ives Consolidated Mines, Ltd., who began production there in April 1911. From November 3 of that year the 20-stamp mill ran continuously on ore from the dumps and upper levels. In June 1912 the 60 and 112 fm. levels were entering virgin ground, and prospects both in the eastern and Robinson's shaft sections looked good. Between the 100 and 112 fm. levels the lode had opened out to a width of 11', assaying 30 lb. of tin oxide per ton over the whole width. To deal with the steadily rising output (valued for the month of May at £1,864) an additional ten head of stamps with a large tube mill were commissioned.

The *Mining World* of July 20 carried an interesting description of Giew. They were then clearing the 122, which was 900' back to Robinson's shaft, where pumping plant would be installed. Robinson's would then be unwatered to the 210, which meant that there would be virtually another new mine underneath on the E. below Frank's shaft, giving a double output from the same ground.

Giew was visited at about this time by members of Cornish engineering and mining societies, whose *Programme* included a detailed description of the mill. This consisted of 20 Californian stamps, of 1,050 lbs. head, driven by two 30 h.p. Westinghouse motors. The principle adopted, both with the pulp in the mill and the calcined concentrates in the tin yard, was thorough classification, followed by treatment of the coarse sands on Buss tables, finer sands on Inhrig vanners, and slimes on convex and concave frames. In the later stages in the tin yard treatment with strong sulphuric acid removed traces of copper compounds and facilitated the final cleaning of the black tin. The surface equipment at Giew also included an auxiliary power plant consisting of three Westinghouse gas engines, each of 140 h.p., coupled to 90 kW generators. This plant was run in conjunction with the one at Consols, and could be run in parallel with it, when necessary.

The exceptionally heavy rain experienced that summer necessitated both skips at Frank's shaft being kept constantly at work baling water, thus preventing the usual tonnage of ore being hoisted for the mill, and output was temporarily reduced. The anticipated eastern ore shoot had been intersected in the upper levels east of Frank's shaft. In the 60 fm. level E. the assay value for the last 7' had risen to 40 lbs. black tin per ton. By May 1913 Frank's shaft had been completed to the 143 fm. level, and was sunk a further ten

Frank's Shaft and headgear, Giew (St. Ives Consolidated)   (Noall Collection)

feet into virgin ground. The North and South lodes made a junction at the bottom of the 142 fm. level; this level had been driven 30′ east into unwrought ground. A footwall branch had been discovered about four feet wide, which assayed the unprecedented quantity of 13.8 cwt., or 1,554 lbs. of black tin per ton of ore. The black tin in this newly opened ground was of very pure quality, the vanners' black tin assaying 73.5% metal pert on of black tin, as against 678% from the ore of existing stopes. The work of sinking the shaft and driving east was being pushed forward with all possible speed to open up this valuable ground for stoping. Stoping had commenced above the 20 fm. level W. in Robinson's shaft section, from where ten tons of ore had been sent to the mill, assaying 34.3 lbs. of black tin per ton.

The lode in the bottom of Frank's shaft continued to look well in November. The cutting of the pump station at the 70 fm. level had been completed, and a large pump was being erected there.[3] A branch lode west of the old level had been discovered at the 122; it looked very encouraging. In Robinson's shaft section, very satisfactory progress had been made clearing and enlarging the 60 fm. level E., the face being within 100' of Frank's shaft. This level had opened up a large extent of profitable ore that could be hoisted through Robinson's shaft.

In January 1914 Capt. Cann, the manager, announced that Frank's shaft had been sunk 60' below the 142. A very extensive block of ground had been opened up by clearing 600' on the 60 fm. level, from Robinson's shaft into Frank's shaft, where the lode was practically intact up to adit level. The mill had established a tonnage record for Cornish milling, and when it had been completed should give an extraction not exceeded by any similar installation at home or abroad. Tests had been made with the latest type of hammer drills for stoping during the sinking of Frank's shaft, with satisfactory results, and the efficiency of the air compressor would be increased to permit these machines to be used on the largest possible scale.

The Power Station, Giew (St. Ives Consolidated)   (Noall Collection)

88

During the sixteen weeks ending February 7, 1914 7,897.6 tons of ore were stamped by the battery, yielding 77 tons 6 cwt. of black tin, worth £7,291. Work on the tin yard extension and mill was proceeding rapidly, and the new plant was expected to be running in April. Additional power had been brought into the mine by the Cornwall Electric Power Company, and would be connected to the plant very shortly.

Group of mine workers (mainly carpenters) at Giew (St. Ives Consolidated) (Noall Collection)

Following the outbreak of war in August, the St. Ives Consolidated Mines ran into financial difficulties, the particulars of which will be found under St. Ives Consols, and the company was wound up in March 1915. Production continued at Giew under a receivership; but in February 1917 the mine was taken over by the Thermo-Electric Ore Reduction Corporation, Limited (registered December 18 1912) which changed its name to Thermo-Electric, Limited, in July 1918. After a receiver had been appointed on April 29 1920, Giew continued to operate under the receivership; the company itself was finally struck off the Register in January 1932. The fall in the price of tin, after the cessation of hostilities in 1918, brought serious problems to the management. In January 1920 all the 180 men employed there went on strike in support of two lorrymen whom they considered had been unjustly discharged. The pumps were stopped for a while, but later re-started, pending negotiations. This dispute was eventually adjusted; but further trouble occurred in July when the management announced a ten per cent cut in wages. A meeting of the men was addressed by Arthur Wilkens, district organiser of the Dockers' Union, when it was unanimously decided not to accept the decrease. The management stood firm, however, and the men eventually accepted their terms.

With the position still worsening, the miners, in December, agreed to follow a recommendation by Wilkens, to hand back £1 per month until the price of tin reached £260 per ton, the current price being only £223. In so doing, they followed the course recently taken by the workers at Tincroft. The latter mine was not saved by this sacrifice, and closed in January 1921, but Giew survived, "the only bright spot on the horizon for the Cornish mines in jeopardy."

General view of air-compressor house, hoist house, Frank's headgear, balance-bob house, and dry at Giew (St. Ives Consolidated) (Noall Collection)

However, the reprieve proved to be only temporary. In September 1922 it was announced that during the previous two months the sales of tin had fallen in quantity, and that as a result the owners found themselves unable to meet more than a few days' pay to the men for a month's work. This led to seventy of the 120 employees withdrawing their labour, and the debenture holders promptly put in a receiver. It had been a gallant struggle while it lasted. Financial co-operation between the men and the company had been a significant factor, the miners and service hands first agreeing to forage ten per cent and afterwards twenty per cent of their modest monthly pay to assist in keeping the mine open, the portion of wages thus given up being regarded as a loan to the company.

Reviewing the situations, James E. Ward, one of the directors, stated that

General view inside the Mill at Giew (St. Ives Consolidated)

Buddles and frames in the Tin Yard, Giew (St. Ives Consolidated)

at the close of 1920 they had to estimate their capital resources and consider whether they could possibly keep the men in employment. Early in 1922 it was believed the mine had turned the corner and could be successfully continued. The recent fall in output had brought on a new financial crisis, and had occurred so suddenly that no negotiation were possible to raise the money for the wages, and so the men could only be paid half what was due to them.[4] He maintained that Giew was paying considerably higher wages than the prevailing rate at Camborne. The mill men, who were the worst paid, and all the salaried staff, refused to join the strikers, and the following week secured a better tin sale than for months past. All this money had been distributed among the workers. Questioned by an interviewer, Ward conceded that the miners' average wages was £2 a week, the unskilled labourers' wages being much less. "Probably, if we had adopted the course of the other mines, we should have had the working capital available at the present time which was spent in the early part of 1921 in keeping the men in employment. We made application to the Government Facilities Board, who informed us that we could employ one of the Government experts to make a report at a cost of a hundred guineas, but we were not encouraged to believe that this expenditure would secure the working capital which was necessary for the working of the mine."

Ward, as receiver, took up the case again with the Trades Facilities Board, and learned that the main obstacle to their providing the assistance which had been given to other Cornish mines was the existence of the first mortgage

The "Buss and Wilfley" separating tables, Giew (St. Ives Consolidated)   (Noall Collection)

debenture, amounting to £5,500; and that if this charge could be removed, the most sympathetic consideration would be given to the requirements of the mine. Efforts were thereupon made to raise the amounts required, so that the mortgage might be redeemed and the mine re-established under a new company. Wrote one commentator: ''When the Patriarch interceded for the Cities of the Plain, he succeeded in securing the promise that they should not be destroyed for lack of five. Mr. J.E. Ward...states that...mortgage debentures to the amount of £5,500 is an insuperable obstacle to the obtaining of Government assistance to keep the mine open, and he appeals to the local inhabitants...to subscribe the sum and not allow the mine to be destroyed 'for lack of five.' The appeal is one which on grounds of self-interest should appeal to the ratepayers who will have to keep the miners who would be thrown out of employment should the mine be closed.''

But, alas, the ''five'' could not be found; and Giew was closed in January 1923. Capt. Shipwright (Sir Edward Hain's son-in-law) and his wife had put £3,500 into Giew to keep her going as long as possible. When the mine stopped, tin was fetching only £144 per ton, but a few weeks after it rose to £188. During the last two years of its existence Lady Hain and other landowners gave up half dues; but under the prevailing circumstances the mine's fate was probably inevitable. It is, however, a remarkable fact that, during the early part of 1921 Giew was the only mine in Cornwall to remain in operation. This, more than any other factor, points to its being still one of the best mining prospects in the county.[5]

The auction of valuable mining machinery and effects by J.R. Buddle was advertised to take place on ''Friday June 8 1923 at 2 p.m. sharp at Giew Mine, Cripplesease, Towednack.'' The items included three-throw vertical pumps by T.H. and J. Daniels, Ltd., plungers 4¾ " diameter by 7½ " stroke delivering 250 gallons per minute at 185 r.p.m. with a head of 500', geared electric drive; five three-throw vertical pumps by the same makers, plungers 3¾ " diameter, delivering 165 g.p.m., at 500'; a steam lorry; and the usual assortment of timber, scrap metal and stores. It is said that the mine's rod mill was removed to the Gwithian Sands plant, and afterwards worked at Treskillard, and at the Hydraulic Tin Works, Bissoe.

Not all the miners who lost their jobs when Giew was ''knocked'' became a burden on the rates, as had been predicted, for just at about this time Capt. Shipwright started the Porthia China Clay Works at Towednack, just a short distance north of the mine, and this afforded employment for a few years to some of them. For others the future proved far less kind. A good deal of overhead drilling had been carried out at Giew, and some of the men engaged in this work, disliking the streams of water that ran back on them when they drilled ''wet'' turned of the water jets. The dry dust then fell on them like flour, and they breathed it in large quantities, the result being that all died of miners' disease soon after.

In May 1965 it was announced in the magazine *Tin International* that the merchant bankers Kleinwort-Benson and Westfield Minerals had joined forces to form a privately owned company, Baltrink Tin, to investigate the abandoned Giew mine at Trink Hill which had closed in 1922. However, two years later the results of the diamond drilling programme were reported to be disappointing, and it was decided not to proceed further with the project. So ended the most recent attempt to restart mining in the St. Ives district.

1. *Royal Cornwall Gazette* March 6 1819
2. *Cornish Telegraph* August 14 1867; October 13 1869
3. An old miner told the author that Giew was an exceptionally dry mine. Only one or two buckets of water per shift needed to be pumped from the section where he worked. Water from the upper levels was trapped on reaching the shaft and then raised by hand pumps; consequently very little found its way to the bottom.
4. A miner employed in Giew at this time informed the author that he was owed £25 in wages when it closed, and that this money was never paid. The men knew it was such a good mine that they offered to keep it working if they were allowed to "pay themselves" out of the tin they raised, but the management would not agree. "This was the *real* cause of the strike which closed the mine."
5. Most of the information relating to the later history of Giew has been derived from files of *The St. Ives Times*. The references to South Providence are: Williams, 1870, p.14. Hunt's Min. Stats. 1869-72. Dines, 1956, p.125. *Mining Journal*, 1874, (19.12), 1889, (25.5). Ore sales, Min. Stats. 1875, 1877-78, 1880-81.

LADY DOWNS

In 1804 1-18th of three pair of tin bounds in "Lady-Downs in the parishes of Towednack, Zennor, Gulval and Ludgvan" were advertised to be sold by auction at the Union Hotel, Penzance, on December 31.[1] At another sale, to be held at the Star Inn, Marazion, on June 15 1813 "1-8th in four Pair of Bounds, in Lady Downs, called the Eastern Pair, the Western Pair, the Northern Pair, and Gamses Bounds," in the same parishes, were offered to the public.[2]

1. *Royal Cornwall Gazette* December 15 1804
2. *Royal Cornwall Gazette* May 1813

WHEAL MONTAGUE (GREAT CLEVELAND)

Close to Towednack Church a small mine was developed on a series of six parallel tin lodes coursing E. 15 deg. N., underlying S., one of which, Great lode, passes within 60 yards of the church; these are cut by three N.-S. cross-courses. The sett was known variously as Great Cleveland and Wheal Montague. In August 1851 was issued the prospectus of "Wheal Montague, Towednack," the sett being granted by "the Duke of Cleveland and the noble family whose name it bears." It had been partially worked by "old men" for more than 100 fms., but nowhere, it was thought, to a greater depth than 30 ft. — "and that some 80-90 years ago" (*i.e.*, *c.* 1760-1770) this being as far as they could go on account of water difficulties. An old shaft, recently cleared, was found to be only 25' deep, the lode being 2'-3' wide, one fathom of which had sampled £16 worth of tin.[1] In September 1853 the mine was said to be nearly paying cost; but in 1855 its materials were offered for sale. These included an excellent 30" cylinder rotary steam engine, 9' stroke in cylinder and 7½' out, with fly wheel, sweep rod, stamps axle for 16 heads, and a 9 tons boiler; two balance bobs; three horse whims; and the account house furniture. All these were "new within the last two years and of the very best description."[2] It is a matter of some regret that no picture survives of Towednack Church Town at this period, as the tiny village must then have presented a very interesting and animated appearance, the centuries-old church with its stubby tower and the peaceful farmstead contrasting strongly with the smoking engine house, thundering stamps and busy dressing floors of Wheal Montague. This mine gave its name to an inn at Towednack, the Montague Arms, now the Church Town farmhouse.[3]

1. *West Briton* August 15 1851
2. *West Briton* March 30 1855
3. Per E.T. Berryman, Beagletodn, Towednack

WHEAL MUSIC AND WHEAL SANDWICH (TRENDRINE HILL)

Although it might be presumed that the high and bulky mass of Trendrine Hill is as highly minerlised as its eastern neighbour, Rosewall Hill, only a minimal amount of mining seems to have been carried out there, and the area may be considered to be comparatively unexplored. Adits have been driven into the north-eastern flank of the hill, a little west of the road fork in the "Wide Gates" valley leading up to Towednack church. These workings apparently belong to an ancient mine known as Wheal Music, whose history was thus related in the *Mining Journal* of June 7 1839:

"About fifty years ago" (1790) "some Miners commenced sinking shafts on the top of the hill, on the back of the lode, and by accounts received from a respectable old man, they there found much tin, but unfortunately their principal shaft ran. They then drove a shallow level and sunk a shaft on the back of it, which shaft is now in good repair. They also commenced a deep level which would bring a depth of 40 fms. below their old workings.

"In 1831 this mine was purchased by James Meacock, Esq., who commenced working at the deep level and drove in 60 fms.; when, for the want of air, he commenced sinking a shaft, which they sunk 6 fms., but in consequence of the Company sustaining great failures in their foreign speculations, the said mine was stopped in the same year. In 1836 the Mine was again purchased by Capt. Francis when he commenced working in Meacock's shaft, but in consequence of the death of Capt. Francis the working was stopped, which at that time was about 3 fms. from the back of the level. Mr. William Daniel, who was fourteen years the sampler of St. Ives Consols, after trying the tin taken from Wheal Music lode and knowing the situation of the mine, states that in his opinion St. Ives Consols was not so promising at the same depth. Wheal Music rises to the W. similar to Rosewall Hill, and her lodes are in the same run as Rosewall Hill and St. Ives Consols. It is the opinion of miners in general that she will make abundance of tin at small depth. She is well situated and worthy the attention of mining speculators.'' Following the appearance of this ''puff,'' interested persons were invited to apply to Richard Penrose, of St. Ives, for further information. Dues of 1/18th were payable to the lord. The flotation was apparently unsuccessful.

There was another old mine on Trendrine Hill located about half-a-mile S.E. of Tregerthen Farm, called Wheal Sandwich (O.S. Survey, 1839). In December 1844 16-256 shares in ''The United Mines of Wheal Music, and Wheal Sandwich, now known by the name of 'Trendrine Hill,' '' were offered for sale, the enterprise being described as ''a most kindly speculation, and likely to prove very productive.''[1]

1. *Penzance Gazette* December 11 1844

WEST PROVIDENCE

See under Wheal Tyringham Consols

WHEAL RANSOM

Wheal Ransom lies sandwiched between St. Ives Consols on the E. and Rosewall Hill on the W. It was combined with St. Ives Consols when that mine started in 1818,[1] but later regained its independence, only to be eventually absorbed by its western neighbour under the name of Rosewall Hill and Ransom United.

Wheal Ransom seems to have been a very ancient bal, its history reaching back to that remote period when miners believed implicity in the existence of ''knockers'' and other supernatural phenomena. In his *Popular Romances of the West of England*, the noted Victorian mining authority and folklorist, Dr. Robert Hunt gave the following story which he had collected regarding this mine.

The ''knockers'' were very active in all parts of Wheal Ransom, and especially so in one particular end, where it was believed the lode was very rich, but despite offers of very high ''tribute'' no pare of men could be found brave enough to venture in the ground of the ''Bockles.'' However, an old man and his son called Trenwith, who lived near Bosprenis, saw the small people at midnight one midsummer eve bringing up the shining ore, and having some secret by which they could communicate with the fairy people, offered to break and bring one-tenth of the richest stuff to grass, leaving it properly dressed for the little miners if they would quietly give up this end. An agreement on these lines was concluded; the Trenwiths took up the pitch, and in a short time realised much wealth. The old man faithfully kept his part of the bargain, and left a tenth of the ore for his friends; but after he died, his son, who was avaricious and selfish, sought to cheat the knockers, and ruined himself by so doing. The lode failed, and nothing else went right with him; disappointed, he took to drink, squandered all the money his father had made, and died a beggar.

Turning from legendary lore to recorded facts, some interesting early references to the Ransom are to be found in the account book of Mr. Nathaniel Anthony, an 18th century St. Ives fish merchant and mine adventurer, from which the following have been selected:

"1775. 3d. June. To Ransom Ball 4 dozn. pick helves 92. 1777 April 12. Ransom ball 5 Kiballs pr. T. Tonkin 17s.6d. Decr. 4th. Pd. Cost to the Ransom ball £2.19s.1¼d. (Further calls were paid to the mine on February 26 and August 31 1778). 1779 July 6. paid Capt. Thos. Michell for Mr. Simons on the Ransom ball £3.17s.4½d. To paid Capt. Michell Cost for Ransom for Mrs. Anthony & self Nathl. Anthony £1.2s.4½d." (Further calls were paid until February 3 1781.) "1781 Febry. 5th. Rec'd from the Ransom for Mr. Symons for tin stuff 8s.3d." (Calls continued to be paid until October 18 1783, the mine apparently having divided no profits during the eight years of Mr. Anthony's connection with her.)

The *Royal Cornwall Gazette* of January 31 1829 carried an advertisement regarding a sale of shares in "Wheal Ransom Tin Mine," the auction to take place on February 14 following at "Bennetts' Hotel in the Borough of St. Ives." The number of shares on offer was given as 18-32nds or more parts of one third in the mine. "This valuable sett lies between Rosewall-hill Mine, and St. Ives Consols, the levels of which to the 57th" — *i.e.*, the 57 fm. level "inclusive, are driven into the Ransom; the latter is now making a profit, and the present state of the mine holds out to the purchaser the prospects of an ample and permanent remuneration, and also may, as the present proprietors have done, take out and return the Tin Stuff of the said One-Third." Enquiries were to be made of Capt. Thomas Lean, of Praze, or Ambrose Oxley, Marazion.

In 1830 there were advertised for sale "one Sixth part of all those Three pair of valuable and extensive Tin Bounds, called the Ransom, Wheal Pink, and Hellesveor-Downs Bounds, all situate within and contiguous to the very productive Mine called The Consols... The *Ransom Bounds* are now in full working and yielding considerable profit to the Proprietors."[2] Wheal Ransom appears to have been amalgamated with its western neighbour in 1857 to form the Rosewall Hill and Ransom United undertaking, *q.v.*

1. Barton, D.B., *A History of Tin Mining and Smelting in Cornwall*, 1967. p.39
2. *Royal Cornwall Gazette* June 1830

97

REETH CONSOLS

This mine lay just to the west of Wheal Reeth, and worked a series of lodes parallel to those coursing through the latter. It seems probable that after Wheal Reeth was suspended in 1772 its name was adopted by its western neighbour, and that the "Wheal Reeth" sett and materials offered for sale in 1818 (see under Wheal Reeth) were actually those of the mine which on its resumption in 1834 employed the designation of "Reeth Consols" to avoid confusion with the original Wheal Reeth which had been restarted in 1822.

In 1840 Peter Matthews Champion was crushed to death under a large stone when working in "Reeth Consols Mine, in Towednack."[1] Mr. Augustus Dalby, of Penzance, invited tenders for the supply of materials for "Reeth Consolidated Mines" in August 1846. These included 40 loads of good Norway balk; 20 loads of dram; 20 loads of longsound; and "180 Dozen of MINE CANDLES of the best quality, stating the price per dozen; one small Box to be sent to the Mine as a sample" — an ingenious ploy for obtaining a free supply from the competing merchants!

Reeth Consolidated Mines,
PARISH OF TOWEDNACK.
TENDERS WILL BE RECEIVED
By Mr. AUGUSTUS DALBY,
TREWARTHA TERRACE, PENZANCE,
Until the 16th of September,
FOR the SUPPLY of the following
Materials for these Mines,
viz:—
40 LOADS of good NORWAY BALK.
20 LOADS of DRAM, specifying the price
per foot.
20 LOADS of LONGSOUND, do. do.
180 Dozen of MINE CANDLES of the best
quality, stating the price per dozen; one
small Box to be sent to the Mine as a sample,
on or before the 18th of September.
The whole to be delivered free of carriage, on
or before the 1st of October.
August 31st, 1846.

Tender for the supply of materials for Reeth Consolidated, August 1846   (Noall Collection)

Another sad accident occurred in 1852 when a 15 year old lad named Thomas Trudgen, of Gulval, slipped out of a ladder whilst descending a shaft and was killed after falling 14 fathoms.[2] An even more shocking fatality was recorded in August 1853. As Robert Berryman, an engineman, was oiling the engine gear, his head came into contact with the fly wheel, which severed it from his body and scattered his brains in all directions. "The poor fellow was drawn among the machinery, and was so dreadfully mutilated that his bowels gushed out and every bone in his body was smashed."[3]

Some curious particulars regarding the manner in which this mine was run were given in a letter signed "A Traveller" Plymouth, which appeared in the *Mining Journal* of July 23 1853:

"Sir: Business having called me into the west of Cornwall lately, I made enquiries into the state and management of mines, having some connection therewith. Amongst other mines *Reeth Consols* came under my notice, respecting which allow me to make a cursory remark. A gentleman at Penzance informed me a little about the expenditure by the *official*. He said at a time (1837) when the expenditure in all did not exceed £200 per month, £45 per month was paid in salaries, and at the same time one agent did all the work for £5 per month! That the late purser had £250 per annum; whereas a responsible purser, such as Mr. R.R. Michell, Marazion, would, I doubt not, perform the duties for £5 or £6 per month. The total salaries *except* the resident agents' salaries, amount to about £600 per annum! My informant said that the working agents are not well paid — their salaries being lower than those of almost any other mine in Cornwall; and the account-house is the most shameful one ever seen in the county, consisting of *one room* for office, etc., and a detached *hut*, which serves for the kitchen. In other mines a fair allowance is made for expenses on pay-days, &c.; but in *Reeth Consols one guinea* per month must cover all these! so that while the directors are extravagant on the one hand, they are parsimonious on the other. I find that *favouritism* has prevailed too extensively in the appointment of purser, &c. The late purser was a relative of a large shareholder. My friend said that but for the heavy salaries paid to purser, directors, &c., the mine would have paid something in dividends. I am a party unconcerned in this matter; but I would recommend the adventurers at their next meeting to introduce *retrenchment* as to the salaries of those adverted to, and to remove all abuses. I advise them to commit the entire management to Cornishmen, who know how to do the thing on the most economical plan. Non-resident directors are useless." (See *Stannary Tales*, by Justin Brooke: p.47: P.V. Robinson.)

In may 1854 a young miner called Michael Curnow, of Lelant Downs, blasted a hole in the back of the 140 fm. level, and against the advice of his comrade, returned to the place before the smoke had cleared; as he was forcing a gad into a fissure in the rock, a large mass of ground fell away and killed him instantly.[4] A sale of spare mining materials held at the mine on November 10 1857 comprised the usual assortment of pumps, timber, air pipes, kibbles and so forth. Prospective purchasers were invited to apply to Capt. Champion on the mine, or to Henry Williamson, Esq., the purser.[5]

Soon after this Reeth Consols was knocked. In 1866 it was said that the mine had been prosecuted to a depth of over 200 fms. From Wheal Reeth, Reeth Consols and the Durlo, not less than £400,000 worth of tin had been raised during their various workings, and the whole range of setts formed collectively one of the most productive fields for tin making in West Cornwall.[6]

Collins asserted that Reeth Consols sold 888 tons of black tin between 1855-80. In August 1867 a proposal was made "to re-work the ancient mines, the Billia, Durloe, Belm, Giew, and Reeth Consols, situate in the far-famed St. Ives, Lelant, and Towednack mining district." Their prospects were said to be unquestionable, the yield in a late working from 1838-58 having exceeded £191,000.[7]

1. *Royal Cornwall Gazette* October 30 1840
2. *West Briton* May 7 1852
3. *Royal Cornwall Gazette* August 26 1853
4. *Cornish Telegraph* May 24 1854
5. *Cornish Telegraph* November 4 1857
6. *Cornish Telegraph* November 28 1866
7. *Cornish Telegraph* August 14 1867

NORTH WHEAL REETH

The *Royal Cornwall Gazette* of October 6 1837 carried the following notice: "North Wheal Reeth Tin Mine, Towednack, near St. Ives. This ancient Tin Adventure, lately resumed, is situate near the Clift, in the midst of the most flourishing Mining Speculations; and from the vast amount of its former produce, the variety of Lodes of Tin and Copper, the Tin now in sight, the small expence of trial, and other peculiar local advantages, this popular undertaking will be found to yield in recommendation to no other Tin Adventure lately commenced in Cornwall. A Specimen of Tin lately taken from the ground, among others, nearly 26 lb. weight, worth 75% in metal, may be seen at Mr. Tregoning's Shop, Truro." A few shares were still available from George Vivian or R. Penrose, St. Ives, or Tregoning, bookseller, Truro.

As North Wheal Reeth was "near the Clift" it must have been located at or near Trevegia, the only place where Towednack parish meets the sea.

WEST WHEAL REETH

In June 1832 the materials and setts of West Wheal Reeth, in Towednack, were offered for sale. The former included a 30' water wheel, 3' breast, with two cranks, sweep-rod, brasses, launders and stays complete; a main bob, with gudgeon-troughs, brasses and braces, and a balance bob; 200 fms. of iron horizontal rods; two horse whims, with 9' and 10' cages; 4½ fms. of 8", 30 fms. of 6", and 7½ fms. of 4" pumps, and the account house furniture. The setts were very extensive, with many lodes passing through them, which had produced immense quantities of tin, such as Great Wheal Reeth North and South lodes, Durlo, Croft Wheal Reeth, Tin Crofts (North and South), Berjow, Gew, Dippa and Lane, with several others, on which little or no trial had been made. Enquiries should be made of Mr. Nichs. Phillips, Penzance.[1]

1. *Royal Cornwall Gazette* June 2 1832

MINE MATERIALS,

FOR SALE.

TO BE SOLD BY AUCTION, on Mon-
DAY the 11th of June next, at Eleven
o'Clock in the Forenoon, at WEST WHEAL
REETH MINE, in the Parish of *Towednack*,

THE FOLLOWING

MINE MATERIALS :—

A WATER-WHEEL, 30 feet diameter, 3 feet
wide on the breast, with 2 Cranks, Sweep-
rod, Brasses, Launders and Stays, complete.
1 MAIN BOB, with Gudgeon-troughs, and
Brasses.
1 V BOB and the Gudgeon-troughs, Brasses,
and Braces of a Balance-bob.
200 Fathoms of I on HORIZONTAL RODS.
2 HORSE WHIMS, 9 and 10-feet Cages, with
Shieves and Shaft-tackle.
About 70 Fathoms of WHIM ROPE, 5½ inches.
An Oak CAPSTAN AXLE-TREE, 11 feet
long, 15 inches diameter.
4½ Fathoms of 8-inch, 3 fathoms of 6-inch, and
7½ fathoms of 4-inch PUMPS.
1 7-inch PLUNGER-POLE-CASE, with
Stuffing-box and Gland.
1 4 inch Ditto, with ditto, ditto,
1 7-inch H-PIECE, with Doors and Bottom
complete.
1 4-inch Ditto with ditto, ditto, ditto,
1 7-inch, 1 6-inch, and 1 4-inch PLUNGER
POLES.
1 12-inch, 2 7-Inch, 1 5½-Inch, 1 5-inch, 1 4½-
inch, and 1 3½ inch WORKING BARRELS.
1 12-inch, 1 5½-inch, 1 5-inch, 1 4½-inch, and
13½ inch CLACK-SEAT PIECES, DOORS
and WINDBORES.
2 6 inch WINDBORES.
26 Fathoms of AIR-PIPES.
Flanch and other Bolts; Staples and Glands
Strapping Plates; Lead and Lead Rings; a
quantity of Round and Flat Iron; six Winze
Water Barrels; two Whim Kibbles; a pair of
double and treble Blocks; two 4-feet Whim
Shieves; two Cisterns; a Grinding Stone and
Trough; Carpenter's Bench; a large Smith's,
Bellows and Anvil; Vice, and other Smiths'
Tools;

COUNTING HOUSE FURNITURE,

With a variety of other articles.

Any Company of Adventurers wishing to
treat for the Materials, together with the
SETS of the above MINE, by PRIVATE
CONTRACT, a treaty may be entered upon
for the same

These sets being very extensive and having
a great many Tin Lodes passing through them,
which have produced immense quantities of
Tin, including Great Wheal Reeth North and
South Lodes, Durlo, Croft Wheal Reeth, Tin
Crofts, (North and South), Berjow, Gew,
Dippa and Lane Lodes, with several others, on
which little or no trial has been made, and being
in the immediate neighbourhood of several of
the best Tin Mines now working in the County,
makes it a most desireable object for a respectable Company of Adventurers.

Application may be made personally, or by
letter, *post paid*, to

Mr. Nichs. Phillips,

Penzance.

May 23, 1832

Advertisement for the sale of mine materials at West Wheal Reeth, May 1832 (Noall Collection)

NEW WEST WHEAL REETH (BALDHU)

In April 1887 a group of gentlemen mostly from the Nancledra district met at the White Hart, Hayle, under the chairmanship of Edward Boase, of St. Ives, to consider the restarting of "New West Wheal Reeth, lately Baldhu Mine, near Nancledra." It was said the mine could be set to work for £2,500, two-thirds of which was already promised. The property contained several lodes, totally unwrought save where they had been opened on successfully for tin on the backs of the adits. Recently a miner had driven 40 fms. of adit on the main lode, passing through 27 fms. of tin ground from which he and a boy broke in one month 180 bushels of tinstuff which yielded13 cwt. 3 qrs. of tin. this was "the best deposit of tin...that has been discovered in the grand old Wheal Reeth district for many years past," and lay only nine fathoms from surface.

Capt. John James, of Redruth, who had recently inspected the mine, submitted a report, stating that the lode was of the same formation and embedded in the same strata as the rich mines of the Lelant district. Adit shaft was sunk about 8 fms. from surface and the adit driven 26 fms. on the main lode to a cross-course. For the whole of this drivage, the load varied from one to two feet wide, and had produced tin in paying quantities. The back of the level had all been stoped to surface. The stuff had shown a fair profit even on the present primitive mode of working. The level had since been extended fourteen fathoms into the hill through a lode producing occasional stones of tin and large quantities of arsenical mundic, which James considered a great feature. The sett was traversed by several other lodes close to main lode, and could be reached by short cross-cuts. The present owners wished to sell the mine as they had no funds to erect an engine to prove the lode twenty fathoms deeper. There was a water stamps and other dressing machinery already on the mine. It could be recommended as a very fair speculation.

The licence to work the mine at present held by Mr. Henry Berriman from the Hon. Mrs. Gilbert would be transferred to the new company. Mrs. Gilbert, being anxious to further employment in the area, would grant a sett on very favourable terms, and also make available further land to the eastward on the course of the lodes. The meeting decided to start the mine in 1,000 £1 shares; but little progress seems thereafter to have been made.[1]

1. *Cornishman* April 14 1887.

ROSEWALL HILL AND RANSOM UNITED: GOOLE PELLAS

Among the more picturesque mine remains in the St. Ives area are the ruined stacks and engine houses of the old Rosewall Hill and Ransom United mine. This is a very ancient bal; and the eastern side of the hill on which it lies is riddled with old shafts, some of which exhibit the most primitive method of working. A zig-zag road runs to the summit to serve some shafts there; and it is said that in calm weather the men on night core walking up in procession with their lighted candles in their hats formed a line of moving lights that made a striking appearance against the dark hillside.

Some interesting references to mining at Rosewall in the seventeenth century are to be found in the records of a court of inquiry held in 1680 into the refusal of Andrew Rosewall to pay tithes to the Vicar, a pluralist who held the livings of Lelant and St. Ives, as well as of Towednack, where the defendant resided. In evidence, James Quicke, of Zennor, yeoman, aged 48, stated that the defendant "doth depasture his cattell on the tenement called Rosewall and on that parte of the tenement called Boreesa" — Breja — "in the posssssion of the defendant," and that Rosewall "doth likewise keepe and depasture on the said premisses three or ffower labouringe horses Nagges or Mares which the defendant hath from tyme to tyme and doth usually imploy them in carryinge of tyn stuffe to the Stampings Mill and allsoe to the bloweinge howse."

William Daniell of Zennor, tinner, aged 37, was in partnership with Rosewall in mining; whilst Morrice Dyer of St. Ives "holdeth by Lease one stampinge Mill with thappurtenances parcel of the said Tenement of Roswall." John Browne, of St. Ives, yeoman, aged 48, described a suit which had been commenced "for the Tryall of the Right of Certaine Tynn works" in which he (Browne), Mr. Edmond Davy, the defendant's daughter, and others appeared as plaintiffs, and William Botteroll and others were defendants. Edmond Davy of Ludgvan, gentleman, aged 55, confirmed that he had "been an adventurers with the sayd Defendant" — Andrew Rosewall — "for divers yeares in adventuringe and workinge for Tynn, and that the said Defendant hath bynn Captaine of considerable Tynn works." A dispute had arisen with one Tredinham when Rosewall was "Captaine of a Tynnworke called Hard to Come by."[1] Clearly, mining, albeit to shallow depths, was being vigorously carried on at Rosewall Hill at this early period.

On January 1 1742 "3-4ths of 1-3rd of 2 pair of Bounds, St. George's Work and the Little Bounds, Common of Rosewall, Towednack," were mentioned in an indenture bearing the names of Thomas Kniveton of Lelant, Abel Angove of Illogan and Peter Carveth, late of Nansalverne.[2] The Rosewall family had by no means lost interest in mining the hill from which they took their name, however; and in 1765 they were working it for tin jointly with the Harrises of Penbeagle. At that period the lodes were exploited at surface in "coffens" or open pits, a number of which still remain on the flat summit of the hill, extending towards Buttermilk. Near Rosewall Farm there used to be a most perfect specimen; it was about thirty yards long, eight fathoms deep, and only a few feet wide. Entry was gained by walking down easy stages of steps at one end set a few feet apart, where the stuff was shovelled to grass. "I well remember," wrote a local antiquarian at the beginning of this century, "walking between its narrow, fungus-covered walls, gazing up to the blue

Valuable Tin Mine and Materials, for Sale.

TO be SOLD by AUCTION, by Mr. WILLIAM RICHARDS, on WEDNESDAY, the 26th day of October instant, at Three o'clock in the Afternoon, at PEARCE'S HOTEL, in the Town of *Penzance*, all that large and valuable TIN MINE, called

Rosewall Hill,

Situate in the Parish of Towednack, in the County of Cornwall, adjoining on the west the very productive Mine called St. IVES CONSOLS, which has for many years past, yielded the adventurers very large dividends of profit.

The Mine now offered is held by the Adventurers under setts granted by the Lords and Bounders for a term of 21 years, about 18 of which are unexpired under the payment of one twenty-second dues.

The Setts are large and upwards of £30,000 have been expended by the present adventurers in the erection of Machinery, and in opening and exploring the western part of the Sett, which has produced several thousand pounds' worth of Tin, and a comparatively small outlay to draw the water from the shaft at the eastern extremity of the Sett, and which may be done by flat rods, will open a large extent of Tin Ground on the very borders of the St Ives Consols, and from which, under ancient workings, former adventurers realized large profits.

With the Mine will be sold all the

MACHINERY AND MATERIALS,

Lying thereon, which are nearly new, viz.:— 1 36-inch Cylinder Pumping Engine; 1 20-inch Whim Engine, and 1 Stamping Engine, of Sims's combined double Cylinder Engine; large Cylinder 48-inch, and small Cylinder 25-inch, with Boilers, &c, complete; about 69 fathoms of 7-inch and 100 fathoms of 6-inch Pumps, with Plunger Poles, &c., &c., Capstan, and Capstan Ropes, Shears, Pulleys, &c., several Horse Whims, 4 Smiths' Bellows, Anvils, and other Smiths' Tools of various descriptions; Iron, Timber, Ladders, Sheds, and a great variety of Materials of the very best description, which the Adventurers have purchased without regard to price, and which are well adapted for carrying on a mine on a large and extensive plan.

On the mine is a large and convenient Account-House, with Material-rooms, Stables, Smith and Carpenters' Shops, and other convenient Buildings, which alone have cost the adventurers in their erection about £1,000.

Persons disposed to treat for the same by Private Contract, may have an opportunity of doing so in the mean time, by applying to Capt. NICHOLAS TREDINNICK, Camborne; or to Messrs. JOHN and RODD, Solicitors, Penzance; from whom any further particulars may be known; and should any Sale take place by Private Contract, due notice will be given prior to the day fixed for the Auction.

For a view of the Mine and Materials, apply to the Agents, and for further particulars, at the office of Messrs. JOHN & RODD, Penzance.

Dated, October 1, 1842.

Advertisement for the sale of tin mine and mine materials at Rosewall Hill, October 1842
(Noall Collection)

104

sky and watching the trees waving overhead. In the damp, close smell of its atmosphere and the soft mellow light and stillness there came creeping over me 'a feeling of old-worldness, as if some strange influence would impress my mind with ghostly messages from the past.'' At the deeper end were more modern workings, and a shaft had been sunk and levels driven to follow up the lode underground to a depth unattainable by the ancients. This interesting coffen was filled in about the year 1896 by Squire Tyringham's steward because of its danger to cattle.[3]

Deep mining at Rosewall Hill probably commenced during the latter part of the 18th century. The shafts had certainly been sunk to some depth by its close, as is evident from the circumstances recorded in connection with two accidents which occurred at the time during the year 1801. In May, three men working in the bottom were drowned when the ground gave way as another party of miners were holing ''a house of water'' (old flooded workings); whilst in August an attendant who was adjusting the engine lost his life when struck by the moving bob.[4]

It is asserted that Rosewall Hill was worked without intermission from 1761 to 1811, and to a depth of 132 fms. below adit. A new company later took over the undertaking, but having incurred heavy debts, ceased operations in 1817.[5] The *Royal Cornwall Gazette* carried an advertisement for the sale of machinery and materials at the mine, to take place on March 25 that year. These included a steam engine, 30″ cylinder, single, ''on Boulton and Watt's plan;'' a steam whim, 12½″ cylinder, double, also on Boulton and Watt's plan, with a new boiler and new cage; a pressure engine, with 12½″ plunger pole and brass cylinder; 60 fms. of 6″ and 7″, 20 fms. of 4½″, and 120 fms. of 4″ pumps; 30 fms. or iron air pipes of 3″ to 4″ bore; 140 fms. of 4½″ and 6″ rods; a horse whim, with whim rope and kibbles; 150 fms. of ladders; two balance bobs; a counter, almost new; and a quantity of winze trees and winze kibbles. Further particulars could be obtained from Capt. Uddy Bray, at the mine.

In 1818 St. Ives Consols lying to the east of Rosewall Hill, and on the same run of lodes, was started. It incorporated the ancient Ransom mine, *q.v.*, situated between Consols and Rosewall Hill, but a part, at least, of the Ransom property was again working independently in the 1820's.[6] Rosewall Hill appears to have remained idle during this period; but in 1838 it was taken up by a new group of adventurers styled ''The Rosewall Hill and Gweans Mining Company.'' The ''Gweans'' in this name refers to Wheal Wens, on the summit of the hill. This company would rework setts forming ''a continuation of St. Ives Consols which had produced considerable profit to the shareholders and are now exceedingly rich. The lodes in the present company's sett have been profitably opened to considerable depth and extent, the produce being of the richest quality.''

Soon after Rosewall Hill's re-opening a miner called John Ninnis had his skull so badly fractured by a stone falling down the sahft that it was necessary to remove several pieces of bone, and he lay in a precarious state.[7] This was a sad event; but the labours of John Ninnis, and his comrades were helping to reveal the riches of the mine. On August 4 1841 the *Penzance Gazette* reported: "We are glad to hear that the enterprising adventurers in (Rosewall Hill) mine, some of whom are resident in Penzance, have been lately raising nearly sufficient Tin to pay Cost. A considerable improvement has again taken place, and Tribute pitches were last week set to twelve men at 3s. in the £, a large and rich *Carbona* having been discovered. Such a discovery must be a great benefit to St. Ives and the neighbourhood, where several thousands of pounds have already been expended in getting the mine in working order." This is the first known reference to a carbona in the mine. These peculiar deposits of tin were a striking feature of Rosewall Hill and St. Ives Consols.

Unfortunately, it appears that financial difficulties hindered the adventurers when prosecuting their promising speculation; and in October 1842 the mine was offered for sale. Rosewall Hill was said to be held under setts granted by the lords and bounders for a term of 21 years, 18 of which were unexpired, at 1-22nd dues. These setts were large, and over £30,000 had been spent by the present company in erecting machinery and in opening and exploring the western section, which had produced several thousand pounds' worth of tin. By making a further small outlay to draw the water from the shafts at the eastern extremity of the sett, which could be done by means of flat rods (presumably from the existing engine) a large extent of tin ground would be opened on the very borders of St. Ives Consols, from which, under ancient workings, former adventurers realised large profits. The materials to be sold with the mine included a 36" pumping engine 1 20" whim engine; and a "Sim's combined double Cylinder Stamping Engine, large cylinder 48 inch and small cylinder 25 inch;" about 60 fms. of 7" and 100 fms. of 6" pumps; several horse whims; ladders; and tools. "On the Mine is a large and convenient Account-House, with Material-rooms, Stables, Smith and Carpenters' Shops, and other convenient Buildings, which alone have cost the Adventurers in their erection about £1,000."[8]

Between 1845-50 the property was managed by the Rosewall Hill Mining Company. Then, in 1857, efforts were made to resuscitate it under the name of "Rosewall Hill and Ransom United mines," Wheal Ransom being added to the sett at about this time to form an enlarged undertaking. A cost-book company wa set up in 6,000 £2 shares, the management committee consisting of John Pool, Riviere House, Hayle; Han. Ellis, Rose Villa, Hayle; Stephen Eddy, Grassington, Yorkshire; Capt. Treweeke, Eden House, St. Ives; and Thomas Treweeke, Uny Lelant. Besides the main lode in the sett, which had been obtained on a 21 year lease from W.B. Praed, Esq., at 1-22nd dues, other parallel lodes were known to exist both north and south of it, which had yielded immense returns to former workers. The length of the rich mineral ground which cropped out at the highest part of the hill varied from 130-150 fms., with a dip E. at an angle of 45 degs., which was followed to a depth of 130

The ruins of Rosewall Hill (Noall Collection)

fms. below adit, where the lode maintained its original diameter, the stuff giving a greater average value than that of any other mine then being worked in the district.

An attempt at re-working the old mines had been made about sixteen years ago, but instead of directing their attention to the original deposit in its eastward dip, operations were confined to the hard, barren rock beneath the productive layer of ore ground, from which it had retreated 100 fms. E. Exhausted funds, and failure to exploit that section which had yielded more than twenty tons of tin monthly for a long period to a former company, soon led to a suspension. "Twenty or even fifteen Tons Monthly must have been a great yield at that time, inasmuch as the labourers did not employ more than two thirds of their time in the excavation of ground, the remainder being occupied in preparing the stuff for sampling, bargaining with the Agents for prices, in some instances watching the returns at the Stamping Mills, and agreeing with the Captains for another three months' contract; in fine, the unsystematical application of the tributer and the whole management tended naturally to deteriorate the condition of the concern, which at length became rotten and ragged, both at the surface and beneath."

The new adventurers proposed to drain the mine by erecting a 40″ pumping engine on the Old Bridge or Sump shaft, now sunk about 130 fms. below adit, at which point, and for a great many fathoms above no levels had been driven in either direction, "excavations being left wholly to the caprice of tributers."

107

A rod would be extended eastwards from this engine to Ransom shaft, already sunk 80 fms. under adit, at which level it intersected the cross-course; on its being driven through that part an immune quantity of valuable ore ground would soon be made available, the ancients not being advanced so far east at that depth. By sinking Ransom shaft to the 90 the cross-course would pass from west to east, and alight immediately on Rosewall Hill Main lode, where the richest portion should be found. Sinking would then be continued, the tin still dipping E. following the underlie of the cross-course. Ransom would eventually become a second sump, thus enabling a complete and economical working of the mine to be speedily effected; and if reports could be believed, there would also be found a lengthening of ore west of the Engine under the slide known to exist there.

At about the 100 fm. level a carbona diverged north from Main lode and produced immense quantities of rich tin stuff up to the time the mine was abandoned, and which would again materially contribute to the returns.

A 40" engine, with 6" pitwork to the 80 and 4" below, would be ample to commend the water to a depth of 300 fms. A 24" whim, with skips and guides for drawing, would effect a saving of fifty per cent over the old method of discharging; whilst an engine of similar size with 32 heads of stamps would suffice for treatment. The century rock and lodes were easily wrought; the tin was of the best quality; the water "marvellously easy;" and the situation all that could be desired. The length of the sett on the run of lodes, in granite, was 400 fms., and of ample width. "There is no old Mine in the neighbourhood offering such prospects of success in so short a period, and lastingly profitable on so small an outlay as £12,000."

The mines could be expected to yield 20 tons of tin monthly, worth, at prevailing prices, £1,700, the working costs not exceeding half that sum. Management of both surface and underground operations would be under the direction of Capt. Treweeke, who was also manager of St. Ives Consols, Wheal Margaret and East Wheal Margaret. Intending shareholders were invited to inspect the original section of the old workings made in 1808, and the old cost book, at Mr. Treweeke's office, Uny Lelant.[9] The flotation proved successful, and steps were quickly taken to put the mine in good working order.

On September 30 1857 a splendid new 40" cylinder pumping engine, of 9' stroke, equal beam, built by Sandy's Vivian & Co., of Hayle, was christened in the presence of a large number of shareholders and gentlemen, the engineers being Messrs, Eustice & Son, also of Hayle. "It was truly gratifying to observe the ease and grace with which the engine moved up and down," commented the *Cornish Telegraph* admiringly. At four o'clock, the party, numbering 22 all told, sat down to a sumptuous meal at the Halsetown Hotel, where "Success to the Rosewall Hill and Ransom United" was drunk in sparkling champagne.

By August 20 1853 the new company had spent £7,110 on re-establishing the mine. The new steam whim had been installed and was performing its duties satisfactorily.[10] The lode in Ransom shaft was valued at £120 per fathom in

June, 1860; other lodes were looking well, worth from £30-60 per fm. "Large dividends will certainly soon occrue."[11] But this hopeful promise was not immediately fulfilled. At the account held in Halsetown Hotel on March 15 1861 Mr. T. Treweeke, jun., reported a loss on the six months' working of £1,824, requiring a call of 6s. per share.[12] Not long after this, however, Rosewall Hill entered the dividend list, and paid regular profits for several years. At the end of 1864, low prices for tin and a falling off in returns darkened the prospects again; and at the account held in the Steam Packet Hotel, Hayle, in January 1865 a call of 5s. was made, amounting to £1,500.[13] There was a further call of 2s.6d. in August. The November account showed that although 25 tons 8 cwt. of black tin had been sold for £1,418 that quarter, the mine was still in the red to the tune of £254, but a call was avoided.[14] Spargo, writing at about this time, opined that the property had the elements of success. He gave adit level as 30 fms., "Rosewall Hill" (? Engine) shaft 170 fms. under adit, and Ransom 130 fms. below, and still being sunk. Mention was made of a 32″ stamping and 24″ winding engine. The labour force comprised 120 men, 20 women and 30 boys.

The 1866 returns showed a considerable improvement; 30 tons 2 cwt. of tin being raised during the June quarterly.[15] Unfortunately, the prices realised were very low, ranging from £45.10s. to £46.15s. per ton, the total amount earned being only £1,394, so the adventurers continued to lose money at the rate of nearly £100 per month. Some of them had already relinquished shares,

Ruinous stack, Rosewall Hill   (Noall Collection)

109

while other shares were declared forfeit, as no less then five calls remained unpaid on them! The total number of shares now amounted to 5,915. The lode at the 100 fm. level in Ransom shaft was worth £12 per fm.; a caunter lode opening at this point had a value of £16, but at the 90 S. this caunter was 4' wide, worth £50-60 per fm. The lode in Engine shaft, 12 fms. below the 170, was worth £35 per fm. It proposed to work the western part of the mine at a depth of 100 fms. to exploit a lode of great size left by former works. This could be done for an outlay of about £500 and would give employment to a number of miners thrown out of work by the stopping of several nearby mines.[10]

With the financial position continuing to deteriorate, a special meeting was called in March 1868 to decide on the future of the mine. At this, it was revealed "that in consequence of the number of relinquishments and the present state of the working, the mine be stopped, the machinery and materials be offered to the lord of the lease, and if not accepted by him, the whole materials be drawn to the surface and sold by public auction or private contract as soon as possible." Over 900 shares were actually relinquished at the meeting, whilst many other adventurers declared their intention to relinquish if the mine was not shut up. Fortunately, matters soon after a turn for the better, and the adventurers decided to carry on.

In the quarter ending November 1868 38 tons of tin were sold at an average price of £57.12s., enabling a small profit of £395 to be shown, but a heavy debit balance remained.[17] By June 1869 this had been wiped off; and the adventurers sat down to a substantial dinner in the account house, under the presidency of Capt. Treweeke, feeling happier than they had done for some time past. Mr. Banfield, proposing the chairman's health, said that the mine, like most others in the county, had passed through a most serious and depressing ordeal, but its prospects had now improved with the price of tin. He described Capt. Treweeke as a man of great energy, perseverance and ability, who was entitled to the thanks of the shareholders for effecting a complete resuscitation of the mine from a calling state to that of one which would soon probably pay a dividend.[18] Later that month Rosewall Hill carbona, in the western part of the mine, was reported worth £20 per fm.

Rosewall Hill rejoined the dividend list in June 1870. It was then in 5869 shares, with an expended capital of £24,000. Future prospects looked cheering, as three St. Ives Consols lodes ran through the sett, one of which they were daily expecting to intersect 150 fms. W. of the boundary.[19] Charles Osborne, a lander, was unfortunately killed during August when he fell 180' in Ransom Main shaft whilst putting a barrow into the skip, which was required by a miner in the adit level.[20] In December 1871, with the mine just meeting costs, it was decided to raise the standard price for tin paid to the tributers from £40 to £60 per ton. On the Standard lode the 100 E. was worth £25 per fm., the tin ground being 27 fms. long. Carbona lode, at the 46 fm. level, worth £10 per cubic fathom, was 12' wide. North lode showed an improvement, being worth

£8 per fm. in the 100 fm. level.[21] Capt. W. Buglehole succeeded Capt. Daniel as agent in September 1872 at nine guineas a month, Mr. J. White, of Halsetown, being second agent at seven guineas.

Soon after this a dispute arose between Rosewall Hill and St. Ives Consols concerning what was described as "a question of underground right;" but on November 28 1872 it was agreed to submit the matter to friendly arbitration. A slight loss was sustained in December. The four months' account included an item of £341.9s.9d. for "coal from vessels at St. Ives." Messrs. W.C. Tyack, N. Pentreath and J. Poole were added to the committee.[22] By June 1873 the mine was again making calls; but in August a newly discovered Carbona lode in the 80 fm. level at the eastern end of the sett was reported to be increasing in size and value. It was 12′ wide, and estimated to be worth £200 per fm. It was thought that four tons of tin would be produced from it that month. Some lucky tributers who ventured upon what they termed "a poor lode in sight," would now earn from £30-40 per man as their month's gettings. Capt. Buglehole also entertained a very high opinion of their new workings at Goole Pellas, in the northern part of the sett, where they had four new lodes, all in virgin ground; these were well defined and highly productive for tin.[23] In December, the lode in the North Carbona in the back of the 100 fm. level was still going up, and worth £120 per fm. The agents, however, now thought that the main part of this carbona was thrown by the Wheal Mary lode to the west of the present workings, and in the bottom of the level, and had put a pare of men to stope the bottom, where the lode was worth £50 per fm. No.'s 2 and 3 Crossings were looking well, and worth £60 per fm. The mine, on the whole, had never looked better.[24]

The year 1874 proved to be a very troubled one for the mine. The first indications of this came in January, when, as a result of a decision by the adventurers to introduce the five weeks' month the men refused their bargains at the following survey. After a deputation of six had met the management to discuss the matter, the latter gave way, the system of twelve pays in the year was restored, and the miners resumed work. A Penzance newspaper commented acidly: "Our mining friends need not waste their time about a four or a five weeks' month, for soon there will be no month at all, unless all classes are prepared to make great sacrifices." But although the tin mining share markets were collapsing in ruins, nine-tenths of the mines having ceased to make profits, the Rosewall Hill wrangle went senselessly on. At the February meeting the adventurers "sturdily took the bull by the horns" and again insisted that twelve calendar, and not lunar months were to regulate pays and settings; moreover, the nominal standard for tin, by which the men were paid, was to be reduced from £80 to £50, and a vigorous effort was demanded "not for more work and less pay, but for more work and the same pay. The feeling grows that *all* must pull in the same boat, or the adventurers will stop all but the best parts of the mines, and speculate for a few months in water charges only. If the lords will not assist they can work their own mines; if the men do not aid they must turn to other sources of employ.''

The men reacted as one might expect to this tough pronouncement. At the following Saturday survey all refused to take their pitches, but the engines were kept working. In the evening, the St. Ives town crier with his bell summoned the men to meet at the mine at eight on Monday morning. At this assembly another deputation of six was appointed to meet the agents, who were supported by Mr. George Treweeke, of Wheal Margaret. An ingenious compromise put forward by one of the men was that there should be a monthly engagement with a settlement on the last day of the month, whatever the day of the week on which it should happen to fall; as this could not occur in any calendar month, the men would never have to wait five weeks for their pay. This failed to win acceptance, and the men remained out. It was said that if the miners could obtain payment for the extra week they would return to work; as it was, they often got less in a five weeks' than in a four weeks' month, especially if they didn't work hard enough. The dispute was eventually resolved, but not before it had seriously jeopardised the future of the mine.

The irony of all this was that Rosewall Hill itself had never looked better than at this time. In the previous quarter it had sold no less than 42 tons of tin and made a profit of about £150, but a debit balance still remained.[25] At the quarterly meeting in October it was announced that an even higher quantity — 43 tons 7 cwt. — of tin had been sold, but this had resulted in a loss of £235, due to the low price obtained. The agents reported a strong masterly lode, very kindly, in the 70 W.; the lode at the back of the 60 was 2½' wide, worth £15 per fm. On North Carbona, the lode was less productive, worth only £14 per fm., but with every prospect of improvement. At Goole Pellas, the new shaft was sunk to the 25 fm. level, lode worth £15-30 per fm. The stopes and pitches here were looking very well, and the returns increasing. Considering they were still at such a shallow depth, these were considered excellent indications for a valuable and productive mine being laid open there. About 100 men and boys were employed on tut and tribute, who were earning fair average wages and working very well.

This account was considerably enlivened by the putting down of a motion to associate Mr. Fitzgerald, of St. Ives, with Mr. Mudge, of Hayle, as mine surgeon. ''It is seldom that such lively meetings take place nowadays, with tin at its present price! As usual, with all matters affecting Hayle, or anyone resident there, at this mine, right or wrong, the Hayle clique rules; and, protesting that the motion was 'frivolous and ridiculous,' it was negatived. (But) it was 'frivolous and ridiculous' not to appoint a surgeon resident in the immediate neighbourhood of the mine, and to retain one living five miles away! To deduct doctor's pence monthly from men who could not consult their doctor, without losing a day's work! There is no question that the *men* were utterly forgotten, or ignored, in the desire to serve a friend.'' Such was the comment by a disgruntled miner on this affair.[26]

The mine continued to look well in November, three stopes being valued at £40 per fm., two ends £22, and New Flat Rod shaft £30.[27] In January 1875 the agents reported Goole Pellas in fork again, following extraordinary rains which had flooded the working; they had resumed the sinking of New Flat Rod shaft below the 25 fm. level where the lode was now 5' wide, worth £40 per fm. The 25 driving E. and W. of the cross-cut on Goole Pellas lode were both producing tin, but they had suspended the cross-cut N., fearing that if the North lode were intersected the mine might be flooded in the prevailing wet weather. In the ''old'' mine — *i.e.*, Rosewall Hill itself — they had 20 fms. of water in, but were forking slowly. A considerable quantity of tributers' tin stuff at the 110 fm. level could not be brought to surface until the water had been forked below that level; because of this, the account meeting would be postponed for a month. North Carbona was now worth £12 per fm. Fair progress was being made in clearing deep adit level; the level, however, was very badly crushed — this may have been a consequence of the heavy rains — and required a considerable amount of timbering.[28] Similar problems had been caused in many Cornish mines by this same torrential downpour, which had actually occurred during the preceding November; the town of St. Ives was badly flooded by rainwater which swept down the Stennack Valley from Rosewall and other hills in the vicinity.

During April two Rosewall Hill miners met with a remarkable piece of good luck. Whilst working in a pitch at 10s. in the £ tribute they cut into a carbona, the lode suddenly increasing to an extraordinary width. The agents offered them £30 to relinquish their bargain, which was refused, the men hoping, by working long ''cores'', to realise double that amount for their month's labour. By October, New Flat Rod shaft at Goole Pellas was sinking below the 35, the lode — now described as Middle lode — getting more settled and defined, worth £15 per fm. North lode in the 25, driving W. of cross-course, was letting out a large quantity of water in the end, inducing the belief that a larger and better lode lay ahead. North Carbona, in the back of the 100 fm. level, had improved, being 3' wide; and No's. 2 and 3 Crossings were worth £11 per fm. In the 100 W. of North Carbona they had splendid tin ground; and from the present appearance of the lode they thought another carbona must lie in the bottom of the level. The lode was now 3½' wide, worth £30 per fm., and a cross-cut was being driven towards it from the 100.[29]

Unfortunately, the company's financial position at this time was giving cause for concern; and the shareholders were issued with a notice convening a meeting for December 1 to consider immediate stopping the ''old mine.'' The agents saw no hope of that section becoming remunerative, and recommended an application to the lords for power to draw all the materials to surface. The ''old mine'' embraced a very extensive run of workings, about 150 fms. deep. For over forty years very extensive mining operations had been carried on there, particularly on the carbonas, which had been most productive. It was proposed, however, to continue working the north or Goole Pellas section, where the prospects were very encouraging.[30] The mine's shares for some time past had been unsaleable, and many of the shareholders would gladly have paid a premium to have been relieved of their burden. "It is, indeed, a wonder that the mine had held afloat so long as she has; and now she is not only under water, but some parts of her are full of water as well." Its stopping would seriously affect the adjoining St. Ives Consols, their drainage systems being interconnected. The underground labour force amounted now to only just over twenty.[31]

The December meeting confirmed the proposal to suspend the "old" mine. It also levied a call of 3s. and decided to dispense with the services of one of the agents. In February 1876 a lode in the new Flatrod shaft below the 32 fm. level was reported 2' wide, worth £39 for tin per fm; but by March no less than 1,600 shares had been relinquished. As a result, a special meeting resolved to offer the mine for sale as a going concern on April 5. The total debit balance then amounted to £3,238. The last lot of tin sold (5¼ tons in February) had realised only £42.15s. per ton. Rosewall Hill was, in fact, one of the many good mines killed off at that time by the appallingly low prices for tin.[32]

At the auction, all the materials, together with the leases, were bought for £1,300 by Mr. Browne, of Buckfastleigh, a shareholder in the former company, for the purpose of re-working the Goole Pellas section only, Mr. S. Abbott, of Redruth, being appointed purser and managing agent of this new undertaking.

The winding-up of the old company's affairs proved to be a protracted and expensive business. In June, the *Cornish Telegraph* reported that the purser and some of the large shareholders had instructed Messrs. Hodge, Hockin and Marrack, solicitors, Truro, to file a petition in the Stannaries Court. The accounts — after crediting the sums realised by the sale of the mine and materials to the new company established to develop Goole Pellas Mine — showed a debit balance due from the shareholders of £2,245.11s.10d. Mr. Glanville, for the trustees of R.W.G. Tyringham, Esq., generously accepted an offer to £100 for all claims for land destroyed by mining operations. In November, the shareholders had to meet a heavy call of £1.17s.6d. per share imposed on them by the Stannary Court; but in October 1877 the official liquidator announced that a return of 6s.8d. per share would be paid to all those who were on the list of contributories, the proportion of the first return on account of the surplus assets which remained after discharging all liabilities.

Meanwhile, work had been proceeding on the Goole Pellas section, where in November 1876 50-60 men were being employed. A good caunter lode was discovered there in 1878. In January 1880 some machinery was purchased from the defunct Wheal Providence; but whilst removing the cylinder cap from an engine two workmen were injured, one of them very seriously. Between 1877 and 1881 Goole Pellas produced 526 tons of black tin. The mine closed in April 1883, when twelve of its discharged miners were obliged to emigrate to America.[34]

One of the old shafts at Goole Pellas adjoining the St. Ives-Land's End coast road now provides water for the town's supply. An old miner — the late Mr. John Curnow — once told the writer that the mine was very wet, and that they did very little there in winter except pump water! An underground stream runs through the workings, so that the shaft overflows in winter, and in summer only requires siphoning. By contrast, Rosewall Hill itself — the "Old" mine — was very dry, there being no water down to 80 fms. Many thousands of tons of good quality tinstuff still remain in that mine, which could be opened at little cost and worked above adit without the expense of pumping. As proof of the richness of Rosewall Hill, he mentioned that, although the dumps had been twice turned over, he had himself turned them over a third time and still found stones containing payable quantities of tin.

Another former miner, also in reminiscent mood, described how a tributer at Rosewall Hill encountered what he took to be "clay granite" but which was in fact a rather unusual variety of tin ore. Thinking the stuff of no value, he threw it away among the "attle" (waste.) Another miner, realising its true nature, obtained permission to work over the spoil heaps and recovered the ore, which he sold at a good price without having had the trouble of mining it. This ore, when stamped, yielded the familiar black tin.

Between 1839-76 Rosewall Hill sold 1,500 tons of black tin worth £245,000 and paid £90,000 in dividends. Some arsenic was also produced. From 1881-3 the western section of the mine, originally known as Wheal Union, or Wheal Wens, was worked as a part of West Providence (Tyringham Consols); whilst in 1908 the sett was taken over by St. Ives Consolidated Mines, Ltd., but they undertook no development there.

1. Exchequer Deposition by Commission (1680) Michaelmas No. 6; (1681) Easter No. 29
2. Per Justin Brooke
3. *St. Ives by the Sea* (1904)
4. *Cornwall Gazette & Falmouth Packet* May 16 and August 15 1801
5. Barton, D.B., *A History of Tin Mining and Smelting in Cornwall*, 1967, p.38.
6. *Royal Cornwall Gazette* June 1830
7. *Royal Cornwall Gazette* February 8 1839
8. *West Briton* October 7 1842
9. *Royal Cornwall Gazette* March 20 1857
10. *Royal Cornwall Gazette* September 3 1858
11. *Cornish Telegraph* June 6 1860
12. *Cornish Telegraph* March 26 1861
13. *Royal Cornwall Gazette* January 20 1865
14. *Royal Cornwall Gazette* November 30 1865
15. *Royal Cornwall Gazette* December 13 1866
16. *Ibid.*
17. *Cornish Telegraph* December 23 1868
18. *Cornish Telegraph* June 5 1869
19. *Cornish Telegraph* June 8 1870
20. *Cornish Telegraph* August 17 1870
21. *Cornish Telegraph* December 20 1871
22. *Cornish Telegraph* December 18 1872
23. *Cornish Telegraph* August 20 1873

24. *Cornish Telegraph* December 24 1873
25. *Cornish Telegraph* February 25 and March 4 1874
26. *Cornish Telegraph* October 14 1874
27. *Cornish Telegraph* November 11 1874
28. *Cornish Telegraph* January 27 1875
29. *Cornish Telegraph* October 13 1875
30. *Cornish Telegraph* November 24 1875
31. *Cornish Telegraph* December 1 1875
32. *Cornish Telegraph* March 28 1876
33. *Cornish Telegraph* October 7 1877
34. *Cornishman* April 19 1883

WHEAL RUBY

The *Mining Journal* (Supplement) of January 27 1872 announced a re-opening of "Old Tin Croft, Ludgvan," under the name of Wheal Ruby. The lode was said to have been worked in a small way "about 65 years ago" by some men of very limited means from Penzance, who drove an adit from the eastern boundary, the deepest point reached being not more than 14 fms. This would appear to be the same mine as West Wheal Tin-Croft, Ludgvan, (*q.v.*), which was active around 1810-12, and *not* Old Tincroft Consols, situated in Towednack and Uny Lelant. Wheal Ruby adventurers were driving the adit end W. on main lode, the part then being worked being 3' wide. This was being forced on to reach the cross-course and the junction of the granite and killas. Samples taken in the cross-cut, shaft bottom and adit end over lode widths from 4½'-5' gave a produce of tin varying from 2 to 13 lbs. per ton of stuff.

OLD TINCROFT CONSOLS (NEW TINCROFT UNITED)

This ancient mine is the most westerly of the Wheal Sisters group, Wheal Henry adjoining it on the N.E. and Wheal Margaret on the S.E., its principal lode, known as Bramble lode, being actually the westward continuation of Wheal Margaret lode. The principal shaft, Dimmond shaft, lies nearly a quarter of a mile S. of Cuckoo Rock.

In 1838 "Old Tincroft Consols, Towednack," possessed a 20″ engine and employed 37 people. Three years later (November 1841) "Tincroft Consols, in the parishes of Towednack and Uny-Lelant," was described as "those valuable, productive and highly improving Tin-Mines" when 4/128ths shares were offered for sale by auction. "The additional powerful Steam Engine, lately erected, and now in complete operation, when considered with other concomitant advantages resulting therefrom...strongly recommended those Shares to public notice."[1] The mine was then about 42 fms. deep.

In August 1874 the "Old Tincroft Consols Mining Company, Limited," was registered in Truro with a London office at 35 Ethelburga House, 70

Bishopsgate Street, E.C. to re-work the mine. It was then drained to the 30 fm. level by Wheal Margaret's engine, and had the continuation of the lodes of Wheal Mary, Wheal Margaret and Wheal Reeth. The lease ran for 21 years from March 1870. The secretary was George Still and manager Capt. James Pope. In September 1874 the manager wrote: "We have erected the whim, and completed the repairs of Diamond Shaft, fixed ladders, etc., 60 fms. from surface, and resumed driving the 30 and 10 fm. levels W. I have taken and assayed samples from both levels, and find the lode in te 10 is 15″ wide, producing 1 qr. 23 lbs. per ton of staff, or 4 cwt. 1 qr. per 100 sacks." This was equivalent to 51 lbs. of black tin to the ton. The manager hoped in a short time to set some men on tribute and bring some quality tinstone into the market.

By June 1875 1,000 shares (of £4 each) had been issued, and a 28″ steam engine bought for £370 drained the mine to 50 fms. below adit. A meeting held in December decided to add Wheal Gilbert to the sett. In order to merge the two concerns a fresh company was registered and took over the properties under the title of New Tincroft United in September 1876. The new company was in 3.500 £5 shares, of which 1,799 went to J.B. Reynolds (managing director of the old company) as purchaser of £1,030 of the old company's debts. The shareholders in the old company accepted shares in the new company in exchange; later George Still claimed the sum of £1,030 should have been paid to him as liquidator.

In March 1876 a meeting resolved to liquidate the company, and the resolution was confined in April, when George Still was appointed liquidator and advertised for claims. In May 1876 the company was fined 5s. with costs for not having a gauge on the boiler and for not having an abstract of the Metalliferous Mines Act posted at or near the mine.

Being unable to obtain £446.8s. plus interest, including a dishonoured acceptance for £359.4s.9d., the liquidator successfully petitioned the Vice-Warden's Court in February 1879 to wind up the company. J.H. Hamley was appointed liquidator. An auction of the mine and materials was held in May, when the 24 inch pumping engine, 16 heads of stamps, rods, pitwork, a horse whim, tools and other items were offered. Only £30.19s.6d. was raised, and a further auction was held in July, after which the liquidator was replaced by the Registrar of the Vice Warden's Court. Another auction took place in October.

During the winding-up it was discovered that a board meeting held in May 1875 had resolved that the directors should issue shares for a deposit of £1 on application, not £2 as at first agreed, and that of this sum 12s. per share should be paid in commission to them. This was illegal, and the directors were ordered by the Vice Warden's Court to repay the sums they had received, of which £184 had been received by J.T. Holden (director from 1875-6). At the time of the merger with Wheal Gilbert debts amounted to £1,717.17s.10d., of which £883.6s.1d. was due to J.B. Reynolds. In part settlement of this sum Reynolds took acceptances for £937.10s. received in payment of calls from

Birmingham shareholders. The acceptances were endorsed "sans recours" by Reynolds, who received them from Still who said that the company could not take acceptances.

The liquidator's final accounts were approved in July 1884 and showed receipts to June 1882 £614.8s.2d., payments £382.5s., and balance £232.3s.2d. Out of the latter sum payments of £216.18s.3d. were made, of which £15.4s.11d. was unclaimed. An order to dissolve the company was amde in November 1884.

The shares were listed in the *Mining Journal* from two days before the company's registration to November 1877.[1]

1. *Mining Journal* September 19 1874; April 22 and May 6 1876; March 29, May 10 and October 18 1879; *Mining World* June 5, June 12 and November 13 1875; April 1 1876; Dines (1956) p.131 (Sisters, including Old Tincroft or Tincroft Consols.) (Per Justin Brooke.)

WEST WHEAL TIN-CROFT

In November 1810 six-sixtieth shares in "Wheal Tin Croft, in the parish of Ludgvan," were offered for sale, together with a quantity of materials. These included a whim (11' cage) and a 5¼" whim rope 60 fms. long.[1] This appears to have been a close neighbour of "West Wheal Tin-Croft Mine, in Ludgvan," referred to in an advertisement in the *Royal Cornwall Gazette* of February 10 1816, which read: "A Meeting of the Adventurers in the above mentioned Mine, by whom the same was carried on to the end of the year 1812, under the direction of Capt. Daniel M'Kenney, will be held at Pearce's Hotel, in Redruth, on Tuesday the 13th day of February instant, at Ten O'Clock in the Forenoon, for the purpose of finally Settling his Accounts, and charging all unsatisfied legal demands of which the said Adventurers, and all others whom it may concern are required to take notice. James Eddy, John Buckingham. Truro, February 1, 1816."

Another "West Tincroft" mine was located to the E. of Chivenhall Moor in the parish of Paul. It re-started in 1822 under the name of Wheal Bal; and in 1864 proposals were issued for working it by a cost book company as West Tincroft.

1. *Royal Cornwall Gazette* November 1810

TOWEDNACK BOUNDS

On August 28 1672 Coskar Bounds, Towednack, was cut by (possibly for) James Praed, jr.; John Newman and Williams Newman (sons of Arthur Newman); and Thomas Hawkins, gent.; "south corner joining lands of Eubla/Embla/ tenement, north corner with William Parson's tenement alias Beagle Tubben, east corner on land of Amall Veor, west corner joining highway from Towednack to tenement of Vosmarrack, alias Vose or Rose."

On 2 September 1672 Gwary-Teage ("fair play)" bounds were cut by John Jackson to the use of James Prade (*sic*) jr., Esq., William Newman, son of Arthur Newman, gent., and Thomas Hawkins, gent, in Amalveor, in Towednack, "south-east corner joining the lands of Tubla tenements, west corner near lands of Voesmarrack, alias Vose or Rose, north corner bounded with the way that leads from Towednack to Vosemarrack alias Vose."[1]

1. DD.J. 1339, CRO, Truro

TREVEGA BAL
(TREVESSA AND BREA; WEST ST. IVES CONSOLIDATED; BREA CONSOLS)

Rising boldly from the coastal plain near the cliff between Treveal and Trevega, the ruined stamps engine house of an abandoned mine forms a picturesque object when viewed from the main road and hills to the south. It belonged to a working best known locally as Trevega Bal, but which has borne a variety of other names at different periods. Near the engine house are several burrows and shafts; and the workings extend down to the cliff and into the valley on its western side.

Trevega Bal must rank as one of the most ancient mines in Cornwall. The late R.J. Noall, who possessed an unrivalled knowledge of the antiquities of the St. Ives district, wrote in 1906; "Half-way between Trevelgia Bal and the field called The Plague in memory of that terrible visitation to St. Ives, there is a flat, rather round, and almost buried rock in the south-west corner of the roadway field, on the face of which there is written part way round the edge the following inscription: M.O. 1674. It is supposed to have been done by Matthew Oates, of Ludgvan, memorising his starting Trevegia Bal as a paying mine. Near one of the burrows of this mine there is a beautiful basin-like hollow in a large rock, said to have been used by the old tinners to bruise down their samples for 'trying' (assaying) purposes."[1]

The technique of blasting rocks was first introduced by some Germans into the mines of east Cornwall during the seventeenth century, but the method was kept secret, and could only be known by persons who paid for it. It was brought into the west — Lelant, Zennor and St. Ives — by two eastern men called Bell and Care, being first used by them in "Trevigha Bal." They permitted no one to see them charge the holes; but a Zennor man, more cunning than the others, hid himself and so discovered their secret. This took place about the year 1700, the story being collected about ninety years later.[2] Apart from its general interest, this affords further striking evidence of the great antiquity of Trevega mine.

Some interesting references to Trevega Bal (under the name of Wheal Brea) are to be found in an old account book, now at St. Ives Museum, kept by Mr. Nathaniel Anthony, an 18th century St. Ives merchant:

1778 Febry. 26. Recd from Brea mine profit £3.11s.6¼d;

1779 Janry. 19th. Recd from Wheal Breay £5.2.11d.

1779 July 6. Cost in Wheal Brea to 1 July 1779 pd. for Mrs. Anthony & self Nathl. Anthony £1.2.4½d.

1780 24th Febry. Setled Wheal Brea mine profits arising from the mine is ye Whole £194.5s.6d.

At 59s. pr. hundred on 65 c. 3 qr. 12 lb.

That is to 3/32 parts is £18.4s.0¼d.

Cost on ditto mine £79.14s.5½d.

Cost to pay on to 3/32 parts £7.8s.9d.

neat profits to 3/32nd. £10.15s.3d.

Rec'd 6th Octr. 1780 from Wheal Brea mine profits £15.13s.5d.

1781 11th April. Paid the Brea Cost to end April £5.19s.7d.

21st Febry. 1782 paid Cost to Brea mine £6.10s.3¾d.

6 Novr. paid Cost to the Brea mine £1.19s.3d.

1783 pd. Cost 29th Janry. to the mine £7.9s.7d.

1783 Octr. 18. pd. Cost to the Brea £9.19s.4½d.

It would appear from these entries that apart from 1778-80 Wheal Brea was earning good profits, but thereafter became a "calling" mine, and seems to have been stopped around 1784.

On September 6 1836 as a young man named Richard Curnow, son of

Crumbling engine-house, Trevega Bal   (Noall Collection)

Capt. Samuel Curnow, of St. Ives, was ascending a ladder in "Trevessa mine," a small stone fell from the shaft's side and struck the front of his hat, driving a part of it into the skull; he lingered for six hours in great agony before expiring.[3]

In 1842 materials of "Trevidgia Mine" were offered for sale, these including a 9″ capstan rope 120 fms. long, four horse whims with shaft tackle, rollers and stands, horse whim water barrels and winze kibbles, 200 fms. of excellent whim chain, 80 fms. of underground ladders, dressing houses, and the account house furniture.[4]

Williams' *Mining Directory* for 1861 lists "Brea Consolidated Tin Mining Co., Ltd.," in 12,000 shares, with offices at Leeds. Between 1860-3 this venture produced 75 tons of black tin. From 1868 to 1872 the Trevessa and Brea Mines worked as "West St. Ives Consolidated;" but were sold, together with their plant and machinery, at the Auction Mart, London, for only £415 in January of the latter year.[5]

The workings then lay fallow until 1907, when they were resumed under the name of "Trevegia Mine." The first parcel of tin was sold in August of that year.[6] At Redruth tin ticketing in late November 1910 a parcel from this mine was purchased by the Cornish Tin Company at the rate of £110.7s.6d. per ton, one of the highest paid to any of the mines in the county. In July 1911 a ton of tin was sold for £113, compared with £103.7s.6d. paid to St. Ives Consolidated at the same time.[7] This reflects the high quality of tin ore for which Trevega was so famed. Unfortunately, the lodes, though rich, were small, an old St. Ives miner who worked there assuring the writer that they averaged no more than three inches in width. This was probably the reason for the mine's closing again after a few years' trial.

Trevega Bal appears to have been formed from an amalgamation of several small mines. Wheal Brea lay on the cliff at Brea Cove, with Wheal Trevega 400 yards S.S.E. of it. Wheal Matthew was situated about 550 yards N.N.W. of Trevega Wartha. The former is an metamorphosed killas and greenstone, the latter in granite. The shafts in Brea were named Bowling Cove, Roger's, Footway, Whim, Old Brea (entirely underground); and in Trevega, Matthew's, Engine and Tabbs. The workings are said to have been anciently carried out under the sea.

In his *History of St. Ives* (1892) J.H. Matthews relates a curious story about Hugh Edwards, whose family resided in an old house on the west side of Fore Street, near St. Ives Parish church. One dark night he had the misfortune to ride down Trevega mineshaft. His body was recovered and buried inside the church, near the chancel rails, with his clothes on. About the year 1840, on the Edwards family vault being opened, the remains of the unfortunate Hugh were found; but of his clothes nothing remained except the yellow tops of his riding boots, which were as good as new.

During the 1939-45 War Trevega engine house suffered some damage when a German aeroplane, seeking to escape from a pursuing British fighter, jettisoned a bomb in a nearby field. The writer visited the scene soon after, and collected some fragments of bomb casing from the crator.

1. *St. Ives by the Sea* 1904
2. *Trans. Roy. Geol. Soc. of Corn.*, vol. iv
3. *Royal Cornwall Gazette* September 9 1836
4. *Royal Cornwall Gazette* April 15 1842
5. *Cornish Telegraph* January 8 1872
6. *Western Echo* August 17 1907
7. *St. Ives Times* December 3 1910 and July 29 1911

WHEAL TYRINGHAM CONSOLS
(WHEAL BUSSAR, BUZZA, BESOW, BUSSOW OR BOSSOM: WEST WHEAL PROVIDENCE)

In a field near Higher Bussow farmhouse on the southern flank of Rosewall Hill may be seen the engine house of an abandoned mine known during its last working as Wheal Tyringham Consols. From this building, partially destroyed for building materials *c.* 1925, a line of flat rods ran a long way S. across the fields to pump an old working called Parc-an-Shafters, and several other shafts lie on the hill W. of the house.

In its early days the mine bore a variety of names based on that of the tenement where it was located. The sale by auction of the materials of ''Wheal Bussar Mine'' in the parish of Towednack was advertised in February 1820 ''by Virtue of a Decree of the Worshipful the Vice Warden of the Stannaries of Cornwall;'' these included a whim, whim rope, kibbles and ladders.[1] Three years later William Trenery, mine broker, Redruth, offered for sale 2/64th shares in ''Wheal Besow, in Towednack,'' at £10 per share;''[2] whilst in 1825 the same vendor had available the like number of shares in ''Wheal Bossom,'' near St. Ives.[3]

In 1860 the property was reogranised as a new adventure under the grandiloquest title of ''Wheal Tyringham Consols,'' derived from the fact that it lay on the Trevetho estate, owned by the Tyringham (formerly Praed) family of Trevetho, Lelant. A lengthy description of the new enterprise was published in *The Review of the Progress of British Mining* for December of that year. This began with an account of the mine's fortunate position, adjoining the rich Rosewall Hill and Ransom United, St. Ives Consols, Providence, Trelyon Consols, and others of proven worth. The sett was very extensive, nearly a mile in length and breadth, and having within its limits a considerable number of lodes, some of which had been worked to a great extent at and above adit level. Shallow operations on Bussow lode had been prosecuted for a lengthy period, and many unsuccessful attempts made for working it with a steam engine by adventurers lacking the necessary capital. The adit was being cleared and secured, and would shortly be completed, when the best position for the engine could be decided on.

The leading cross-courses of the district traversed the sett, from Rosewall Hill to Wheal Reeth, and as the granite was alike, there could be no doubt of similar results being obtained as in these mines. ''Probably there is scarcely a piece of mining ground in the...district that has more promise of ultimate and permanent success.'' South of Bussow lode they had recently cut a large lode 2' wide containing tin, and its appearance for the depth seen (only 7 fms. from surface) was most promising. It was intended to develop the mine with spirit, and a call of £1 per 1,024th sharre had been made a few months previously. Probably £5,000 would be sufficient to develop the mine, and as the operations had only been a few fathoms below adit level, upon the bunches of tin, the cost of clearing it would be trifling. The shares, at around £2 each, were an excellent speculation, for there were great chances of the mine being a good one. A highly favourable report on Tyringham Consols was also issued at this time by Capt. John Brown, of Wheal Buller.

Ruined engine-house, Wheal Tyringham Consols   (Noall Collection)

J.H. Murchison, F.G.S., who wrote the flattering account quoted above, acted as the mine's secretary from 1860-63. The *Mining Journal* gave some details of development carried out during this period. Work began in April 1860, and by February 1861 the adit had been cleared for its full length of 320 fms., of which 120 fms. had to be ''made new'' before the end could be driven. One shaft was then being cleared out and another sunk to the adit, where Bussow (or Bussoe) lode was 1' to 2' wide and extensively wrought down to this depth. The lode lay parallel to those of Rosewall Hill and Ransom United and 7 fms. N. of South Bussow lode, which was 18″ wide and promising. Drysack lode lay 34 fms. S. of South Bussow and had been worked down to adit, 20 fms.

In February 1861 Capt. Thomas Richards, the Purser and Manager, bought a steam engine for £150, which he sold to the company at the same price. Work continued until about November 1864 without their having gone below adit,[4] the shares were listed in the *Mining Journal* from July 1860 to October 1863. The property worked by this cost-book company included Bussow, Lower Bussow and Chytodden, held from Mr. Praed, and Breja, held from the Duke of Cleveland.

A re-working of part of the sett began in 1880 under the name of "Bussow Mine." In April, upon the completion of a new engine house and installation of the engine, a dinner was given to about 60 labourers masons, carpenters and others by the owners, Messrs. Brown.[5] In the spring of 1881 a cost book company with offices at Station Hill, Redruth, was formed to work, as "West Providence," on adjacent mine whose northern part had formerly been included in Rosewall Hill and Ransom United. This property, which appears to be identical with the ancient Wheal Union or Wheal Wens mine (q.v.) on the summit of Rosewall Hill, was held from Reginald C. Glanville of Truro at 1-20th or 1-22nd dues (probably on renewable licences), another part held from Mr. Praed. Messrs. Brown (of whom M.G. Brown, of Stannon House, Dawlish, was one) held a majority of the 2,500 £1 paid shares. Certificates were issued in July 1881, and Samuel Abbott, who only held the post of purser for a few months as he had "not been A1 lately," dealt in them.

The manager reported in June 1881 that a hard bar of ground had been met with in Cooper's shaft in the south part of the mine. The South Carbona had been opened by Parka Shafts, and the lode in the carbona to the north of the winze showed promising further improvements as they got under the old men's workings. The main body of the lode seemed to be dipping northwards. In Ada's shaft they were still cutting down the old men's winze below the adit, preparatory to sinking a shaft on the course of Drysack's lode. In the north mines the 20 fm. level W. of Ivy's shaft was being cleared, and the mine was looking exceedingly rich E. of the cross-course, once through which an improvement was looked for.

At about this time Capt. Bugelhole (the manager) applied to the mineral lord for the sett of Bussow, which adjoined West Providence, on behalf of another company (presumably the "Bussow Mine" concern) but he refused to transfer the lease, which led R.S. Teague, the purser, to ask him to reconsider his decision. A new company to work Bussow was in course of formation, with a capital of £2,000, of which Mr. Bain (a West Providence committee member) was willing to buy 110 shares at 2s. per share from Capt. Bugelhole.

In August 1881 the sinking of Cooper's shaft in the south mines was resumed, and the lode in the 30 fm. level W. of shaft was improving in size.

At Park O'Shafts (*sic*) the carbona N. and S. of the winze was yielding better quality tinstuff than for some time past. In the northern mines the 20 fm. level was still being driven W. of Ivey's (*sic*) shaft, but was not yet enough the great cross-course. Wheal Winze shaft was down to the 30, which was being cleared E. and W.; and seven or eight tons of tin had been sold.

Cooper's Engine shaft was 2 fms. below the 30 fm. level in November 1881, New Flat-Rod or Brown's shaft was 5 fms. down on Montague lode, some hundred yards S. of Cooper's lode, and Ada's shaft was 12 fms. under adit. At the Northern Mines there were horse whims on Wheal Winze (or Wenze) shaft and Ivey's shaft, which were both being worked at the 20 and 40 fm. levels. Elsewhere Brown's shaft was about 140 fms. N. of Parkins (Parka, Park O'Shafts.)

A meeting held in February 1882 was told that the Brown brothers had declared their intention to relinquish their shares, 120 of which they sold through H. Waddington, a London sharebroker. The meeting resolved that the purser, with Messrs. Abbott and Bain, be instructed to sell the mine as a going concern. After receiving an inspection report from Captains Ritchie and White, an adjourned meeting held in March unanimously agreed to wind up the company, reconstruction being mentioned. At this time it was noted that the Ransom section lay E. of Wheal Winze (shaft), and that Ransom shaft was drained to near the 30 fm. level or 50 fms. from surface.

A circular issued after the meeting at the end of March 1881 showed that Messrs. Brown had sold their share to others, who wished to continue the working, and it was consequently resolved not to sell the mine. The lord's agent had given liberal concessions, and it was resolved to work the Ransom, Wheal Winze and Wheal Mary lodes.

In April 1882 Capt Bugelhole resigned, and Messrs. Bain and Rich, members of the committee, agreed to run the mine. In August the steam engines, boilers and machinery on Bussow Vean sett were offered to Capt. Bugelhole for £1,666, and in October the property was put up for sale. The machinery included a 40″ pumping engine, a 24″ stamping engine, boilers, 48 heads of stamps, dressing machinery, seven whims, pitwork, about 100 fms. of ladders, a 42′ x 12′ timber shed used as an office, and the account house furniture. The rich tin leavings throughout the mine, ''for the return of which a convenient time will be allowed,'' were included in the sale. The notice stated that the mine was formerly known as Rosewall Hill and Ransom United.

The machinery does not appear to have found a buyer, since meetings held in February and March 1883 resolved to suspend operations and to offer the machinery and materials to the lords. A meeting held in October the following year made a distribution of 11d. per share, the accounts not having taken credit for the 40″ pumping engine and two boilers, stamping engine and odd materials, against which some £140 or £150 was due for damaged land.

Martin Edwards, jr., of Redruth, a sharebroker, was caught with five shares on his books, whose cost, £5, he wrote off after the liquidation. The sale of materials continued until the middle of 1891, when Mr. Glanville was asked for permission to leave them on the mine for another six months to aid a person about to purchase them.

During this working the mine sold 63 tons of black tin for £3,368.3s.8d.[6]

Some confusion appears to have been made between the records relating to this mine (as West Providence) and the similarly named West Providence at Gwinear. Dines, for example, gives exactly the same output statistics for both mines between the years 1851-62 and 1881-3, whereas these should probably be credited only to Gwinear Wheal Providence.

1. *Royal Cornwall Gazette* February 12 1820
2. *Royal Cornwall Gazette* November 3 1823
3. *Royal Cornwall Gazette* October 8 1825
4. *Mining and Smelting Magazine* November 1864, p.295
5. *Cornishman* April 22 1880
6. Company's printed reports *penes* J.H.T. (1966). Letter book, R.I.C. (1966). MJ 1881 (18.6, 24.8), 1883 (22.9). MW 1882 (25.2, 18.3), 1883 (17.2). M. Edwards, jr., Dealing Book 1883, pp.22-25, *penes* J.B. (1955). Dines (1956) p.113 (Rosewall Hill, etc., including West Providence). Ore sales: Company's printed reports (above).

Editors' Note:
Gerald Williams has argued that Cyril Noall was misled by Dines' confusion over the identity of West Providence and that, like Dines, Noall has mistakenly intertwined details of Towednack's West Providence with those of the mine of the same name in Gwinear parish. Mr. Williams has kindly supplied the following notes to help put the record straight:

On the southern slopes of Rosewall Hill, and running nearly parallel with the hill lay a series of lodes which were worked in and around Bussow Moor. Here the "Old Bussow Mine" had been active prior to 1820, when in February of that year the mine and materials were offered for sale by virtue of a decree of the Vice Warden of the Stannaries Court.[1] There appears to have been another attempts to work the mine shortly afterwards, as in 1823 2/64th shares in 'Wheal Besow' — Towednack were offered for sale.[2] This was followed in 1824 by the sale of 8/64th shares in 'Wheal Bossow'[3] and in the latter part of the same year 2/64ths in 'Wheal Bescow' were advertised.[4] According to Hamilton Jenkin the three northerly lodes, Bussow, South Bussow, and Drysack, were worked by the old men above adit level, and bunches of tin had been followed to below that level as far as it was possible to achieve by manual labour. The main adit, brought up from Bussow Moor, was 20 fathoms deep at Drysack Shaft which was to the north Chytodden farm, and had been driven westward from this point.[5]

The mine worked in the early 50's as the *Mining Journal* for the 23rd of Oct. 1852 reported an accident in which a miner, in the act of freeing a kibble in a shaft at Wheal Bussow, fell about 4 fathoms and was severely injured.

In 1860 the mine was re-started under the name of Tyringham Consols, and by June the adit was being cleared and secured.[6] Captain Thomas Richards, the manager in his report of February 21st 1861 said that although the adit had to be renewed for about 120 fathoms, and firmly secured with good timber, it had been fully accomplished, and now the adit had been cleared and secured on the different lodes nearly 200 fathoms beyond that point last mentioned (the 120). In carrying forward this work a shaft had been sunk to the adit, and three other shafts had been cleared and secured. Bussow Lode had been very extensively worked at adit level and the indications of good ore producing ground at a greater depth, fully warrented the purchase of a steam engine. At present the adit was being driven west by four men at £7 per fathom, in which the lode was from 3 to 4 feet wide.[7] A 40″ engine had been purchased for £150 and erected on the north of Great Bussow Lode, which was later called 'Tyringham's', and from here flat-rods were extended to the Park Lode in the southern part of the sett.[8] At the shareholders meeting in February the accounts showed:

Preliminary expenses	£256. 0s.0d.
Mine Cost from April-June 1860	£443.18s.0d.
Merchant' bills	£194.17s.0d.
Engine etc.	£150. 0s.0d.
Total	£1,044.15s.4d.

From this a call amounting to £1,024.0s.0d. was deducted, leaving a balance of £20.15s.4d.[9] Two years later the mine closed, as Spargo remarked, "having not been effectually tried".[10] Collins stated that Tyringham Consols was worked afterwards as 'Bossow Mine', but stopped working before 1865.[11] This was partly correct as the mine was worked *after* 1865 as Buzza or Bussow. In 1879 Mr. Brown, the proprietor of Goole Pellas and Rosewall Hill Mine, acquired the property where in November it was reported that the first sod of a new shaft had been cut,[12] and in 1880, following the completion of a new engine-house and the erection of the engine, a dinner was given to about 60 labourers, masons, carpenters, miners, etc. by the mine owners.[13] In 1881 the name of the company had been changed to 'West Providence' — still under the same management. During the previous fifteen months 400 fathoms of adit had been cleared and secured and a 40″ engine with two boilers erected. As in the previous working the Park Lode, or Park-o-Shafts section was pumped via flat-rods.[14]

A special meeting of the shareholders was called in February 1882 for the purpose of auditing the accounts, and to consider the future working of the mine. This was due to the fact that Messrs. Brown had relinquished their interests in the mine. The accounts showed:

Labour costs	£1,942. 3s.8d.
Merchant's bills	£1,154.16s.8d.
	£3,097. 0s.4d.

Balance against the mine £2,404.3s.10d. less a call of £1,157.11s.9d. left a balance against the present shareholders of £1,246.12s.1d. After Captain Buglehole, the agent, had presented an encouraging report on the working of the mine, Mr. Brown explained that he and his brother would have to relinquish 1,375 shares, as they could not meet with the constant demand on their purses. A call of 5s. per share was then made and another special meeting was called for the 9th of March.[15]

The report for November stated that the men were making progress in driving the 80 fathom level east in Wheal Wenze, which suggests that further exploration in the Rosewall Hill and Ransom Mines was in operation. Also it was reported that the ladder-road had not yet been completed at Frank's Shaft, which indicates that possibly the recently abandoned Giew/South Providence Mine, or at least a part of it had been taken up with the Bussow sett, although there is no documented evidence to support this. Moreover, Frank's Shaft at the Giew Mine is one mile from Bussow Moor. What is certain is the fact that the Ransom section of the Rosewall Hill mines was being worked, as the report concluded by stating that the four stopes at the Ransom part of the mine were maintaining values of £9 per fathom.[16] By December the three stopes on the old Ransom Lode, in the back of the 40 fathom level east, were valued at £8 per fathom.[17] In October 1883 the mine closed,[18] having according to Collins, produced 790 tons of black tin from 1881-83.[19] However both Collins and Dines have confused this mine with its namesake in the parish of Gwinear, the output figures being identical in both cases (see Dines pp.119 and 166). Furthermore an output of 1,535 tons of copper ore were also recorded in the working of West Providence for the years 1851-62 which again is related to the mine of that name in the parish of Gwinear, and not Towednack.

1. *Royal Cornwall Gazette* 11 February 1820
2. Ibid. 1 November 1823
3. Ibid. 5 June 1824
4. Ibid. 27 November 1924
5. A.K. Hamilton Jenkin, *Mines & Miners of Cornwall vol 1*, p.19
6. *Mining Journal* 30 June 1860
7. Ibid. 23 June 1861
8. A.K. Hamilton Jenkin *Mines & Miners of Cornwall vol. 1*, p.19
9. *Mining Journal* 23 February 1861
10. Thomas Spargo, *The Mines of Cornwall*, 1865 p.12
11. J.H. Collins, *Observations on the West of England Mining Region*, 1912 p.604
12. *Cornish Telegraph* 19 November 1879
13. Ibid. 22 April 1840
14. *Cornishman* 24 March 1881
15. Ibid. 23 February, 1882
16. *Cornish Telegraph* 9 November 1882
17. Ibid. 14 December 1882
18. *Cornishman* 24 March 1887 — inquest on fatal accident at St. Ives Consols
19. Collins 1912 p.604

WHEAL UNION (WHEAL WENS)

On the summit of Rosewall Hill lies a small mine which at different periods enjoyed an independent existence under the name of Wheal Wens, or Winze, and Wheal Union. In 1804 "1-24th of one pair (of bounds) in Wheal Wens or Rosewall Hill in Towednack and St. Ives" were offered for sale by auction at the Union Hotel, Penzance.[1] It was later merged with Rosewall Hill mine, but following the demise of the latter it was again revived as a separate undertaking under the name of West Providence in the 1880's. (See under Wheal Tyringham Consols.)

Wheal Union developed Wheal Winze lode lying about 60 yards N.W. of Main lode in Rosewall Hill by a series of shafts — Wheal Winze, Footway, Ivey's and Old — running roughly in line with one another up to 290 yards S.W. of the Logan Rock at the N.E. point of the hill. Henwood apparently refers to Wheal Winze lode as "Gwens" in his 1843 account of Wheal Union; it was up to 1′ wide carrying cassiterite, quartz, tourmaline, chlorite and felspar in granite country.

1. *Royal Cornwall Gazette* December 15 1904

THIRD SECTION
ZENNOR DISTRICT

CARNELLOE (ZENNOR CONSOLS)
WHEAL CHANCE (ROSEMORRAN, ROSEVALE) ZENNOR
CLEVELAND
WHEAL DOLLAR
WEST WHEAL FANNY
WHEAL FORTUNE
NORTH WHEAL GRYLLS
GURNARD'S HEAD (WHEAL TREEN, NORTH UNITED MINES)
WHEAL HOPE, ZENNOR
WHEAL MALKIN: NEW WHEAL MALKIN
WHEAL SPERRIS (GREAT SPERRIS CONSOLS)
TREGERTHEN
TREVAIL
TREVEAL STAMPS
TREWEY DOWNS
WICKOW
ZENNOR BOUNDS

CARNELLOE (ZENNOR CONSOLS)

Carnelloe mine lies on the coast in the vicinity of Porthglaze Cove and Carnelloe Cliff, where a number of lodes outcropping along the shore were opened on at an early period, possibly around the beginning of the 18th century. On the NE side of the headland small heaps of slag have been discovered which when crushed and washed show small beads of metallic tin, proof of the existence here at some period of an old "blowing house" or smelter.[1] Mining at Carnelloe was certainly well developed by the early 19th century. In July 1830 "all that valuable Tin and Copper Mine, called or known by the name of Carnellow, Situate in the Parish of Zennor, about four miles West of St. Ives," was advertised for sale by private contract. The materials comprised a pressure engine, with brass cylinder, capstan, shears, whim, ropes, tools, with 24 fms. of 7" and 24 fms. of 6" pumps. "On the said Mine there had been an Office, Carpenter and Smiths' Shops erected, the whole forming a desirable speculation."[2]

In 1851 proposals were issued for reviving the mine on a greatly extended scale, under the name of Zennor Consols. It would then have taken in all the coast between Boswednack Cliff and Zennor Head, within which area at least twelve lodes were known to exist. The outcome of this proposal is not known; but the mine was again worked as Carnelloe Consols from 1853-56. In December 1853 the manager reported that he had set the Engine shaft to sink then fms. below the 10 fm. level to make good the place already sunk and as much more as would complete it to the 20 fm. level for the sum of £73 by six men. The lode in the shaft was valued at £60 per fm., and the lode in the 10 fm. level W. of the shaft was expected to yield a ton of black tin per fm., worth £60; it was being driven on for £6 per fm. The lode in the E. was about 3' wide, and the hydraulic pressure engine only needed to work an hour a day to draw the water. Two years later Engine shaft had been sunk and completed to the 21 fm. level below adit, 15 fms., and a road about a quarter of a mile long had been opened to the main road. Over £150 worth of tinstuff had been raised, and about £1,500 laid out on the mine. In January 1856 two-thirds of the company's capital (£4,500) was offered for sale at £1 per sharre, the remaining 1,500 shares being kept by the properties. The name of the manager of Carnelloe Consols (in 1854) was given as Capt. J. Hallon.[3]

Carnelloe was taken over by a new company, divided into 3,000 shares, in 1862. Spargo stated in 1865 that the dues were 1-20th, payable to the Duke of Cornwall and another. As the Duchy owned the foreshore, it seems clear from this that the workings were then being carried out beyond the cliffs. Depth of adit was given as 30fms., and depth under adit 30 fms. Pumping was effected by a hydraulic engine, and stamping (12 heads) and winding by a water wheel. Fourteen men, two women and two boys were employed. The prospects were described as good.

This company failed in 1866; but in 1871 it was reported that "Carn Ella, a pretty little sett, four or five lodes in which may be seen in the cliffs not far from Gurnard's Head, is being re-worked.''[4] The company involved was composed of local men and working miners, and it would appear that the greater part of the work in Porthglaze Cove was done between then and 1876. In June 1872 the South lode was said to have been opened in places for 60 fms. in length; it was fully 5′ wide, and yielded tin close to surface. The lode in the bottom of Engine shaft was worth £30 per fm. for tin and fine stones of copper intermixed.[5] By November 1872 Engine shaft had been sunk to 26 fms. from surface on the lode which, at the deepest point, was 2½′ wide and worth £15 per fm. Assuming a sale value of £87 per ton of tin oxide, this would be equivalent to 62 lbs. of tin oxide per ton. The 20 fm. level W. of shaft had then been extended 11 fms. and the lode in the end of the level was valued at £10 per fm., or 41 lbs. of tin oxide per ton. This Engine lode was the only one then being worked on, though there were three other large lodes within a distance of 30 fms. S. of the shaft, and an equal number N. of the shaft. The agents (W. Rich and W. Ennor) stated they were anxious to prove the mine deeper, and with this object in view had been pressing on with the sinking on one lode first. All the tin they were raising had come from Engine lode, chiefly in sinking Engine shaft and driving one end. "We have a strong opinion the mine will open out profitably productive if we persevere in sinking deeper, and open out on the course of the lodes." All the machinery for pumping, hauling and stamping was being driven by water power, and was in first rate working order. A small profit of £56.12s. was shown during the three months period ending in September. The general meeting of shareholders to whom this information was presented was held on November 27th at the Red Lion Hotel, Truro, W.G. Nettle occupying the chair.[6]

An independent opinion of the mine was given by Sir Warington W. Smyth in his annual report to the Duchy of Cornwall on the undersea mines of Cornwall, on which certain foreshore dues were payable to the Duchy. Writing on December 28 1872 he stated: "The little mine now re-opened on this picturesque headland labours under the disadvantage of remoteness from the centres of mining activity; and I feel consequently a little anxious whether the fair but not very rich appearance of the lodes will obtain them a suitable trial."

In 1872-3 there is a record of Carnelloe having produced six tons of tin oxide. Unfortunately, the mine was abandoned before January 1876 owing to the rapidly falling tin prices which closed so many other Cornish mines around this time. Its machinery advertised for sale in November 1877 comprised one wooden water wheel 37′ in diameter and 2′ 6″ on the breast, with wrought iron shaft, cast iron axle and crank, nearly new; one iron water wheel, 24′ diameter, 3′ breast, with 8 heads of stamps attached; and 12 4½″ pumps. All the material was in good condition.[7]

Little further interest seems to have been taken in Carnelloe until 1937 when the late Mr. W.T. Harry, a West Cornwall mining engineer who had a lifetime's experience of the industry both in this country and overseas, being most favourably impressed with its potential, obtained an option on the mineral rights. In 1960 he applied for planning permission to open up the old shafts and explore and extend the existing workings so as to obtain sufficient samples and information to assess development prospects. There were from 14 to 16 mineral bearing lodes in the application site, some of which extended under the sea; he believed they would prove to be rich in tin.

Wheel-pit below the Count-house at Carnellow; photographed in April 1956 by H.G. Ordish
(Courtesy Royal Institution of Cornwall)

Mr. Harry's own description of the district is interesting and worth quoting at some length: "The application site is at Carnelloe Farm, Zennor, on the N.W. coast of the Land's End peninsula about 0.5 mile W. of Zennor village. It is about 5 miles W. of St. Ives and 5 miles slightly W. of N. of Penzance...Carnelloe Farm...has an area of about 84 acres and lies between the coast road route B3306 and the sea. Access to the farm is by two rough tracks which joint the coast road at Poniou, where there is a group of three cottages set well back on the N. side of the road. One track passes to the E. of these cottages and leads to the farmhouse; the other passes to the W. of them and leads to Carnelloe Cottage, which stands on...Carnelloe Cliff, near the disused Carnelloe Mine. The southern part of the farm is above the 400' contour, and the land falls towards the NW, the average gradient becoming progressively steeper until it reaches the cliff edge. There are a number of arable fields and fields in permanent pasture on the higher ground in the southern part of the farm, but the northern part is steep, rocky and uneven, and of little agricultural value. The coastline within the agricultural area comprises Porthglaze Cove, Carnelloe Cliff and part of Veor Cove. The cliffs vary in height and steepness and are very broken and rugged.

"There are at least four disused mineshafts on the application site, but this application mainly concerns the two shafts of the former Carnelloe Mine, which were sunk in the cliffs just to the W. of Carnelloe Cottage. The former No. 1 shaft is only a few feet above high water mark and is filled, or blocked, with small rocks. The former No. 2 shaft is about 100' above high water mark at the top of the cliff and an adit from this shaft emerges from the cliff just above high water mark. Both the shaft and the adit appear to be filled or blocked. It is possible to clamber down the cliffs to the entrance to No. 1 shaft but Porthglaze Cove is not easily accessible.

"There is a public footpath through the application site somewhere near the top of the cliff, but without a track to identify its position. A stream, from which the applicant proposes to obtain water supplies, runs down the western boundary of the site. Carnelloe Cottage, which stands in a prominent position about 225' above sea level, is an old bungalow formerly used as a mine office, and let for holiday use. Zennor Cliff, which is owned by the National Trust, is about 0.5 mile to the N.E. of Carnelloe Cliff. It overlooks the north-eastern part of the application area, but the area W. of Carnelloe Cottage, on which the applicant proposes to erect mine buildings and plant, cannot be seen from Zennor Cliff.''

Mr. Harry's application resulted in a public enquiry being held at Penzance on May 10-13 1961. His proposals met with widespread support in the county, many local authorities and organisations interested in the promotion of mining appearing on his behalf; but strong opposition was expressed by conservation groups who argued that if the application succeeded, damage would be caused to a particularly beautiful stretch of unspoilt coastline. The Inspector who conducted the enquiry recommended that permission be granted to work Carnelloe, subject to condition designed to secure the preservation of amenities. However, the Minister rejected his Inspector's advice, and the application was refused. This decision evoked a great deal of resentment throughout Cornwall, and 25 out of the 30 local authorities in the county combined to make representations to the Prime Minister that it was in the public interest that this mining development should be allowed to proceed.

Mr. Harry subsequently submitted a further application on modified lines, which received the support of the County Council. This also was opposed by the same small but vocal minority who had contested the earlier application, and the new Minister felt obliged to call it in. A local enquiry was held on March 20 1963, as a result of which permission was granted to prospect for minerals on the site, subject to certain restrictions.

Consolidated Gold Fields, Ltd., of London, now began to take an interest in the matter; and in June 1963 Professor K.F.G. Hosking drew up a report on the Carnelloe mine area, a second report also being prepared by Mr. John

H. Trounson, Chairman of the Cornish Mines Development Association. These reports, thaken in conjunction with some observations made by Mr. Harry, provide an excellent description of the site and its potentialities. Mr. Trounson defined Carnelloe and the adjoining Dollar working as "two small and obscure tin mines on the north coast near Zennor, about mid-way between Pendeen and St. Ives." Their lodes occurred in a narrow coastal strip of metamorphosed killas and greenstone resting on the northern flank of the Land's End granite mass. It was in precisely the same assemblage of rocks that the lodes of the celebrated Levant and Botallack mines occurred in the Pendeen — St. Just area, five to six miles further west. Although the latter lodes did not appear to be particularly promising in the greenstone at surface, in depth and beneath the sea they proved to be some of the finest tin and copper producers of Cornwall. "It is because of that fact that these hitherto small mines at Zennor are potentially important and deserve thorough examination both in depth and seawards."

At Carnelloe the principle shafts were sunk on the sloping cliff face of Porthglaze Cove, the collar of the lower shaft being only just above high water mark. Although mining was thought to have commenced here early in the 18th century, it was not until about 1871 that these shafts were sunk on the cliffside to develop two N.E.-S.W. striking lods which were there about 150' apart. These lodes ran right across the headland, but converged eastwards so that in Veor Cove, 700' distant, they were only 35' apart.

The No. 1 or northernmost lode dipped S.E. at about 55-60 degs. towards No. 2 which dipped steeply S.E. so that the two were soon likely to junction in depth.

Harry described both lodes as strong and well mineralised, showing cassiterite, chalcocite, chalcopyrite and pyrites, varying in width, where exposed, from 12" to 42". No. 1 shaft, sunk on No. 1 lode, was believed to be 150' deep. The ends of the shaft had been stoped away for a length of about 20', the lodes there being 42" wide exhibiting coarse crystals of cassiterite. The walls of the lode were hard and firm. Samples cut there in 1937 gave 26 lbs. of tin oxide over a width of 30", this value being *exclusive* of the coarsely crystalline cassiterite.

No. 2 shaft on No. 2 lode was situated about 150 ft. S.E. of No. 1 shaft, its collar being 70 ft. above that of the latter. The mine section showed that its workings were 120 ft. deep below adit and extended a few yards seaward. The shaft collar has collapsed, but it was possible to reach it by going in through the adit which meets the shaft at a depth of 75 ft. The lode as seen in the adit was also a strongly mineralised one, varying in width from 16 to 21 ins. Both lodes were exposed on the other side of the headland and adits had there been driven on them for a distance of up to 200 ft. and a little stoping done on No. 1 lode which varied from 15 to 24 ins. in width and exhibits both tin and copper mineralisation. Mr. Harry commented that both these lodes were similar in every respect to those of Levant which he knew intimately.

On the western side of the headland, in Porthglaze Cove, there were two other lodes striking approximately N.W.-S.E., which would thus cross Nos. 1 and 2 lodes out under the sea, almost at right angles. No. 3 lode, on the western side of Porthglaze Cove, was best seen at low tide, as it was partly covered by a raised beach. It was a strong lode with massive quartz varying in width from 3 to 6 ft. and exhibiting a few specks of cassiterite in the quartz, but it would appear that the ore-bearing channel alongside the quartz had either been worked away or denuded by the sea. About 250 ft. of the lode was exposed at low tide.

No. 4 lode, about 250 ft. E. of No. 3, was only exposed on the beach for about 80 ft., its seaward extension being covered by pebbles. It too was a strong lode, 3 ft. wide, consisting of lenses of quartz and hematite, with low tin values in stringers of chlorite. It lay in a wide band of reddish rock through which ran numerous stringers of quartz and calcite. The lode itself was similar to several which have been worked in the St. Just district, especially that at Wheal Cock where the workings reached a depth of 1,300 ft. below sea level.

Prof. K.F.G. Hosking commented that half-way up the cliff, where the ore from the mine was broken, tin-rich and copper-rich specimens can be collected. The former consists of crystals of cassiterite associated with chlorite in a quartz matrix, whilst the latter consist of masses of chalcopyrite, together with some chalcocite and pyrite in a chlorite — quartz matrix. On the beach of Porthglaze Cove boulders are occasionally found as large as a human head composed of large aggregates of cassiterite associated with quartz and chlorite and which have, doubtless, been broken from the backs of the lodes by marine activity. These emphasise the fact that the potential of the lodes in this region cannot be determined by the appearance of the outcrop, and suggest that within the Carnelloe area there may well be lodes with considerable economic potential.

In addition to the foregoing lodes, there was a large formation known as the Great Guide (''guide'' being a local term for a cross-course) on the eastern side of the headland which emerged on the cliffs at Veor Cove. Dines states that this strikes N.N.E., but it probably trends a few degrees W. of N.

Prof. Hosking observed that in Veor Cove there were a number of wide highly-altered and sheared lode zones. Haematitisation was the dominant type of alteration exhibited by these, though there was, locally, a certain amount of kaolinisation. These ''lodes'' were penetrated by numerous quartz veinlets (sometimes containing tourmaline) while at least one of them contained ¼ inch wide veinlets of cassiterite.

W.T. Harry described No. 5 lode as a very wide zone on the east side of the headland, from 60 to 80 ft. in width, through which were scattered numerous quartz veins. This was at one time very extremely worked at surface, but had become overgrown, making sampling impossible, though one cut put across 24 ft. showed low tin values. A little to the N.W. on the beach, and separated from this by a small tongue of greenstone, values had been obtained as high as 37 lbs. of tin oxide per ton over 7 ft. This was apparently caused by the inclusion of some small stringers of cassiterite which can sometimes be seen up to ⅛ inch wide.

"It might be argued," wrote Prof. Hosking, "that sufficient rich tin-ore to support a mine was not encountered at Carnelloe during the time of its operation, nor in other small mines in the district, and so, although the area is mineralised, this is not very strong. However, it must be stressed that all these small mines were operated by companies with very limited capital, and these were never prepared to continue unless really good ore was struck almost immediately. Furthermore, if they ran out of ore they were never prepared to spend anything but a pittance to look for more. I think, therefore, that it can be fairly contended that the area has never been adequately examined and I am of the opinion that the best way to determine its potential would be to unwater Carnelloe Mine, and, in the first instance, to sample the N.E. trending lodes for distances of at least 600 or 700 ft. along the strike." He believed this would be a much better way of tackling the problem than by attempting to diamond drill these particulars lodes, a view with which Mr. Trounson concurred.

Encouraged by these favourable observations, Consolidated Gold Fields, Ltd., of London, took an active interest in the matter, and submitted an application for planning permission on a more extended scale to explore for tin during a three year period both at Carnelloe and the adjoining Dollar Mine. This application was called in by the Minister of Housing and Local Government for his decision, and an enquiry would have been held; but in 1965 the application was withdrawn, Consolidated Gold Fields stating they were unable to proceed with their plans because a local farmer had refused to grant mining rights, although he had previously indicated his willingness to do so. The land in question adjoined Carnelloe, and the company considered its acquisition essential for their purposes.

Explaining their attitude in a letter to Mr. Harry, they stated: "Our preliminary investigation of the Carnelloe Farm, in conjunction with Dr. Kenneth Hosking, has left us in no doubt whatever that the potential of this area rests primarily on the Dollar Lode system. The north-south veins, which could be linked with the Great Guide, together with the east-west veins appearing on the cliffs, would, in our opinion, be interesting targets for subsequent exploration; but unless a worth-while tonnage of ore can be proved by drilling on the Dollar Lode system, we would not be prepared to go ahead. Therefore our first drilling target must be the Dollar Lode, and until we have rights to prospect (there) we could not be justified in drilling at all."[8] The importance of the Dollar lode system in regard to this project will be found more fully discussed in the section on the Dollar Mine.

The farmer who occupied the land where the Dollar lode was situated subsequently withdrew his objection to the mining proposal, but by then it was too late, and the opportunity to establish what might have proved a very successful mine was, for the time being, lost. Despite the furore caused by conservationists, there can be little doubt that the mine envisaged in Mr. Harry's original application would have caused very little impact on the environment, the buildings and other surface erections connected with it being almost invisible from the scenic coastal road which passes from St. Ives to Land's End. Had the initial prospecting proved successful, further development would have been carried out by a company of high repute. A new shaft would have been sunk to the south of the old shafts with headgear about 36'-40' high. The mine would have been brought into full production in 2½-3 years, and employed up to 200 men, producing 50-60 tons of tin concentrate per month.

1. Report by J.H. Trounson, per W.T. Harry
2. *Royal Cornwall Gazette* July 31 1830
3. *Mining Journal* January 7 1854 and January 12 1856
4. *Cornish Telegraph* October 25 1871
5. *Cornish Telegraph* June 5 1872
6. *Mining Journal* December 7 1872
7. *Cornish Telegraph* November 7 1877
8. Letters, documents and other material, per W.T. Harry

WHEAL CHANCE (ROSEMORRAN, ROSEVALE) ZENNOR

On a headstone at Zennor Church appears this inscription: "Sacred to the Memory of Matthew Thomas of this Parish, who was kill'd in Wheal-Chance Tin-Mine in Trewey Downs near this Church-Town, by a fall of Ground ye 16th of August 1809, aged 44 years.

> Belov'd by most, through all his well-spent life,
> He left seven children and a loving wife,
> Mourning their loss, their hearts with grief oppress'd.
> Weep not, but hope he's mingled with ye blest.
> By sudden death, his life's short days are o'er,
> A loving father and a friend no more."

The mine where Matthew Thomas met his sad end lay on the western side of the valley extending south towards Foage Farm about a third of a mile from Zennor village. It was worked by adits, which went by the somewhat unusual name of "Tunnels" — Main and Upper. Wheal Chance was working in 1844, when 10-134th shares in that "desirable adventure" were offered for sale. In 1887 intending mine investors were urged to turn their attention to Zennor, where large lodes of tin and copper were known to exist; "competent authorities who have examined the ground recently declare that speedy returns could undoubtedly be made at Wheal Chance, which is already sunk about 23 fms. The mine was worked 40 years ago by poor men who could not afford to purchase the necessary machinery, and who gave up the workings with reluctance because they had full faith in her appearance. Sperre's shaft, near to Wheal Chance, is 30 fms. deep, and there are at least three lodes in the sett.''[1]

Dines states that this mine was tried unsuccessfully in the 1930's. During its later phases it bore the names of Rosemorran, and Rosevale. Recently the workings were rehabilitated by a mining club as an example of a small scale Cornish mining enterprise.

1. *Cornish Telegraph* December 1 1887

CLEVELAND

The workings of this mine lay on the western side of Treveal Valley 250 yards E. of the farm. The plan, dated 1844, shows 11 lodes and several shafts. An adit driven S.E. from River Cove was not connected to the Cleveland workings; this adit presumably drained Trevail Copper Mine, *q.v.* No records have been traced relating to operations at Cleveland.

WHEAL DOLLAR

This mine, lying south of Carnelloe mine near Carnelloe Farm, and very close to the granite-invaded rock contact, apparently took its name from one of the lodes coursing through the sett, the Wheal Dollar lode, others being known as the Copper Gozzan, South Tin and North Tin.

An interesting legal case concerning Wheal Dollar, which reveals some curious details of its early history, came on in the Stannary Court in 1838. In this, the Rev. William Hockin, of Phillack, filed a petition against John Rosewarne, Gentleman, and Thomas Pearce, mine agent, both also of Phillack. It appears that on June 1st 1834 Hockin granted Rosewarne and Pearce a sett of Wheal Dollar for 21 years at one-fifteenth dues; but being dissatisfied with their method of working — or not working — the mine, formally took possession of it on April 26th 1837, as he claimed to be entitled to do under the conditions on which the sett had been granted. In reply, Rosewarne and Pearce denied Hockin's allegations, and described in some detail how they had proceeded since acquiring the mine.

The extent of Wheal Dollar was given as ''All those parts of the Estates or Tenements of Kerrowe and Carnelloe situate in the pariah of Zennor...which are bounded on the West by the Lands of Davies Gilbert Esquire, on the East by the Estate or Tenement of Trewey, on the South by the Road leading from Zennor Church Town through the Village of Kerrowe to Saint Just, and on the North by a straight line supposed to be drawn from the South Wall of an old Stamps in Carnelloe Crofts Eastward to a Stone set up at the Tail of the middle Addit, and thence Eastward to the Extremity of the said Estate or Tenement of Carnelloe, Together with the use of the sea level Addit and the old mans Addit.''

Pearce was unable to recall the discovery of Wheal Dollar about sixty years before (around 1780), but believed it was worked by a party of adventurers about the year 1823. A steam engine was then erected; he did not now whether the mine was carried to any considerable depth, or whether there were three adits there, but the enterprise was abandoned in 1824 or 1825 "because they had prosecuted their Search for Metals, Ores and Minerals in an unproductive part of the limits...and had worked the same limits and erected the said Steam Engine within and on a disadvantageous portion of the same limits.''

Pearce claimed that Rosewarne and himself began to work the sett within three months of its being granted to them; and from August 30th 1834 worked it constantly in accordance with the terms of the agreement. However, they did not carry out any operations on the old mine, because they understood the former adventurers had not found any lodes or veins there which would warrant further prosecution. He and his partner had nevertheless effectually worked other parts of the sett, kept the shafts and adits properly sollared, fenced and secured, and done no wilful or unnecessary damage to the land.

Hockin was evidently dissatisfied with the adventurers for not re-working the old mine; and on October 21 1836 he served a written notice on them warning that unless they immediately commenced and continued to work Wheal Dollar Sett in conformity with the terms under which it had been granted to them, he would get the sett worked by others. This failed to have the desired effect; and so on April 26 1837 he took formal possession of the sett in the presence of William Michell of Zennor, as a witness; and on May 2 served notice on them that the indenture had been made void.

However, during the following September, Pearce and Rosewarne "entered on a certain field within the said limits, in the occupation of one Richard Nicholls, a Tenent of the said Complainant, and there caused to be stripped of the soil and meat earth in two several places to the extent of about seventy feet long and twelve feet wide and to the depth of about sixteen inches.'' They also "caused to be dug certain small pits commonly called Costeen pits at intervals within the place so stripped.''

Pearce denied Hockin's allegation that these pits were dug as a pretence and without any real intention of searching for tin there, declaring it was in accordance with "the invariable custom and practice of good miners in the said County of Cornwall'' to carry out such stripping and costeening operations. He also claimed that the "said soil and meat earth'' which had been stripped off was at once carefully laid aside in heaps and that no ores or rubbish was afterwards laid on them, "and that the same Mining Operations were carried on not with a view to injure and annoy the said Complainant or his said Tenent.''

The costeening had disclosed indications of metallic veins and lodes, and

Pearce had expressed an intention of carrying out further stripping in the field in order to develop these discoveries. He denied, however, that he had expressed himself in a threatening manner, or had threatened to injure other lands occupied by Charles Matthews, another of Hockin's tenants.

Following a rehearing, the Court's verdict was given on January 23 1841 in favour of the complainant (Hockin) with damages of £10.1s. against Rosewarne.[1] It would seem that the law suit did not result in a final abandonment of Wheal Dollar, for an advertisement published in September 1842 offered for private sale shares in "Wheal Dollar, Wheal Edward and Carnelloe" in the parish of Zennor.[2]

When the late Mr. W.T. Harry, put forward proposals in 1960 for re-working Carnelloe, it soon became evident that in order to give the area a fair trial, it would be necessary to investigate the adjacent Dollar Mine in conjunction with it. Accordingly, Consolidated Gold Fields, Ltd., who later became associated with these plans, sought planning permission to work both setts, but were frustrated in their intentions when a farmer withdrew permission to mine on his land. (See under Carnelloe.)

In connection with this scheme, reports were drawn up in 1963 by Mr. J.H. Trounson and Professor K.F.G. Hosking on Carnelloe and Dollar in which both mines were fully described and their prospects carefully assessed. Writing of the Dollar Mine, Mr. Trounson stated that the surviving plan of it was a very crude one, and it was not clear whether the North shown on it was true or magnetic. However, as the "Great Guide" of the Dollar mine was almost certainly the same as the cross-course of that name in Carnelloe, it was possible to orientate the Dollar plan approximately. It then seemed that the five N.E.-S.W. striking lodes (not four, as given by Dines) ran roughly parallel to the No's. 1 and 2 lodes of Carnelloe.

A note on the plan stated that two deep adits were driven side by side from the cliff on the course of the (Great) Guide, nearly 150 fms. S. to a point about 180 fms. from the main shafts (not 150 fms., as per Dines.) These deep adits must also be at least twice the depth of 25 fms. from surface at their southern extremity given by Dines.

Mr. Trounson continued: "The two principal shafts of the tin are thought to be those in the rough ground 150 yards E. of Carnello Farm. Harry states that from the amount of water flowing from them the workings would appear to be very wet, and this was probably the reason for the driving of the deep adits. The mine was known to have been working between 1838 and 1840, but the mineral owner was dissatisfied with the rate at which the deep adits were being driven and he revoked the company's lease. This led to a law suit and the stoppage of the mine before the deep adits could reach and drain the workings."

Mr. Trounson considered the Dollar lodes well worth renewed investigation by unwatering the old workings and doing all the exploratory work (including diamond drilling) underground. As, however, there were numerous small lodes both here and in Carnelloe mine, the whole area should be regarded as a single unit and prospected accordingly. He concluded: "It cannot be too strongly stressed that, in view of the similarity of the geology and the lodes of this area and of the great St. Just — Pendeen district, this mineralisation west of Zennor deserves far more attention than it had yet received."[8]

Dr. Hosking described the E.-W. trending lodes in Wheal Dollar as lying within a belt of ground 200 yards wide, crossed by the N.W.-S.E. striking caunter lode in the vicinity of the main shafts, and by the Great Guide, a N.N.E. trending cross-course. In addition to the main shaft E. of Carnelloe Farm, the plan indicated several adit shafts, some on the middle adit to the N. and others on the shallow adit ot the N.E. of it.

The longitudinal section showed, within a distance of 40 yards, four shafts, each 10 fms. deep and connected by drives at 3 fms. and 10 fms. below surface. "The true strike lengths of the E.-W. lodes, their mineralogical characteristics and economical potential are quite unknown; they are, however, very favourably situated near the granite-invaded rock contact, and their strike approximately parallels that on the Carnelloe Mine lode which is known to be tin and copper bearing. It is probable, therefore, that these two groups of lodes were developed at the same time and their mineralogical characteristics are qualitatively, though not necessarily quantitatively, similar.[2]

"Nothing is known of the nature of the Caunter lode, but it may well be mineralised. It is probably somewhat later than the E.-W. lodes, but the plan gives no reliable indication concerning either the effect of the development of this lode or of the still later — probably barren — Great Guide, on the early lodes."

Dr. Hoskin considered the E.-W. Dollar lodes, and possibly the Caunter lode, to be favourably situated and might well have some economic potential. He thought that here diamond drilling might well be used in order to determine their precise positions, to trace them along the strike and down dip, to discover something of their width which might be variable, and to determine their broad mineralogical characteristics. Should this work yield encouraging results it should be followed by exploration in driving along the lodes and intensive sampling.[4]

1. Stannary Court Records, per Justin Brooke
2. *Royal Cornwall Gazette* September 21 1842
3. Typescript per W.T. Harry
4. Ibid.

WEST WHEAL FANNY

The West Wheal Fanny Tin Mining Company wa formed in May 1852 in 1,024 shares, on which a £2 deposit was paid. The mine itself, about half a mile square in extent and situated about three miles W. of St. Ives, was held for 21 years at 1-18th dues from the Dowager Countess of Sandwich and the Duke of Cleveland. It was near Bray (Brea), St. Ives Consols and Trowan Consols, and lay in Zennor parish. It adjoined Trevisa (Trevessa) on the E., which seems to place it on Treveal Farm, where there are several shafts on the W. side of the valley. The manager was William Fitze, the agent Capt. Joseph Richards, and the London treasurer and purser Frederick Leith. The buildings were completed and the engine shaft sunk, cased and divided to the adit (7 fms.) by September 1852; a meeting held in November was told there was a credit balance of £693.10s.6d. The meeting instructed the purser to apply for a lease in exchange for the letter of license, the existence of which was not mentioned in the offer for sale. In February 1853 the manager reported that the lode in the adit level S. of the trial shaft was small and somewhat disordered, but that the lode in the adit N. of the trial shaft was small but regular and very kindly. The mine was put up for auction in London in one lot in November 1853, after about £1,900 had been expended. The property was knocked down at £105.[1]

1. *Mining Journal* 1852 (1.5, 8.5, 18.9, 27.11), 1853 (19.2, 13.8, 1.10, 5.11). (Per Justin Brooke.)

WHEAL FORTUNE

In the account book of Nathaniel Anthony, of St. Ives occurs this entry: "1774. August. 9th. To Wheal fortune Zunor (Zennor) pr. Capt. Michel 6 pick halves 1s.1½d."

NORTH WHEAL GRYLLS

In December 1860 a number of miners summoned Capt. John Retallack, of North Grylls Mine, Zennor Cliff, for unpaid wages. William Boase, spokesman for himself and several others, said they had worked for four months and been paid very little, one man not having received a halfpenny for three months. The secretary of the mine (in London) promised the amount due in a few days, and Capt. Retallack said the materials and tinstuff would pay all the wages, the tin being worth £100, though the men valued it at only £30. The miners agreed to wait a little longer for their money on the magistrates making an order forbidding any attempt to move articles from the mine. Capt. Retallack expressed confidence that the money would be paid, and that Wheal Grylls would prove to be a good speculation.[1]

An amusing story relating to this mine (in which, however, it appears under a different name) was given to the late Richard John Noall, of St. Ives, by Mr. William Blight, J.P., and is now presrved among the Hamilton Jenkin MSS. It illustrates very well to what shifts the unfortunate Capt. Retallack and his friends were put to try to prevent the bal from being "knocked" through lack of funds:

"Zennor Church Town Mine, on the Zennor Cliff, had been working for some time, but was now (c. 1860) stopping for want of funds. Capt. Retallack had applied to the 'venturers, with little result. Some of them were from Penzance; one was a Mr. Sam Higgs. Now, Sam Higgs and party wanted specimens of tin from the mine to carry to London to show as samples of the richness of the mine and influence people to adventure, and so raise working capital. So they came out one Sunday from Penzance on a wagonette to Zennor Church-town, put up at the Tinners' Arms, and called for volunteers to go down in the mine and bring up the best specimens they could find, promising a half-crown each and a pint of gin.

"Some were not willing to go; for, though they could drink their pint of beer or glass of gin on a Sunday, they drew the line at digging up specimens from a mine, which might prove unlucky on the Sabbath Day, and seemed a bit too much like courting fate.

"At last a party was got to go. They went underground, the specimens of tine were broke, brought up and delivered to Sam Higgs and party at the inn; they had their money, drank their gin, and everything went off all right.

"But a boy, who, for the fun of the thing, went with them, split the gaff on the Monday morning to his master, Mr. Blight, who was the smith at Trevidgia Mine, and he, for a spree, wrote some verses and chalked them up behind the smithy door. Everybody who came for their tools naturaly read them; in a short time the yarn was all through the mine, and before long all over Zennor parish. The smith had the fault for writing the verses, and was threatened to be killed by Bill Retallack, who was son to the Capt. Retallack of Zennor Church-town Mine, and he only escaped by denying all knowledge of the scamp who tried to cast a slur on honest folks by writing such scurrilous verses.

"And these are the verses he wrote:'

"RAISING OF SPECIMENS OF TIN AT ZENNOR CHURCH TOWN MINE, ON THE SABBATH DAY

"On Sunday last to Zennor came
Some gents, and they were not ashamed
Of asking men to break some tin
And bring it up to them again.

A person walking to Zennor Church
Did meet a party on the lurch;
He watched a while, and saw them drift
For they were going down the clift.

144

Carmen was there, and Turner too,
But Josey said he would not go,
Retallack went, also Jack Quick,
Edwin Bamfield and landlord's Dick.

Says Carmen to Josey, "Come tha wast down,
We all shall have a haalf-a-crown,
We'll bore the hoal, and break the tin,
And that will do the quaart of gin."

Carmen soon made an alarm
For fear that Quick would break his arm;
The mallet-hilt brawk whilst giving a lick,
And they made en into a swabbing-stick.

They bored the hole and brawk the tin
And at the landlord's drank their gin,
They had their money without delay,
That's the rig in Zennor on the Sabbath Day."

In 1862 a company was formed in London to re-work this property, which it purchased from John Escott and John Jory. In February 1864 a new venture, styled the North Wheal Grylls (Zennor) Mining Company, Limited, was registered in 300 £10 shares, their offices being in Worcester. A total of £6 was called up on each share, but the company worked at a loss; and it was resolved at an extraordinary general meeting in June 1865 that it should be voluntarily wound up. However, the liquidator was unable to get in the company's assets, not one single call in arrear being forthcoming. Accordingly, one of the shareholders petitioned for a winding-up order, which was granted in August 1867.[2]

1. *Cornish Telegraph* December 12 1860
2. *West Briton* August 8 1867

GURNARD'S HEAD (WHEAL TREEN, NORTH UNITED MINES)

The ruined engine house of Wheal Treen is one of the most romantically situated in this part of Cornwall. Standing a short distance back from the cliff edge just below Treen Coastguard Station and with the bold, unusually shaped Gurnard's Head providing a dramatic western backdrop, it seems to symbolise the spirit of Cornish coastal mining. Indeed, there is some evidence that in its early days — before 1822 — some of the workings were actually carried below the sea. The shaft was then sunk in a rock near high water mark, its mouth protected by a ten feet high wall to prevent the waves breaking in. There

145

was only one level, at a depth of 13 fms. below the sea bed, driven 20 fms. E. and 10 fms. W.

Soon after this the mine seems to have closed; but in 1828 it was stated that Wheal Treen copper mine had recently been set to work in the parish of Zennor, and that it promised to turn out an advantageous concern.[2] In 1835 the sale was advertised of 10-128th shares "of all that Valuable and well-known Copper Mine called The Gurnet's Head...Considered to be one of the best Speculations in Cornwall; she is of the same Strata of ground as the Levant Mine, and the Ores are equally rich." Further particulars could be obtained from Capt. John James at the Golden Lion Inn, Penzance.[3] During that year the mine sold 25 tons of copper ore. In 1838 it employed 24 persons and possessed a 20′ water wheel which seems to have been replaced by a larger one soon after; for the materials, when auctioned in 1843, included "a capital Water Wheel, 40′ diameter and 2½′ over the Breast." Also offered were a whim, 30 fms. of 5″ pumps, 50 fms. of ladders, 30 fms. of flat rods, and the account house furniture.[4]

Gurnard's Head Mine, circa 1890s (Courtesy Royal Institution of Cornwall)

Despite the failure evidenced by this sale, the property was considered worthy of another trial; and before the end of the year it was taken up again by a new company using the name of "The North United and Gurnet's Head Mine." This enterprise lasted until 1847, when the materials were sold. These were described as being of superior quality and nearly new. The most interesting

146

item was "a First Rate Pumping Engine (from the manufactory of Messrs. Harvey & Co., at Hayle Foundry, in 1843), 30-inch 9-ft. stroke Cylinder, 7 in the Shaft, with a Boiler 8½ Tons." There were also 20 fms. of 5″ and 18 fms. of 4½″ pumps, and a miner's dial, by Wilton. The quality of the engine was particularly stressed, it being described as "one of the best in the County of Cornwall."[5]

No doubt the surviving engine house had been erected to accomodate this paragon.

There was one further phase of activity a few years later, 25 tons of copper ore being raised in 1853. The workings of this mine lay in metamorphosed killas, and exploited two intersecting lodes coursing E. 20 deg. N. and E. 30 deg. S. It seems to have been carried to a depth of about 90-100 fms. below adit level.

In conclusion, it is interesting to recall that the Cornish historian Davies Gilbert was so impressed with the bold appearance of the headland which gave this mine its name that he purchased the manor of Treen and Boswednack "chiefly for the purpose of acquiring the property of a mass of rocks so geologically interesting."[6]

1. Carne, Joseph, (in *Trans. Roy. Geol. Soc. Corn.*, ii)
2. *Royal Cornwall Gazette* September 27 1828
3. *Royal Cornwall Gazette* May 16 1835
4. *Penzance Gazette* July 26 1843
5. *Penzance Journal* October 20 1847
6. Gilbert Davies, *Parochial History of Cornwall*, 1838

WHEAL HOPE, ZENNOR

This little mine commenced operations in 1843, but it does not appear to have lived up to the promise of its name. At a meeting of the adventurers held in Liskeard on October 29 1846 the accounts for the four months ending August showed; labour £234.8s.1d., materials £61.13s.4d., total £296.1s.5d.; by call made at last meeting, £218; balance of last account, £22.13s.4d.; present adverse balance, £55.8s.1d. — to reduce a further call of £2 was made. Clearly, there was very little "hope" to be derived from those figures! The 60 fm. level was reported driving west of Engine shaft by six men and a boy at £6.10s. per fm., in granite, towards the killas; the lode when last taken down consisted of mundic, iron, and spots of ore. This level had been driven about 60 fms., the lode throughout being large — 3′ to 6′ — and seldom without some ore. It was expected the quantities of ore would increase when the killas was reached. The New lode, coursing 30 degs. S.W., had begun to take more of a N.-S. direction; it was now split by a horse of killas in the end, but had previously been 2′ wide, consisting of spar gossan, iron and spots of ore. The lode was driving at £5.10s. per fm. by four men and two boys. They expected soon to intersect and E.-W. lode. The workings here were only at adit level, in which, 50 fms. back from the present end, a little bunch of grey ore had been passed through. The productive lodes of Levant and Botallack being in a N.-W. direction, and in similar ground, led them to believe this lode would turn out well. The water and stuff continued to be drawn by a water wheel.[1] Unhappily, Wheal Hope continued to disappoint her optimistic investors, and two years later was knocked. The location of this mine is not known; but from the fact that it was worked by water power, one may deduce that its workings lay in or near one of the little valleys which run down from the high moors towards the sea.

1. *Penzance Gazette* November 11 1846

WHEAL MALKIN: NEW WHEAL MALKIN

On January 1 1742 Peter Carveth, late of Nansalverne, made an assignment of three quarters of one pair of bounds in "Whele Malkin, Bosuljack Downs, Maddern."[1] This name figured again in a list of mine shares advertised for auction at the house of John Bryant, innkeeper, Penzance, on May 12 1813, which included "7-9ths Parts of New Wheal Malkin, in the Parish of Zennor. — There are several Copper Lodes in this Set." At the same time, the whole of Wheal Malkin mine, in the parishes of Gulval and Madron, was also offered for sale; this had been very productive, its tin being esteemed of the first quality.[2] Wheal Malkin was again sold up, this time by order of the Stannary Court, in July 1820, when its materials included engines of 21″ and 18″ cylinders, and a horse whim.[3]

Although the precise location of these mines is not known, they would appear to have been situated at one or other of the places where the somewhat complicated parish boundaries of Zennor, Gulval and Madron conjoin.

1. Senior 73. C. 107. 73. P.R.O. (Per Justin Brooke)
2. *Royal Cornwall Gazette* May 1 1813
3. *Royal Cornwall Gazette* July 1 1820

WHEAL SPERRIS (GREAT SPERRIS CONSOLS)

On the high moors just south of Eagle's Nest in the parish of Zennor stands the gaunt ruin of the account house of Wheal Sperris, a name which, in Cornish, means "spirit mine;" and indeed the building, set in this lonely solitude, with the sinister-looking granite carns standing around, has a truly ghostly aspect, particularly when mist, or darkness, is settling on the scene. Wheal Sperris, like others in the parish, is a very ancient mine, whose early history is now irrecoverable. What seems to have been its principal phase of working came to an end in 1837, when the mine was offered for sale privately as a going concern. It then possessed a 24″ (double) stamping engine, with crank for flat

148

rods, and all necessary materials, everything being new and of excellent quality. "The attention of Capitalists is particularly invited...as the Mine is offered under peculiar circumstances, the prospects being very good, and but a small further outlay necessary to try effectually a most promising lode."[1]

Another working, under the name of "Great Sperris Consols Tin Mining Company, Zennor," was projected in 1853. According to the prospectus, the sett contained three distinct mineral properties extending over the estates of Tremeader, and Tregerthen, and ranging from Zennor Church Town towards Towednack, with part of an estate bordering to the south on Wheal Montague. It included six promising E.-W. lodes from which considerable returns of tin had been made. Several shafts had been sunk, Engine shaft being down to about 33 fms., and levels driven on the two principal lodes, the Great Sperris and the Red.[2]

The Count-house, Wheal Sperris (Noall Collection)

In October 1930 Dr. Hamilton Jenkin was informed by Mr. Osborne, of Tremeader, then aged 85, that although he could not remember the Sperris mine working he knew the engine-driver there who told him "a braa while ago" that the mine produced good tin going 8s. to the barrow at the bottom of the 20 fm. shaft located near the S. side of the old mine road leading up from Eagle's Nest, just across from the 'count house. The shaft had been sollered with granite slabs, but was now "covered with browze and brimbles." The should be little difficulty in identifying this shaft, as it lay in "Tregerthen

149

right," the other shaft on Sperris being considerably to the W., about half way between the 'count house and Zennor Quoit. He said the workings must have been stopped "nearly ninety years ago" — around 1840.[3]

1. *Royal Cornwall Gazette* September 1 1837
2. *Mining Journal* May 14 1853
3. MS Hamilton Jenkin Coll., Redruth Library

TREGERTHEN

In the summer of 1872, when a limited revival was taking place in Cornish tin mining, the following story appeared in the Cornish press: "Some months since a gentleman from London was travelling in Cornwall when an old miner, Capt. Retallick, told him of a wonderfully rich tin lode near the Eagle's Nest, Zennor, that was discovered and worked by four miners some forty two years ago, from which *in two days* they raised and sold £80 worth of ore, tin being then £40 per ton. They continued working the lode with unabated success until they began to follow it four fathoms below the adit, when an influx of water overpowered the limited means at their disposal. Believing the statements made, a licence was acquired of the Tregerthen sett, and active operations have been lately carried on, exploring and clearing the old workings, and so far they have been amply verified...Mining in the parish of Zennor has ben somewhat neglected for many years. It being a very rough country, and no society near, mining captains have objected to reside there, but lately mining setts have been taken up all over the parish, and active operations are likely to be carried out on every available lode."[1]

In 1959 the late Mr. Hocking of Tregerthen Farm told the author that opposite the ruined cottage which adjoins the St. Ives-Zennor footpath a little east of Tregerthen Farm, may be seen the opening to a tunnel, which extends under the nearby field. The entrance is obscured by vegetation during the summer, but at other times is plainly visible. It is now rather dangerous to enter. In olden days kegs of smuggled brandy were stored in this old mine working after being secretly landed on the coast below.

1. *Cornish Telegraph* July 10 1872

TREVAIL

The pretty, sheltered valley of Trevail (or Treveal) which opens out on the coast near the Western Carracks (Seal Island) was the scene of some early mining operations. Certain very primitive workings may still be seen in the area, but little is know of their history.

In December 1804 one third of two pairs of bounds in "Treveale-Clift," Zennor, came up for sale by auction at Penzance.[1] Ten tons of copper were sold from Treveal mine in 1823 for £92. When 32/64ths shares in "Trevail Copper Mine, in the parishes of Zennor and Towednack," were put on the market in 1830, it was stated that an adit from sea level had been driven 130 fms., with another 30 fms. more to cut the copper lode. This was "about ten fathoms big, the Copper worth £40 per ton," and lay 50 fms. from surface. There were 20 tin lodes within about 100 fms. to the S., many of which were productive when formerly worked at a shallow level.[2]

The early "Tinners' Stone" at Trevail (Treveal), used for the crushing of stone
(Courtesy Royal Institution of Cornwall)

In a fuller description of the mine published in 1836 the sett was said to extend about 700 fms. E. to W. and 40 fms. N. to S. It included a great number of lodes, and several considerable workings had been made, generally open to the surface, varying from 7 to 15 fms. in depth. In the eastern part lay an old mine 40 fms. deep called "Trevidgia" (otherwise Trevega Bal, *q.v.*) known to have been very profitable when last worked. About ten years previously (1826) in order to work the sett effectually and discover all the lodes contained in it a deep adit was opened about 2-3 fms. above high water mark about the centre of the sett where the valley runs southward from the coast, and on a cross-course which facilitated its speedy development. This adit had been driven 170 fms. entirely through killas, and in another 12 fms. would cross the killas-

151

granite junction. One of the most kindly lodes in the sett was called "The Great Copper Lode," from which at about 5 fms. from surface (the greatest depth to which a shaft had been sunk on it) were raised large stones of ore, making a produce of 25%. This lode lay immediately at the junction of the granite and killas. By continuing the adit southward it would gradually increase in depth, and by driving E. or W. would attain a depth of 60 fms. In the course of 150 fms. S. of the copper lode the adit would cross no less than 28 lodes, all of which had been worked to greater or less extent from the surface.[3]

1. *Royal Cornwall Gazette* December 15 1804
2. *Cornubian* October 8 1830
3. *West Briton* 1 July 1836; *Mining Journal* 2 July 1836

TREVAIL STAMPS

On 17 July 1809 Treveal Stamps, Zennor, were granted by Lord Hinchingbroke to George Alexander Stevens, the fine being £15 and common rent 2s.6d. The land comprised "part of Thomas Phillips's Tenement, Manor of Ludgvan Leaze and Porthia, at Treveal." A term of 99 years or any of three lives (45, 22 and 20) would determine the lease. Co-owners were the Rt. Hon. Henry, Earl of Darlington and the Hon. Lady Amelia Powlett.[1]

1. D.45/T.87, County Record Office, Dorchester

TREWEY DOWNS

Trewey Downs or Common, lying about a mile south of Zennor Churchtown, was traditionally the scene of some of the earliest streaming operations in Cornwall. William Bottrell recounts that about "Trewe" there could still be seen (in 1870) the remains of old bals which were worked before the Flood; whilst Trewey Bottom, which runs up towards Zennor from Nancledra, had been streamed for tin over and over again. He gives a fascinating account of the way of life of the dozen or so men who worked for Uncle Matthew Thomas in streaming the moors. These tinners came from Ludgvan and Towednack, miles away from the work, and so they built a large moor-house more than thirty feet long and twelve wide where they could sleep overnight, and also store their tin and liquor, for they frequently engaged in smuggling expeditions to Roscoff, the goods being landed on the Eastern Green, near Long Rock, and taken up to the moors by waiting horses. No riding officer dared to venture among the stream leats and bogs at Trewey, where scores of ankers of brandy were often kept among the burrows till the innkeepers, gentry and other regular customers wanted them. The moor house itself was a kind of fortress, with a low door, so that if unwelcome visitors stooped down and poked their heads in, "one could crack their skulls as easy as so many eggs into the frying pan."[1]

The Trewey Downs mine was sometimes referred to as Edward and Kerrow. In an indenture dated March 31 1764 reference was made to tin bounds called Whele an Crude, Whele (an) Crease, and Whele an Croft, on Cerow Common, Zennor. An advertisement dated December 15 1804 offered for sale a twelfth part of one pair of bounds in Trery Downs in Zennor. Another advertisement of 1856 mentions Wheal an Vere, Dreek Kerro and Little Wheal an Pool bounds on Kerro Common; and Wheal an Creek, Bounds Triangle, Bounds Quivavo, Great Wheal Pool, Wheal an Teese, Wheal Marrack, Little Bounds and Wheal Menor, on Kerro and Truoy Commons.[2]

The early workings at Trewey were on a very limited scale, but more systematic development seems to have taken place there during the late 19th century. Then, in 1906, the sett was taken up by the Trewey Downs Tin Mining Company. In June of that year they discovered a rich lode 2' wide in No. 1 Prospect shaft, and another 18" wide in Edward's shaft. No. 1 shaft was down about 10 fms., and after driving a cross-cut the lode was struck, which they were driving E. and W. A main shaft would be put down in the middle of the sett. It was also intended to erect steam stamps, but in the meantime they had taken the stamps of a Mr. Thomas.[3] In November a valuable lode was struck in the north cross-cut of Main shaft which assayed 90 lbs. of black tin per ton. Prospecting work had begun on the cross-cut in a southerly direction in anticipation of cutting Hocking's lode, which had formerly yielded good results.[4]

Unfortunately, during the following year the company ran into financial difficulties, and in May the directors recommended that it be wound up in voluntary liquidation.[5] Instead, the shareholders decided to consolidate it into a new company with a working capital of £15,000. In connection with this, some interesting particulars were given about the origins of the earlier company. About a year previously six or seven local gentlemen, all of whom had been brought up as miners from childhood, returned to Penzance and settled down with a competence for life. They clubbed together to take up Trewey Downs, and decided to develop and work it with their own means. Having cleared the old shafts, which had been sunk to water level only, and sunk new ones to prove the value of the property, they formed themselves into a company. In May 1907 some London financiers interested themselves in the mine, and agreed to put up the money for a stamps with about 40-50 heads. So the new company was formed, the majority of the old directors remaining on a new management committee, with Mr. J.B. Cornish as local secretary.[6]

This injection of fresh capital led to renewed activity. In August a correspondent who visited the mine reported that the adit to the main shaft was being pushed ahead, though a bar of hard ground impeded progress. They intended to expedite this work by sinking several intermediate shafts between the present end of the adit and the shaft. These shafts would be to the level of the tunnel, thus enabling driving operations to be continued simultaneously at six faces. Moreover, these intermediate shafts would be sunk on one of the rich intervening lodes, and the drift, instead of being dead work, would open up lode matter ready for stoping. The object of this adit, which would strike Main shaft at 110', was to serve as a permanent water conduit, and as the ancient workings went to a depth of only 50' (water level), the tunnel would give 60' of ore reserves in dry ground beneath the old levels, which had a run of several thousand feet. In this connection, it is very interesting to note that Dines says that in the 1890's an adit was driven 2,000' from the Zennor valley to meet the lodes 120' below surface, the crop workings being said to extend to 70' depth. This must be the same adit, but Dines' dating of it may be inexact.

A powerful new pump and boiler had been fixed at Main shaft, to enable the shaft to be continued from its depth of 92' to tunnel level (110'), but it also drained the water from Edward's, Hocking's and Junction shafts, the last being more than a quarter of a mile distant. This afforded satisfactory evidence of the co-relation of the lodes. Junction lode was looking remarkably well, and a phenomenal strike had been made on Edward's lode, stone having been raised giving over 500 lbs. of tin to the ton. The dump of about 20 tons at this shaft was expected to give from 100-200 lbs. to the ton throughout; the lode averaged about 2' wide.[7]

During November 1907 a fire destroyed the wooden dry, the cause being presumed to be the ignition of some of the men's clothing placed near the fire. The mine was still in existence in 1909, congratulations being offered to the adventurers in January on the private sale of their first parcel of tin. Hopes were expressed that Trewey Downs would soon appear in the ticketing list. The company does no appear to have had much success, however, and the mine was in due course "knocked."

1. Bottrell, William, *Traditions and Hearthside Stories of West Cornwall*, vol. i.
2. *Royal Cornwall Gazette* September 26 1856
3. *St. Ives Weekly Summary* June 2 1906
4. *St. Ives Weekly Summary* November 10 1906
5. *Western Echo* June 1 1907
6. *Western Echo* June 29 1907
7. *Western Echo* August 31 1907

WICKOW

At various places in the parish of Zennor small mining enterprises were set to work during the nineteenth century and earlier. When one considers the remote, inhospitable character of the district and the difficulty of communications, the courage and determination of their promoters can but command great respect. One of these little mines was located at Wicca Farm. In 1823 William Trenery, mine broker, Redruth, offered for sale 8-60th shares in "Wickow, in Zennor," at £10 per share. The mine was then producing tin.[1]

1. *Royal Cornwall Gazette* November 8 1823

ZENNOR BOUNDS

An indenture dated January 1 1742, renewed on March 31 1764, lists (among others) the following tin bounds in Zennor parish: 3-4ths of 1-9th of 9 pair, Venton Nigoe (Niger); Whele an Minor, Common of Boshporth Enys, Zennor and Gulvall.[1] (See also under Trewey Downs.)

Several tin bounds "in Zennor Church-town" were advertised for sale privately in 1815. They included "one 4th in Two Pair...called the Cliff Bounds; one 4th in another Pair there, called the Little Bounds; (and) one 4th in another Pair, near the Garland."[2]

In 1856 a large number of bounds was advertised for sale, mostly within the limits of Ding Dong mine, but including the following from Zennor: 1/3 Ventanego, Tredennack & Boskednan Commons (Gulval and Zennor); 1/3 Nine Maids, or Mine-an-Daunce, Lanyon & Vosperings Commons (Madron and Zennor); 1/3 Wheal an Vere, Kerro Common; Wheal an Creek, Truey & Kerro Commons; 1/2 Dreek Kerro, Kerro Common; 1/2 Little Wheal an Pool, Kerro Common; 1/2 Bounds Triangle, Kerro & Truoy Commons (Gulval and Zennor); 4/6 Bounds Quivavo, 1/3 Great Wheal Pool, 1/4 Wheal an Teese; 1/4 Wheal Marrack, 1/4 Little Bounds, 2/3 Wheal Manor, all on Kerro and Truoy Commons.[3]

1. Senior 73. C. 107. 73. P.R.O. (Per Justin Brooke.)
2. *Royal Cornwall Gazette* January 1815
3. *Royal Cornwall Gazette* September 26 1856

APPENDIX

ST. IVES MINES USED AS A WATER SUPPLY

Several references have been made in the preceding pages to efforts made in the past to utilise abandoned mine workings in the St. Ives district for supplying the town with water. The arrangements in use at the time of writing were as follows:

A submerged 90 h.p. electric pump 420' down in Victory shaft at Trenwith pumps water to the covered reservoir near Knill's Steeple to supply all parts of St. Ives.

Trenwith deep adit, which also drains St. Ives Consols and Rosewall Hill mines, formerly terminated at Dale's shaft, near the steps leading from the Parc-an-Roper Coach Park to the Stennack, from where the water ran in an open leat behind the present Trenwith Place to the Fountain at Royal Square. Some of this water drove the wheel of a grist mill situated at the eastern end of Trenwith Place. When Trenwith Place was built the leat was covered with large stones.

On several occasions schemes were introduced for supplying the lower part of St. Ives with water from Wheal Trenwith. The most comprehensive was that installed during the 1930's under the direction of Mr. H.E. Phillips, the then Borough Surveyor, which involved the construction of a dam in Dale's Shaft. The adit started at a depth of 54' below ground level in this shaft and came out at ground level at the Royal Cinema, water being conveyed through the adit by a pipeline.

Early in 1964 a fall of stone and earth damaged the 6" main, and the work of repairing it proved to be very difficult and hazardous. A wall of the Royal Cinema had been erected about 4' from the adit portal some years after the pipeline was laid, making it impossible to pass a normal length of pipe into the adit. At a point about 40' underground and 130' from Dale's shaft the main was split over a length of 4'. An inspection made by Mr. J.H. Hodge of the West Cornwall Water Board (since merged with the South West Water Authority) wearing a frogman's suit, showed that the fall in the adit had dammed back the overflow water, so that it was above the 6" main, leaving only about 1' between the water level and the roof of the adit. Where the main was damaged the adit was only about 15"-18" wide, leaving the rock side of the adit only 4"-6" distant from either side of the main.

The men who effected the repair thus had to lie prone in the tunnel to cut the main, which was about 2' below roof level, carrying out the work in most uncomfortable conditions even after the water had been pumped out. Ventilation was also a problem, as the fall had decreased air circulation.

This difficult task was undertaken by Messrs J.H. Hodge and W. Freestone, of the Water Board, assisted by Mr. T. Waters, an experienced miner loaned by Geevor Tin Mines, Ltd. Because of lack of space, Hodge went into the adit first, crawling backwards, and Waters followed, so that they faced one another in prone positions, manoeuvring their equipment between them, whilst an ambulance equipped with oxygen stood by.

The old pipe was cut with a Wheeler Pipe Cutter and a new PVC main inserted and jointed. The work, which was carried out in October, took about 7½ hours to complete, and the men were bruised and exhausted when they eventually returned to surface. They received high praise for their efforts under such dangerous and unpleasant circumstances, reminiscent of those which Cornish miners of an earlier generation sometimes had to endure. Their action ensured a continuation of the Trenwith supply, which otherwise might have been lost to the town.

At the bottom of Trenwith Burrows Hill, in the Coach Park, is an old shaft known as Allotment shaft, a name which commemorates the allotments at Parc-an-Roper before the field was excavated; this is connected to an adit terminating at Tye Shoot, in the Stennack, at the 'bus shelter opposite Alma Terrace. It was found that this adit caused water to be lost from the main Trenwith adit, so Tye Shot was plugged to stop the waste.

Joby's mine, at Amalveor, supplies water by gravity both to Nancledra and the Steeple reservoir, which is actually 100' lower than Amalveor. Steeple reservoir is also linked by pipeline with Drift reservoir and with Camborne.

Goole Pellas shaft was once equipped with a pump, but this drained the water too fast; and the supply is now provided by a siphon.